Dickens and Switzerland

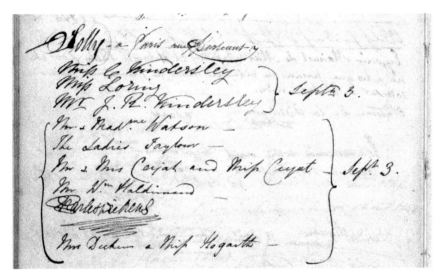

Frontispiece Signatures in the St Bernard 'Registre des Passants' by Charles Dickens and his travelling party from 1846. Sourced from the Archives of the Congregation of Gd-St-Bernard. Copyright: Maison Hospitalière du Gd-St-Bernard – CP 679 – CH 1920 Martigny.

Dickens and Switzerland

Christine Gmür

Edinburgh University Press is one of the leading university presses in the UK. We publish academic books and journals in our selected subject areas across the humanities and social sciences, combining cutting-edge scholarship with high editorial and production values to produce academic works of lasting importance. For more information visit our website: edinburghuniversitypress.com

© Christine Gmür 2025

Edinburgh University Press Ltd
13 Infirmary Street
Edinburgh EH1 1LT

Typeset in 11/13pt Adobe Sabon by
Cheshire Typesetting Ltd, Cuddington, Cheshire, and
printed and bound in Great Britain

A CIP record for this book is available from the British Library

ISBN 978 1 3995 3565 6 (hardback)
ISBN 978 1 3995 3567 0 (webready PDF)
ISBN 978 1 3995 3568 7 (epub)

The right of Christine Gmür to be identified as the author of this work has been asserted in accordance with the Copyright, Designs and Patents Act 1988, and the Copyright and Related Rights Regulations 2003 (SI No. 2498).

Contents

Preface and Acknowledgements	vi
An Introduction to Dickens and Switzerland	1
1. Performing Switzerland	16
2. Narrating Switzerland	63
3. Uncovering Switzerland	119
More Perspectives on Dickens and Switzerland: A Conclusion	169
Bibliography	186
Index	201

Preface and Acknowledgements

Dickens was not a household name where I grew up. I was not fascinated by his words and plots during my early years. Even his name was unfamiliar to me in my youth, and unlike many admirers of Dickens I cannot look back upon the experience of having enjoyed his books since the earliest days of my reading career – though I have always been a keen and fond reader. As a child, I did not know about *A Christmas Carol*, arguably his most well-known work, and only made the acquaintance of Oliver Twist in my early twenties and that of David Copperfield several years later. At secondary school, busy learning English language and grammar, we read plays by Wilde and Shaw, and I distinctly remember writing a rather dilettante essay on Wordsworth's 'I Wandered Lonely as a Cloud,' but no Dickens, who was considered too difficult, too long and too moralistic to be of interest to us. The height of achievement in our EFL class was ploughing through a bilingual edition of Shakespeare's *Hamlet*; nobody understood the purpose or meaning of the work except that it was famous and probably belonged to the same category of 'noble' literature as the texts we had been asked to read by Goethe. Only when I came to England did I realise – not without some astonishment – that here, Dickens's place was generally acknowledged to be second only to Shakespeare in the 'Best of' list of the World's Supreme Literary Heroes. Until this point, I had dutifully accepted that Shakespeare's other rivals were Homer, Goethe, Schiller, Molière and Dante. When I moved to the UK, I became acutely aware of my non-English upbringing and that the focus of my education, in a firmly rooted Continental fashion, had generally tended towards breadth rather than depth.

My first encounter with Dickens was at an open day at one of the Swiss universities I visited during my last year of school. A doctoral candidate was trying to impart one of the early chapters of *Great Expectations* to her students. I found the book rather dull and could not help but think how odd a name Pip was. In my second or third year of university I was asked to read *Oliver Twist*, but did not understand its play with the melodramatic mode, and had no sympathy for poor Oliver whom I found terribly bland and insipid.

I have come a long way since. This tome is the – hopefully convincing – proof that one is never too old to be introduced to and start appreciating Dickens.

There have been many people who supported, helped and encouraged me on this journey, and it is impossible to pay all of them their due tribute here. First and foremost I would like to thank John Bowen who made me *read* and enjoy Dickens, and encouraged me to research this project. I could not have wished for a more dedicated, critical and kind supervisor. He guided me through the intricacies of writing such a project with interminable perseverance, encouragement and optimism, and remained an invaluable source of optimism and support when the time came to turn the thesis into a book. Thank you.

I am very grateful to the Swiss National Science Foundation for their doc.mobility stipend and the extremely helpful responses which my application triggered. My special thanks go to Lisa Wildi, for making me aware of this stipend and ensuring that I would apply.

In 2015, the University of York's English Department granted a scholarship which allowed me to spend a wonderful and inspiring week at the *Dickens Universe* conference at the University of California in Santa Cruz, for which I am extremely grateful.

Steve Martin from the Dickens Fellowship's Kent branch went out of his way to turn my trip to Kent in autumn 2015 into an unforgettable one. I cannot thank him enough for the extremely educational visit to the docks, the trip to Cooling and the comprehensive tour of Gad's Hill. My thanks also go to Stephen Nye from the Medway Council and in particular Sarah Belsom, who made a dream come true by spontaneously agreeing to grant me access to Dickens's chalet at Rochester's Guildhall Museum on a very cold and wet day.

The recent discovery of a complete list of contributors to *All the Year Round* has not been made public at the time of submission of this book. I am, however, extremely grateful to Jeremy Parrott, who dealt with my repeated enquiries with kindness and understanding, and has generously shared his knowledge with me.

Teaching and the many conversations with my students helped me develop as a scholar. Many of their critical questions and lively discussions provided me with important insights and valuable input. I would also like to thank Hans-Ueli Schiedt for his help and information about transport systems in nineteenth-century Switzerland,

and Roger Rosset from the *Archives de l'Etat de Genève* for the rectification of a mistake in Raymond Tschumi's article on Dickens and Switzerland.

Last but not least I would like to thank the whole team at Edinburgh University Press for their confidence in me and this project. I am particularly indebted to Elizabeth Fraser, Emily Sharp, Fiona Conn, Llinos Edwards and Sarah Sturzel.

Many wonderful friends, old and new, contributed to this venture in some form or other, sometimes without, perhaps, being aware of it. Thank you! I could not have persevered without the endless encouragement, optimism and advice from the brilliant Emily Bell, Boriana Alexandrova and Linda Walz. Thank you for your friendship, support and faith. I stand in your debt.

This book would not have been possible without the unconditional support of my parents, Regula and Pius Gmür, and my partner, René Kuster, without whom I would not be where I am today. I am more deeply indebted to you than I can say, and cannot thank you enough for your love, guidance, patience, as well as your seemingly endless confidence in me and this project. I can only hope to be an equally sympathetic and understanding adjuvant to your own endeavours. This book is for you.

Some very special canine friends made sure I would occasionally leave my desk, enjoy the beautiful Yorkshire countryside and let my thoughts roam. How surprised I was to find in the course of my research that Dickens too had liked taking his dogs out on a good walk. He and I may not have many things in common, but the happy experience of walking our dogs is a pleasure we share.

To my Parents and Pip

An Introduction to Dickens and Switzerland

The bright morning sun dazzled the eyes, the snow had ceased, the mists had vanished, the mountain air was so clear and light that the new sensation of breathing it was like the having entered on a new existence.

Little Dorrit, Book 2, Chapter 3

Missing, or the Absence of Switzerland

In Dickens's works, the appearance of Switzerland is frequently treated as a chance or an accident, even though John Forster, Dickens's friend and his appointed biographer, gave it some prominence in his *Life of Charles Dickens*.[1] Forster himself had been opposed to the idea of Dickens's going to Switzerland in 1846 and may not be an entirely reliable source.[2] He is, however, certainly the most detailed and major contemporary authority we have. Surprisingly, Switzerland is rarely considered in works dealing with the author's trips abroad. If it is, the discussion often does not extend beyond a short note. Even some of the more recent studies suggesting comprehensive overviews, such as Anny Sadrin's *Dickens, Europe, and the New Worlds* and John Jordan and Nirshan Perera's *Global Dickens*, do not discuss Switzerland.[3] While everything else

---

[1] John Forster, *The Life of Charles Dickens*. The Fireside Edition (London: Chapman & Hall, Ltd.; and Henry Frowde, *c*.1904 [undated]), 410–72; 631–44.

[2] Ibid., 408.

[3] Anny Sadrin, ed., *Dickens, Europe, and the New Worlds* (Basingstoke: Palgrave Macmillan, 1999); John Jordan and Nirshan Perera, eds., *Global Dickens* (Farnham: Ashgate, 2012).

2 Dickens and Switzerland

connected to Dickens seems to be considered relevant – from his adaptation and reception in the Netherlands and Finland to his connections with the history of the Battersea Dogs Home – Switzerland, for the most part, has been marginalised and ignored.[4] Yet, Michael Hollington is quite right, when he concludes that 'Switzerland [...] figures quite frequently in Dickens's imaginative work' in his entry on the country in *The Oxford Reader's Companion to Dickens*.[5]

Dickens's relationship with and attitudes towards France, Italy and the USA have been explored much more widely, particularly during recent years. Michael Slater's *Dickens on America and the Americans* from 1978 and Nigel Gearing's *Dickens in America* from 1998 indicate a long-standing engagement with the topic.[6] Scholars' unbroken interest in Dickens and America was also confirmed in 2015 by the week-long Dickens Universe conference on *American Notes* and *Martin Chuzzlewit*, Dickens's 'American' novel, at the University of California in Santa Cruz.[7] John Edmondson's *Dickens on France* appeared in 2006 and *Charles Dickens, A Tale of Two Cities and the French Revolution* in 2009.[8] The same year, Michael Hollington and Francesca Orestano published their *Dickens and Italy: 'Little Dorrit' and 'Pictures from Italy'*, which was the result of an international conference on 'Dickens, Victorian Culture, Italy' in Genoa.[9]

In 2013, Michael Hollington released *The Reception of Charles Dickens in Europe* in two volumes. In his chapter on 'Dickens in Austria and German-speaking Switzerland', Herbert Foltinek claims that there are 'many studies that concern themselves with Dickens's visits to Switzerland' and quotes Raymond Tschumi's article with his 'detailed bibliography of writings on Charles Dickens in Switzerland'

---

[4] Michael Hollington, ed., *The Reception of Charles Dickens in Europe* (London: Bloomsbury, 2013), vol. 2, 283ff, 388ff; Jan Lokin, 'Realism and Reality in Dickens's Characters: Dickens Seen through the Eyes of Dutch Writers', *Dickensian* 105, no. 477 (2009): 21; Beryl Gray, 'A Home of Their Own', *Dickensian* 107, no. 484 (2011): 151.

[5] Michael Hollington in Paul Schlicke, ed. *The Oxford Reader's Companion to Dickens*, s.v. 'Switzerland' (Oxford: Oxford University Press, 2000), 558.

[6] Michael Slater, *Dickens on America and the Americans* (Austin, TX: University of Texas Press, 1978); Nigel Gearing, *Dickens in America* (London: Oberon, 1998).

[7] I would like to express my gratitude to the University of York's Department of English and Related Literature for their very generous scholarship which enabled me to attend this event.

[8] John Edmondson, *Dickens on France* (Oxford: Signal, 2006); Colin Jones, Josephine McDonagh and Jon Mee, eds., *Charles Dickens, A Tale of Two Cities and the French Revolution* (Basingstoke: Palgrave Macmillan, 2009).

[9] Michael Hollington and Francesca Orestano, eds., *Dickens and Italy:* Little Dorrit *and* Pictures from Italy (Newcastle upon Tyne: Cambridge Scholars, 2009).

An Introduction to Dickens and Switzerland 3

as an example.[10] Yet, Tschumi himself noted rather apologetically that for his study, 'the necessary research work had to be conducted within a very short time'.[11] He speaks of a 'fair amount of biographical material related to Dickens's stay in Switzerland', but states that at the same time, '[i]n the field of academic articles, material is again lacking'.[12] Tschumi's 'detailed biography', which Foltinek highlights, is an extensive list of translations of Dickens's works and reviews of his life in general, but not a collection of specific studies on Dickens's use of and references to Switzerland in his work.

In fact, Tschumi's study is a prime example of how little critical work has been done on the subject. His choice of vocabulary shows the relative lack of sources: Gustav Schirmer's book from 1929 contains 'a very short account, mainly derived from Forster's *Life of Charles Dickens*, of the 1844 and 1846 stays', one of his essays from 1912 'briefly recounts Dickens' Simplon crossing of November 1845 and Dickens' stay at Lausanne in 1846' while Gavin de Beer's work from 1949 'very briefly records the four visits'.[13] He correctly notes that Liselotte Thalmann's study which appeared in 1956 is 'marred by some uncritical or inexact references'.[14] The longest account which 'evokes, in detail and with the help of suggestive illustrations, Dickens' travels and stays in Switzerland' is Paul-Emile Schazmann's *Charles Dickens, ses séjours en Suisse* from 1972.[15] At fifty pages, however, it is still comparatively short.

Tschumi's study itself is not flawless either. It is the general consensus that Dickens visited Switzerland in 1844, 1845, 1846 and 1853. Yet Tschumi's article makes the odd claim that

> One might also briefly note, at this point, that the Geneva archives record that [Dickens] arrived in Geneva on his way from Lausanne on September 27th, 1856, and returned to Lausanne on October 2nd of the same year.[16]

Tschumi does not comment on this any further – nor have later critics picked up on it. The date of the year is a typographical mistake, however, and refers to Dickens's stay in Geneva in 1846.

---

[10] Herbert Foltinek, 'Dickens in Austria and German-speaking Switzerland', in Hollington, *The Reception of Charles Dickens in Europe*, vol. 2, 255; 256.

[11] Raymond Tschumi, 'Dickens and Switzerland', *English Studies* 60, no. 4 (1979): 456.

[12] Ibid., 459; 460.

[13] Ibid., 459–60.

[14] Ibid., 460.

[15] Ibid.

[16] Ibid., 459.

4 *Dickens and Switzerland*

Tschumi's source is a register of a depot of passports and according to Roger Rosset, Geneva's current State Deputy Registrar, this seems to be, surprisingly enough, the only reference to Dickens in this archive.[17]

Family Affairs, or the Importance of Biography

In *Charles Dickens and Boz*, Robert L. Patten points out that 'Dickens has with considerable success controlled how we read him'.[18] Dickens actively created a powerful image of his persona, which also explains why the periodically resurging scandal about his love affair with Ellen Ternan never fails to stir public outcry – not so much against Dickens, but the indecent scholar who decided to shed some new light on it. Dickens's interest in Switzerland was a private rather than a public matter and it is only in some of his semi-autobiographic and smaller, 'minor' pieces from the 1860s that he reveals his fascination with the country in his fiction. It is mainly from his letters to the most intimate of his friends and family – first and foremost those to his biographer John Forster, of course, but also those to his wife Catherine, his sister-in-law Georgina and the families he met in Switzerland, the Cerjats and the Watsons – through which we learn of his heartfelt appreciation, his revelling in memories and, occasionally, even his desire to return.

In 1856, Dickens replied to a letter written to him by a German author. She had asked whether Dickens would allow her to dedicate her first novel to him. He was delighted. A short but very cordial correspondence began. One of the letters he sent to his admirer reveals how closely, and perhaps inadvertently, he linked Switzerland with his identity:

> I write every word of my books with my own hand, and do not write them very quickly either. I write with great care and pains (being passionately fond of my art, and thinking it worth any trouble), and persevere, and work hard. I am a great walker besides, and plunge into cold water every day in the dead of winter. When I was last in Switzerland, I found that I could climb as fast as the Swiss Guides. Few strangers think I look like one who passes so many hours alone

[17] Roger Rosset, email message to author, 30 March 2016. The source is held at the Archives de l'Etat de Genève under the signature 'CH AEG Etrangers H vol. 19', p. 232, no. 12'658.
[18] Robert L. Patten, *Charles Dickens and 'Boz': The Birth of the Industrial-Age Author* (Cambridge: Cambridge University Press, 2012), 20.

in his own Study. You would be disappointed perhaps, to see me with a brown-red color [*sic*] in my face?

I very seldom write or talk about myself, but you express your interest so naturally and unaffectedly, that I feel I ought to describe myself in the same spirit.[19]

Even though by the time of writing he had already travelled large parts of his own country, had lived in Italy for a year and frequently visited France, he drew on a memory from Switzerland to describe his physical prowess. Dickens claims to 'seldom write or talk about myself', but his perhaps surprising identification with the Swiss guides is a part of it. Chapter 2 of this book will touch on questions of biography and identity which occupied Dickens when he was in Switzerland. The letter above already provides a glimpse of how important Switzerland would become to him. His reference to Switzerland seems to appear out of the blue, and yet the memory is triggered by a request made to Dickens to think about and describe himself.

There has been the occasional acknowledgement of Dickens's journeys to Switzerland, but these are mostly limited to practical information without a great deal of literary critical ambition. All the accounts of Dickens and Switzerland – newspaper and journal articles as well as booklets and pamphlets – are characterised by their brevity: they never exceed fifty pages. This is because they often limit themselves to the most straightforward connections and do not go beyond the obvious links.

However, more details of Dickens's biography have emerged since most of these accounts were written. The vast majority of his texts and a great number of his letters have not only been published and edited but also digitised. Digitisation has transformed the way in which we read, perform research and process data. Keyword searches have become routine and yield a great number of results in very little time. Yet, the beauty of a topic such as Dickens and Switzerland is that despite the – justified – advance of the Digital Humanities, a focus on the number of mentions alone is not enough. What is required instead, is a careful qualitative approach combined with a thorough review of contextual resources. This study does therefore not attempt to reproduce a comprehensive account of

---

[19] To Sophie Verena Alberti, 30 April 1856, in Madeline House, Graham Storey, Kathleen Tillotson et al., eds., *The Letters of Charles Dickens*. The Pilgrim Edition (Oxford: Clarendon Press, 1993), vol. 8, 104.

6 *Dickens and Switzerland*

what Dickens did in Lausanne, whom he met and how he spent his day. Paul-Emile Schazmann has elaborately done this before me.[20] Neither will it touch upon every single reference to Switzerland in Dickens's works. Rather, it will select those which it deems most unexpected and enlightening. There are connections which had to be excluded due to their breadth, and these will be briefly touched upon in the Conclusion.[21] This book is interested in a literary and more than biographical approach, even though biography will play an important role. Its main aim is to uncover the literary and cultural connections between nineteenth-century Switzerland and Victorian England in Dickens's work. In doing so, it will occasionally touch upon the same themes and passages more than once. These different perspectives are understood as readings through different lenses. Often, they will complement each other, but they might, on occasion, contradict each other as well. If they do, it is a sign of Dickens's rich and multi-layered writing and the various readings they allow. The author rejects the idea of a single 'truthful' or 'correct' reading and encourages a multitude of interpretations as long as they can be supported by evidence from text and context.

In 'Dickens in Francophone Switzerland', Neil Forsyth and Martine Hennard Dutheil de la Rochère provide a good overview of publications on the reception of Dickens, which Herbert Foltinek complements with his study on Dickens in German-speaking Switzerland.[22] However, these surveys adopt a different methodology from the one taken in this present work. Whereas Hollington's book deals with the image of Dickens *in* Switzerland and the mostly posthumous reaction to his works, our interest lies in the topic of Dickens *and* Switzerland, no matter where the material was published. These two approaches sometimes merge, of course, as in Gustav Schirmer's 'Charles Dickens und die Schweiz' from 1912. Beautifully set in old German type, Schirmer somewhat gloomily asserts that Dickens's three stays in Switzerland were not nearly as inspiring as those in America, Italy and France. In contrast to the 'powerful' and 'extremely famous' works which deal with the other places Dickens visited, Switzerland has to content itself with some pages in *Little Dorrit* and *David Copperfield*, 'some references' in his letters and a novel of 'doubtful

---

[20] Paul-Emile Schazmann, *Charles Dickens in Switzerland*, transl. H. P. B. Betlem (Lausanne: Swiss National Tourist Office, 1972).
[21] See Conclusion, 169.
[22] Neil Forsyth and Martine Hennard Dutheil de la Rochère, 'Dickens in Francophone Switzerland' in Hollington, *The Reception of Charles Dickens in Europe*, vol. 2, 272; ibid., 252.

quality and origin' – by which he means *No Thoroughfare*, which Dickens wrote in collaboration with Wilkie Collins.[23]

In many ways, Schirmer's assessment is representative of other discussions of Dickens and Switzerland: facts are often incomplete, misrepresented or distorted. Dickens visited the country at least four times and left more references to Switzerland than have been mentioned so far. Because critics did – and often still do – not know what kind of evidence to look for, they abandon or dismiss the subject prematurely. Yet, the topic of Dickens and Switzerland takes many forms which transcend or trouble the distinctions between the biographical, fictional, narrative and epistolary. Experience and imagination often merge in memories which find an outlet in novels, short stories, articles and letters. Dickens's attitudes towards Switzerland are frequently found in remote and unexpected places. Some of the material which can tell us more has only recently been made accessible or deemed interesting enough for research. One such example is Susan Rossi-Wilcox's re-publication and study of Catherine Dickens's book of recipes, *What Shall We Have for Dinner?* Her analysis shows that the Dickens's journeys abroad also had some long-term impact on what they ate. She states that 'Lausanne provided a wealth of experiences and at least one recipe for Catherine, Swiss Pudding, an apple dessert'.[24]

Switzerland, or rather, a particular group of Swiss people, also figure in Dickens's *A Child's History of England*, which appeared in his magazine, *Household Words*, in 1853. Here, he says of Cromwell that

> Over and above all this, Oliver found that the VAUDOIS, or protestant people of the valleys of Lucerne, were insolently treated by the Catholic powers, and were even put to death for their religion, in an audacious and bloody manner. Instantly, he informed those powers that this was a thing which Protestant England would not allow; and he speedily carried his point through the might of his great name, and established their right to worship God in peace after their own harmless manner.[25]

---

[23] Gustav Schirmer, 'Charles Dickens und die Schweiz', offprint from *Neue Zürcher Zeitung* (1912), 1; 2. The author's translation.

[24] Susan Rossi-Wilcox, *Dinner for Dickens. The Culinary History of Mrs Charles Dickens' Menu Books. Including a Transcript of* What Shall We Have For Dinner? *by 'Lady Maria Clutterbuck'* (Trowbridge: Prospect Books, 2005), 153. Unlike in Italy, the Dickenses hired a local cook in Lausanne, named Fanchette. Dickens mentions her in a humorous letter to Forster, but nothing more is known of her. See to Forster, 9 and 10 August 1846, *Letters*, vol. 4, 601.

[25] Dickens, *A Child's History of England* in *Master Humphrey's Clock and A Child's History of England* (London: Oxford University Press, 1963), 490.

8   *Dickens and Switzerland*

In his own 'history', Dickens redefines 'vaudois', which describes the inhabitants of the canton the Vaud, rather than the Protestant people from Lucerne. In an echo of the story of William Tell, a plot with which he had been familiar since his youth and which will be discussed in Chapter 1, Dickens replaces an English freedom fighter with the Swiss one. He also reviews the only revolution he had ever witnessed himself, the first skirmishes of the Sonderbund War, through a historical perspective. This links his personal experience, the 1846 stay in Lausanne, with the histories of his native England and that of Switzerland through Cromwell and the Lucerne Protestants, respectively.

Something Wrong Somewhere, or Amendments

The lack of critical studies on Dickens and Switzerland may explain two recent and rather inaccurate comments. In 2014, it was claimed that

> Dickens often had to race to finish the latest instalment of his serially published novels on time. Despite the urgency of meeting a deadline, he couldn't simply sit at his desk and write until he was finished. He needed to walk every day. Dickens wrote the novel *Dombey and Son* – released in twenty monthly instalments starting in October 1846, then published as a single volume by Bradbury & Evans in 1848 – at a painstakingly slow pace while he stayed in Lausanne, Switzerland. The speed at which he wrote was a direct reflection of how little he exercised at the time. He blamed his creative difficulties on 'the absence of streets and numbers of figures'. Without somewhere to walk, it was impossible for Dickens to maintain his daily work regimen.[26]

This assessment is flawed on several levels. First of all, there is ample evidence that Dickens walked extensively in Switzerland. One of the first things he reported back to Forster was that there were 'all manner of walks' in Lausanne.[27] Forster confirms that Dickens went on 'Regular evening walks of nine or ten miles [...] and thoughts of his books were already stirring in him'.[28] In July, Dickens told Forster that he had set off 'last night at six o'clock, in accordance with my usual custom, for a long walk'.[29] At the height

[26] Celia Johnson, 'Pedestrian Adventures', *Poets & Writers* 42, no. 1 (2014): 51.
[27] To Forster, ?13–14 June 1846, *Letters*, vol. 4, 561.
[28] Forster, *Life of Dickens*, 414.
[29] To Forster, 5 July 1846, *Letters*, vol. 4, 580.

of his personal troubles in Switzerland, Dickens still reported to have 'walked my fifteen miles a day constantly, at a great pace'.[30] As late as 1869, Dickens told an acquaintance that during his stay in Lausanne he 'scoured the whole neighbourhood perpetually. I know every foot of the ground about Vevay [sic], and have scaled all the hills thereabout, and enjoyed all the weathers'.[31] In Switzerland, Dickens was missing his 'magic lantern' of a large city's crowded streets, but not the opportunity to walk as such.[32] Walking was not the problem in Lausanne, nor was *Dombey*. In fact, as I will argue in Chapter 2, Dickens's unsettled mood and restlessness were not caused by Lausanne's rural setting, but had other origins.

A more seriously tendentious reading can be found in Lillian Nayder's otherwise wonderful *Unequal Partners*, which deals with the professional relationship and friendship between Dickens and Wilkie Collins. In her discussion of *No Thoroughfare*, the 1867 Christmas novel and play which Collins and Dickens wrote together, she points out:

> Frequently compared to the Arctic regions explored by Franklin, the Swiss Alps were considered a largely unknown and perilous territory to be charted and conquered, a 'wild' landscape suggesting 'moral savagery.'[33]

The undiscussed connection between *No Thoroughfare* and *The Frozen Deep*, another co-written play by Dickens and Collins, is certainly justified, yet other aspects of her argument are quite misleading.[34] Nayder also connects the composition of *No Thoroughfare* to the 'manly regiment of Alpine adventure' when Dickens returned to Switzerland in 1853 with Wilkie Collins and Augustus Egg.[35] She reads the play through the lens of

> an extensive collection of narratives in which manly character is revitalized and manhood inspired – in which English mountaineers, at once patriarchs and imperialists, band together to conquer a savage, feminine land.[36]

---

[30] To Forster, ?30 November 1846, *Letters*, vol. 4, 671.
[31] To Charles Eliot Norton, 26 June 1869, *Letters*, vol. 12, 372.
[32] To Forster, 30 August 1846, *Letters*, vol. 4, 613.
[33] Lillian Nayder, *Unequal Partners. Charles Dickens, Wilkie Collins, and Victorian Authorship* (Ithaca, NY: Cornell University Press, 2001), 151.
[34] Ibid., 151.
[35] Ibid.
[36] Ibid., 150.

10 *Dickens and Switzerland*

However, by 1853 Dickens had already visited Switzerland three times, and neither his letters nor his fiction suggest that any of the journeys were undertaken to impact the 'manliness' of either Dickens or his travelling companions. Dickens's remarks in his letters from 1853 about 'a variety of gymnastic exercises with a pole, superadded' and being called 'A strong Intrepid' by one of the guides are humorous and mock the mountaineering pioneers rather than support them.[37] As far as we know, Dickens never wandered off the 'beaten track' in Switzerland, and his admiration for Albert Smith, the famous mountaineer and one of the founding members of the Alpine Club, was rather limited. In a letter to Mark Lemon he called him 'the bothering Albert', though Dickens employed Albert's brother, Arthur, as the manager for his amateur theatrical tour and the public readings.[38]

If Switzerland is Dickens's equivalent to Rider Haggard's feminised African landscape in *King Solomon's Mines*, he is certainly less explicit, more cautious and less simplistic in drafting a gendered environment. As will be explored in Chapter 2, the Swiss valley in which David Copperfield finds a 'long-unwonted sense of beauty and tranquillity' and a rich fertility certainly suggests 'feminised' qualities. The 'forests of dark fir, cleaving the wintry snow-drift, wedge-like, and stemming the avalanche' of the higher regions, however, are rather 'masculine'. Rather than the resisting, relentless female which Nayder sees, the Switzerland described in *David Copperfield* is a compound of 'masculine' and 'feminine' qualities:

> The bases of the mountains forming the gorge in which the little village lay, were richly green; and high above this gentler vegetation, grew forests of dark fir, cleaving the wintry snow-drift, wedge-like, and stemming the avalanche. Above these, were range upon range of craggy steeps, grey rock, bright ice, and smooth verdure-specks of pasture, all gradually blending with the crowning snow.[39]

From a 'feminised' place the glance rises upwards, towards an oddly mixed landscape, in which grey rock and smooth verdure-specks of pasture blend with each other and climax in snow. The most explicit feminine landscape in this description is probably the gorge, in which the little village, human life, lies. This enclosure offers safety, comfort and domesticity, but, at the same time, it is threatening and mortally dangerous, due to the avalanches that occur. The feminine

---

[37] Dickens quoted in ibid., 151.
[38] To Mark Lemon, 21 April 1855, *Letters*, vol. 7, 597.
[39] Charles Dickens, *David Copperfield*, ed. Nina Burgis (Oxford: Clarendon Press, 1981), 697.

An Introduction to Dickens and Switzerland   11

is helplessly exposed to this ever-lurking male threat – a topic not entirely new to Dickens scholars. The combination of the 'masculine' and 'feminine' spheres which is accomplished in this landscape explains its inherent attraction.

Nayder further claims that 'In traveling to Switzerland at mid-century, Dickens and his countrymen imagined themselves journeying to a savage region with ties to the East, a land they were destined to chart and develop'.[40] This certainly goes too far. Thanks to his connections and love for the theatre, Dickens was familiar with some of the traditions and customs of the country, even prior to his first visit in 1844. The country was in no need of being charted and developed – it had been one of the most popular travelling destinations for the English since the rise of the Grand Tour in the 1750s and was neither under-developed nor savage. All of the major passes which Dickens crossed, the Simplon, the Gotthard and the St Bernard, had been in use for centuries.

The connection Nayder is trying to establish between savage Switzerland and the East dwells on an archaeological article on 'primitive' finds in Lake Moosseedorf as well as a story called 'Grandfather Blacktooth' which appeared in *All the Year Round* in 1864.[41] Primitive, however, does not equal 'savage' and the author of the Moosseedorf piece – Chauncey Hare Townshend, Dickens's close friend who had lived in Switzerland for a long time – points out that the finds are 'indubitably of a period far anterior to the Roman conquest' and that the skulls he was shown were 'unintellectual, but not cruel like some of later savage nations'.[42] In fact, the article puts great emphasis on the relative advancement of the colony from Moosseedorf, outlining that 'the ingenuity displayed in the structure of these peculiar instruments betokened a people already somewhat advanced out of the first state of barbarism' and that they 'were already sufficiently advanced in civilisation, to have made the first step towards commerce by import, or barter'.[43] In the article, Homer is invoked and the discoveries admiringly turn into the 'subaqueous Pompeiis of Switzerland', the remains of which seem to have the same 'touching and human effect' on the modern spectator, like those from their younger Roman counterpart.[44]

[40] Nayder, *Unequal Partners*, 152.
[41] Ibid., 152.
[42] Chauncey Hare Townshend, 'Subterranean Switzerland', *All the Year Round*, 5 November 1859, 26; James Hamilton Fyfe, 'Grandfather Blacktooth', *All the Year Round*, 10 September 1864.
[43] Townshend, 'Subterranean Switzerland', 27.
[44] Ibid., 29.

12   *Dickens and Switzerland*

The frequency of German vocabulary in 'Grandfather Blacktooth', the protagonist's consultation of 'his Berlepsch' instead of John Murray's *Handbook for Travellers in Switzerland* and the plot's setting in the Grisons, a region which Dickens never visited, strongly suggest that someone else, and not Dickens, wrote the tale.[45] The alpine hunter's 'Chinese aspect' which Nayder alludes to is not likened to the man as an 'Alpine hunter', but merely describes his 'keen wild restless look about the eyes'.[46] Dickens was impressed with Swiss prisons, the country's education system and its charitable institutions, such as the Asylum for the Blind, of which he became a frequent visitor. He did, however, also become interested in the notion of the 'savage' while in Switzerland – not in relation to the Swiss population as such, but the children and young adults he met at the asylum.[47]

I cannot agree with Nayder's claims that 'in *All the Year Round*, Dickens flaunts the technological prowess of the English, which will domesticate the Swiss "wilds"' and that 'While the Alpine peaks are represented as savage, so too are those living in the valleys'.[48] Neither in Dickens's fiction nor in his letters are the Swiss described as degenerated, ill or savage. Quite the opposite is the case. Even before travelling to Switzerland in the 1840s, he had become familiar with some of the most famous Swiss theatrical plots of the time and had made friends with Jean François Degex, the Swiss landlord of the Prince of Wales Hotel off Leicester Square, and his sons.[49] In 1846 he told Forster that it was

> *unjust to call the Swiss* the Americans of the Continent. They have not the sweetness and grace of the Italians, or the agreeable manners of the better specimens of French peasantry, but they are admirably educated (the schools of this canton are extraordinarily good, in every little village), and always prepared to give a civil and pleasant answer. [...] I never saw more obliging servants, or people who did their work so truly *with a will*. And in point of cleanliness, order, and punctuality to the moment, they are unrivalled.[50]

---

[45] John Murray, *Murray's Handbook for Travellers in Switzerland 1838*. The Victorian Library (Leicester: Leicester University Press, 1970). Fyfe, 'Grandfather Blacktooth', 112.

[46] Ibid., 113.

[47] To Forster, ?12 July 1846, *Letters*, vol. 4, 585.

[48] Nayder, *Unequal Partners*, 151.

[49] To W. H. Ainsworth, 30 October 1837, *Letters*, vol. 1, 325, 325n1.

[50] To Forster, ?28 June 1846, *Letters*, vol. 4, 574.

An Introduction to Dickens and Switzerland   13

Just six weeks later he revised his view of the Swiss for the better:

> They are a genuine people, these Swiss. There is better metal in them than in all the stars and stripes of all the fustian banners of the so-called, and falsely called, U-nited States. They are a thorn in the sides of European despots, and a good wholesome people to live near Jesuit-ridden Kings on the brighter side of the mountains.[51]

This is hardly the 'savage' population of a 'wild' country which Nayder presents. By the end of his stay, he wrote to another friend:

> The Newspapers seem to know as much about Switzerland as about the Esquimaux Country. I should like to shew you the people as they are here, or in the Canton de Vaud – their wonderful education – splendid schools – comfortable homes – great intelligence – and noble independence of character. It is the fashion among the English to decry them, because they are not servile.[52]

Dickens, at the conclusion of his stay in Lausanne, admitted that 'Something of the *goître* and *crétin* influence seems to settle on my spirits sometimes, on the lower ground'. Yet, he exclaimed afterwards: 'How sorry, ah yes! How sorry I shall be to leave the little society nevertheless. We have been thoroughly good-humoured and agreeable together, and I'll always give a hurrah for the Swiss and Switzerland' and, more theatrically in another letter, 'my hat shall ever be ready to be thrown up, and my glove ever be ready to be thrown down for Switzerland'.[53] In this matter, Nayder's assessment is therefore too simplistic and one-dimensional. It is true, however, that Dickens's representation of the Swiss in his fiction sometimes differed in interesting ways from that in his letters. As will be discussed in Chapter 2, many of his fictional accounts display a fascination with goitres and 'idiots', but by no means does he represent all Swiss citizens in this way.[54] The 'idiots' and goitre-ridden characters are mostly found on the Alpine foothills. They are beings who live in the in-between area of the 'masculinised' higher regions and the 'feminiscd' lowlands. Intriguingly, the latter also have a childlike dimension, with Dickens frequently likening the objects in the valleys to toys.

---

[51] To Forster, 9 and 10 August 1846, *Letters*, vol. 4, 601.

[52] To Douglas Jerrold, 24 October 1846, *Letters*, vol. 4, 644–5.

[53] To Forster, 13 November 1846, *Letters*, vol. 4, 656 and to Landor, 22 November 1846, *Letters*, vol. 4, 661.

[54] The author acknowledges that the use of these terms is no longer acceptable and, rightly so, deemed offensive. As these words are from Dickens's original text, the decision has been made not to change them, but to use quote marks to indicate the fact that they are inappropriate in a contemporary context.

Dickens's most autobiographical novel, *David Copperfield*, is an exception in its representation of the Swiss, as it is closest to that of Dickens's letters. In Switzerland, Copperfield says:

> It was not long, before I had almost as many friends in the valley as in Yarmouth: and when I left it, before the winter set in, for Geneva, and came back in the spring, their cordial greetings had a homely sound to me, although they were not conveyed in English words.[55]

Dickens's treatment of the Swiss and their country is therefore a great deal more layered and deserves a more careful treatment than Nayder is allowing here. She is certainly right to point out that 'Alpine explorers speak of the mountains as "virgin peaks" to be "taken"'[56] thus attributing to mountain travel the vocabulary of both sexual conquest and military campaigns – yet Dickens himself never does it. According to the Hyper-Concordance of Dickens's works, the word 'virgin' appears less than forty times in his fiction.[57] Not one of these moments stands in connection with mountains or climbing. Even though Dickens may have published – but not written – an article in *All the Year Round* in 1865, 'reminding us that the valleys and lakes are the proper region for women in Switzerland, not the mountain peaks and passes, where wives and daughters are all-too-apt to lose their footing', we know that Catherine as well as the wives of his Swiss friends accompanied their husbands on the mountain excursions.[58] Switzerland was a popular country for female travellers, not only because of its picturesque scenery but also because of its pre-established and well-trodden tracks. This is also reflected in the relatively large number of Victorian novels in which women travel to Switzerland. Even though her idea may be somewhat too extravagant, Paulina tells Lucy Snowe in *Villette* that she would like to go 'to Switzerland, and [climb] Mount Blanck; and some day we shall sail over to South America, and walk to the top of Kim-kim-borazo'.[59]

This book cannot make up for all the lost opportunities to integrate Switzerland into Dickensian discourse, nor touch on every single aspect which connects Dickens and his writing with the country.

---

[55] Dickens, *David Copperfield*, 699.

[56] Nayder, *Unequal Partners*, 152.

[57] The Victorian Literary Studies Archive, Hyper-Concordance, Graduate School of Languages and Cultures, Nagoya University, Japan, accessed 31 January 2024: http://victorian-studies.net/concordance/dickens/

[58] Nayder, *Unequal Partners*, 155; the article referred to is E. S. Dixon, 'Foreign Climbs', *All the Year Round*, 2 September 1865, 135–6; on his friends' wives being part of the travelling party, see, for example, to Forster, ?6 September 1846, *Letters*, vol. 4, 618.

[59] Charlotte Brontë, *Villette*, ed. Helen Cooper (London: Penguin, 2004), 34.

Nonetheless, I hope that this study will contribute to showing that the author's examination of the country, his several journeys and his five-month stay were meaningful both for his career and his writing. In my research I have touched on some topics related to Switzerland which I find particularly noteworthy, either because they have been so far neglected or not considered with the critical assessment they deserve. Dickens's involvement with the place and its inhabitants was deeper both on a personal and professional level, and was more relevant to his work, than has generally been admitted so far. In fact, Dickens came to love the country with an incomprehensibly obstinate determination that puzzled friends and critics alike. He let himself be carried away with prejudice far too favourable and generous. Dickens's journeys in the 1840s and 1850s shaped his attitude towards and perception of the place, but, as Chapter 1 will show, his introduction to Switzerland had started much earlier. This (undoubtedly sometimes exaggerated) admiration and infatuation for the country and its people had its dawn in Dickens's childhood where his one great passion, the theatre, provided numerous opportunities to familiarise himself with popular images of the country. It was in theatre pits and other entertainment venues that the young Dickens was introduced to late Romantic and early Victorian images of a country that had been identified as a place of beauty, adventure and the sublime.

Chapter 1

Performing Switzerland

'In the name of wonder, idleness, and folly!' said Mr Gradgrind, leading each away by a hand; 'what do you do here?' 'Wanted to see what it was like,' returned Louisa shortly.

Hard Times, Chapter 3

A *Loophole*, or Switzerland and Nineteenth-Century British Entertainment

At the symbolic heart of the British nation, between Buckingham Palace and Downing Street, stands a building inspired by an architecture that is foreign. Since its construction in 1841, it has, just as many others of its kind, become so consolidated with British culture that hardly anyone would perceive it as alien or exotic. This building is Duck Island Cottage, a Swiss chalet-style edifice, planned by John Burgess Watson. Originally used as the Bird Keeper's Cottage, it now houses the London Historic Parks and Gardens Trust. From the beginning of the nineteenth century, Swiss architecture, folklore and traditions had experienced a phenomenal surge in popularity. Dickens, who owned a Swiss chalet at Gad's Hill from 1865 onwards, found it 'a very pretty thing', and they became fashionable as picturesque objects of prestige throughout the nineteenth century.[1] Between 1803 and 1804 an inn called 'The Swiss Tavern' was built in the part of London which is still known as Swiss Cottage today, and in 1853, Victoria

---

[1] To Forster, 7 January 1865, *Letters*, vol. 11, 3.

had a chalet erected for her children at their holiday retreat on the Isle of Wight.[2]

Long before he visited Switzerland for the first time in 1844, Dickens had had ample opportunity to familiarise himself with Swiss iconography, traditions and way of life – or at least with what the English of the first half of the nineteenth century perceived them to be. In 1842, Dickens wrote from America:

> So far, we have had this Hotel nearly to ourselves. It is a large square house standing on a bold height, with over-hanging eaves like a Swiss Cottage; and a wide, handsome gallery, outside every story. These Colonnades make it look so very light, that it has exactly the appearance of a house built with a pack of cards; and I live in bodily terror, lest any man should venture to step out of a little observatory on the roof, and crush the whole structure with one stamp of his foot.[3]

This passage is doubly remarkable: on the one hand, it demonstrates Dickens's knowledge that the comparison of the hotel to 'a Swiss Cottage' would trigger a very specific set of associations in the recipient of his letter. 'A Swiss Cottage' is the more familiar, better-known term in this description. Despite its foreignness – it is not English, after all – it is the more intimate and ordinary of the two. On the other hand, when he wrote this letter, Dickens had, in fact, not yet set foot on Helvetic soil. Nonetheless, he had already had numerous encounters with Switzerland and met some of its citizens without having left England.

David Copperfield recollects how his father 'had left in a little room up-stairs [...] a collection of books' and Forster asserts that it is 'one of the many passages in *Copperfield* which are literally true'.[4] Some of these books feature Swiss characters, most of them marginal in the extreme, but present nonetheless: a Swiss valet appears in *Roderick Random*, who helps the narrator find his friend Strap in France; there is a Swiss *valet-de-chambre* who appears on several occasions in *Peregrine Pickle*; and in *Humphry Clinker*, Tobias Smollett's last picaresque novel, we learn that 'a Swiss talking French was more easily understood than a Parisian'.[5] But Dickens is often particularly interested in these figures, as John Bowen points

---

[2] Christopher Hibbert, *Queen Victoria: A Personal History* (London: HarperCollins, 2001), 191.

[3] To Henry Austin, 1 May 1842, *Letters*, vol. 3, 229.

[4] Dickens, *David Copperfield*, 48; Forster, *Life of Dickens*, 8.

[5] Tobias Smollett, *The Expedition of Humphry Clinker* (London: Harrison and Co., 1785), 114.

out: 'Dickens's fiction is repeatedly drawn to figures – like Smike in *Nicholas Nickleby*, or Barnaby Rudge – who are at or beyond the margins of the communities of the novel they inhabit.'[6]

Dickens was 'first taken to the theatre at the very tenderest age' by the family friend and 'a sort of cousin' James Lamert, and this visit kindled a lifelong passion for acting, performing and the stage in the young child.[7] Dickens edited the memoirs of the theatre clown Joseph Grimaldi in 1838, who had entertained generations of nineteenth-century children and adults.[8] Throughout the nineteenth century, a large number of performances drawing on all things 'Swiss' appeared. Between the mid-1820s and the 1840s, when Dickens would go 'to the theatre nearly every night for three years', 'Swiss' performances reached a peak.[9]

Thérèse, the Orphan of Geneva was among those performances which became very popular, with no less than four, probably five, versions debuting between spring and autumn 1821 in various London theatres. Clarkson Stanfield, one of Dickens's close friends, was a 'professional designer and painter of stage scenery' and provided the scenery for the play.[10] He was 'elected to the Royal Academy in 1835' and 'highly esteemed by Ruskin as one of the finest realists among the English painters'.[11] 'Stanny', as Dickens called him, illustrated some of the Christmas Books, including *The Battle of Life*, which Dickens wrote in Switzerland. He created the backgrounds for 'a number of Dickens's private and public amateur theatricals', and Dickens dedicated *Little Dorrit*, which features one of the most prominent Swiss scenes in his writing, to Stanfield.[12]

Stanfield was also known as a painter of dioramas and panoramas, another popular art form at the time.[13] Swiss scenes as examples of spectacular landscapes were part of the genre from

---

[6] John Bowen, *Other Dickens* (Oxford: Oxford University Press, 2000), 20.
[7] Forster, *Life of Dickens*, 10.
[8] Paul Schlicke, *Dickens and Popular Entertainment* (London: Allen & Unwin, 1985), 52.
[9] Ibid., 234; see also Allardyce Nicoll, *A History of English Drama 1660–1900. Vol. 4: Early Nineteenth-Century Drama* (Cambridge: Cambridge University Press, 1955) and *A History of English Drama 1660–1900. Vol. 5: Late Nineteenth-Century Drama* (Cambridge: Cambridge University Press, 1962).
[10] Malcolm Andrews in Schlicke, *Oxford Reader's Companion to Dickens*, 550.
[11] Ibid., 551.
[12] Ibid.
[13] Katie Trumpener and Tim Barringer, eds., *On the Viewing Platform. The Panorama between Canvas and Screen* (New Haven, CT and London: Yale University Press, 2020), 97.

Performing Switzerland   19

the beginning.[14] A 'fairly successful' example was the *Panorama of Geneva and Its Lake* by Barker and Burford in London, which was shown around 1826 and had become popular enough to be exported to the United States.[15] Barker and Burford also exhibited other panoramas showing Swiss scenes, such as *A View of Mont Blanc* in 1837 and *A View of the Bernees Alps* in 1852. Whether Dickens saw any of them, however, is not clear.

Dickens recalls some of the many plays with Swiss plots, perhaps even *Thérèse*, when, in a piece called 'A Few Conventionalities', which appeared in *Household Words* in 1851, he wondered:

> Who knows how it came about that the young Swiss maiden in the ballet should, as an established custom, revolve, on her nuptial morning, so airily and often, that at length she stands before us, for some seconds, like a beautiful white muslin pen-wiper? Why is her bed-chamber always immediately over the cottage-door? Why is she always awakened by three taps of her lover's hands? Why does her mother always spin? Why is her residence invariably near a bridge? In what Swiss canton do the hardy mountaineers pursue the chamois, in silkstockings, pumps, blue breeches, cherry-coloured bows, and their shirt-sleeves?[16]

The Swiss maid and peasant became veritable types. This is also reflected in many titles of plays performed on nineteenth-century stages: there were *Linda of Chamouni, Geneviève, the Maid of Switzerland, Judith of Geneva, Julian and Agnes; or, The Monks of the Great St. Bernard, Linda and Gertrude; or, The Swiss Chalet, Mariette; or, the Maid of Switzerland, Nathalie; or, the Swiss Milkmaid, The Sisters; or The Heroines of Switzerland, The Flower of Lucerne, The Outcast of Lausanne; or, Claudine of Switzerland, The Swiss Cottage; or, Why don't She Marry Him?, The Swiss Girl; or, The Parricide, The Lover and the Avenger, Pauvrette; or, Under the Snow* and many more.[17]

Some 'Swiss' pieces, like *Thérèse*, became so popular that they were corrupted and adapted, and found further life in farces and burlesques, such as *Tereza Tomkins; or, The Fruits of Geneva.*[18] However, this process would also work the other way: Daniel

[14] Richard Altick, *The Shows of London* (Cambridge, MA: Belknap, 1978), 166; Bernard Comment, *The Panorama* (London: Reaktion Books, 1999), 59.
[15] Ibid., 57.
[16] Dickens, 'A Few Conventionalities', *Household Words*, 28 June 1851, 314.
[17] See Nicoll, *History of English Drama*, vols. 4 and 5.
[18] Nicoll, *History of English Drama*, vol. 4, 359.

Defoe's *Robinson Crusoe* – one of Dickens's favourite books – became the model for *The Swiss Family Robinson* (1812), written by Johann David Wyss, a Swiss pastor.[19] Due to the English original and despite, or perhaps because of, its foreign origins, the book became very popular in nineteenth-century England, and was also adapted for the stage in various shapes and forms. Dickens knew the story and jokingly claimed in a letter that some family friends were 'getting up an involuntary representation of the Family Robinson Crusoe. I understand that Mrs. Eaton is strong in pantomime, but is seldom easy in her words'.[20]

There was also a range of stage adaptations of Byron's *Manfred*, partly set in Switzerland, but most popular of all was indubitably *William Tell*. In 1852, Albert Smith, the famous traveller and entertainer, opened his extravagant show *The Ascent of Mont Blanc*, sometimes described as a series of dioramas or a moving panorama, at the Egyptian Hall in London, just as the Barker and Burford panorama was presenting another Swiss scene near Leicester Square.[21] Smith had imported real chamois and some St Bernard dogs from Switzerland, which he put on display for his audience. Two of their offspring were presented to the Prince Consort and another one was given to Dickens, who must have been very familiar with the show.[22] Dickens's St Bernard dogs (or crosses) feature frequently in his letters and were an integral part of his life at Gad's Hill until his death.[23] With a nod to the earlier and very popular Swiss-themed stage performances as well as to Smith's own show, the dog was called Linda. The *Ascent*, Richard Altick claims, was 'one of the biggest hits of the whole Victorian era'.[24]

As an avid theatre-goer, Dickens must have been familiar with most of these plays. Reference to Swiss performances in Dickens appear in different shapes: some are well disguised and implicit, such as that to Josephine Sleary's 'graceful equestrian Tyrolean flower-act' in *Hard Times*, which we will discuss in detail below. In some cases, we know what Dickens saw due to references in his letters, such as

---

[19] Johann Wyss, *The Swiss Family Robinson*, ed. John Seelye (Oxford: Oxford University Press, 1991). The story was first translated into English from a French version by William Godwin and his second wife, Mary Jane Clairmont.

[20] To Mark Lemon, 26 September 1847, *Letters*, vol. 5, 168.

[21] Kunst- und Ausstellungshalle der Bundesrepublik Deutschland, ed., *Sehnsucht: Das Panorama als Massenunterhaltung des 19. Jahrhunderts* (Frankfurt and Basel: Stroemfeld/Roter Stern, 1993), 241; Stephan Oettermann, *The Panorama. History of a Mass Medium* (New York: Zone Books, 1997), 131.

[22] Oettermann, *The Panorama*, 477.

[23] Beryl Gray, *The Dog in the Dickensian Imagination* (Farnham: Ashgate, 2014), 37; 65.

[24] Altick, *The Shows of London*, 475.

in the case of 'The Merry Swiss Boy', a popular song, which was frequently performed at the time.[25] Others are unmistakeable, such as Maître Voigt's 'large musical box' in *No Thoroughfare*, which 'often trilled away at the Overture to Fra Diavolo, or a Selection from William Tell, with a chirruping liveliness'.[26] Dickens's fascination with waterfalls and automatons reflects a common Victorian craze with representations of Switzerland. Among an abundance of other images, there was a panorama of eighteen Swiss cantons in Piccadilly in 1825, which intended to make visitors feel 'as though they were actually traversing' the country and made reference to William Tell, Voltaire, Gibbon, Rousseau and Kemble.[27] Dickens's letters are a treasure trove for finding out what he saw. From Paris, he wrote to a friend:

> At the Cirque, there is a new show-piece called the French Revolution, in which there is a representation of the National Convention, and a series of battles (fought by some five hundred people who look like fifty thousand) that are wonderful in their extraordinary vigor [*sic*] and truth.[28]

Nothing seems to point to Switzerland in this description, yet the editors of Dickens's letters quote a review in the notes, which confirms that the piece ended with the lavishly staged Battle of Zurich in Switzerland.[29]

In this chapter, I will argue that many of Dickens's allusions and references to Switzerland can and should be read within the context of the many stage performances with 'Swiss' subjects. Switzerland in Dickens's writing becomes a repertoire for representation, performance and reproduction, which he uses in order to explore some of the themes that haunt so many of his texts: the arbitrary distinctions between human and inhuman, nature and the supernatural, sanity and insanity, sickness and health, living and dying, affluence and barrenness, excess and restraint. Dickens found some inspiration for his writing on Switzerland in the popular entertainment of the time and performances on stage. After the brief encounters he had had with Swiss characters in the books he read as a child, these performances were the next and likely most intense point of contact

---

[25] Charles Dickens, *Hard Times*, ed. Kate Flint (London: Penguin, 2003), 18; to David Roberts, 19 June 1860, *Letters*, vol. 9, 265.
[26] Wilkie Collins and Charles Dickens, *No Thoroughfare* (London: Chapman and Hall, 1890), 213.
[27] Altick, *The Shows of London*, 395.
[28] To the Countess of Blessington, 27 January 1847, *Letters*, vol. 5, 14.
[29] Ibid., 14n5.

22 Dickens and Switzerland

with representations of 'Swiss' culture before he visited the country itself. The theatre taught him about the scenes and characters which an audience – potentially his audience – would be able to identify with Switzerland, and it also gave him an insight into their possible response. In playhouses, Dickens learned what was familiar and unfamiliar to a British audience in terms of 'Swiss' characters and stage settings, what they would or would not expect.

If Dickens's books are performative, his writing on Switzerland must be too – and visibly so, as I will argue, because many of them draw creatively and richly on the stage performances Dickens saw, in character, form and plot.[30] The wealth of context on Dickens and Switzerland has largely remained unexplored, which explains this chapter's relative descriptiveness and focus on context. I will construct a narrative of how English popular culture adopted a range of specific Swiss plots, the way they were presented to a British audience and how they influenced Dickens's writing.

It is unsurprising, then, that Dickens employed descriptions, comparisons and allusions connected to the stage when writing from his two first, very short visits to Switzerland. Typical for both the pantomimic mode and Dickens's work are the comedy, a fondness for grotesque distortion and the focus on food. In 1844, his first visit, he wrote to his wife:

> The weather was perfectly fair and bright; and there was neither difficulty nor danger – except the danger that there always must be in such a place, of a horse stumbling on the brink of an immeasurable precipice. In which case, no piece of the unfortunate traveller would be left, large enough, to tell his story in dumb-show. [...] And the Inn (with a German bedstead in it, about the size and shape of a baby's linen-basket) is perfectly clean and comfortable. Butter is so cheap hereabouts, that they bring you a great mass, like the squab of a sofa, for tea.[31]

On the second visit in 1845, Dickens describes to Forster that at an inn,

> a woman in short petticoats, a stomacher, and two immensely long tails of black hair hanging down her back very nearly to her heels, is looking on – apparently dressed for a melodrama, but in reality a waitress at this establishment.[32]

---

[30] Bowen, *Other Dickens*, 1.
[31] To Catherine Dickens, 23 November 1844, *Letters*, vol. 4, 228–9.
[32] To Forster, 15 June 1845, *Letters*, vol. 4, 321.

At the end of this same letter, seemingly out of the blue, Dickens asks: '*Did* I ever tell you the details of my theatrical idea before? Strange, that I should have forgotten it.'[33] Not strange at all, however, that he should have remembered it in Switzerland, which was so strongly connected with the theatre in his mind!

Yet, encounters with Swiss culture in Victorian England also extended beyond the stage. During the nineteenth century many Swiss immigrants settled in England. Some gained fame, such as Madame Tussaud with her waxworks, whereas others kept the courts of justice and the newspapers busy, such as Mrs Manning or François Courvoisier, who both murdered their employers. Although they too managed to offer the English some sort of entertainment, theirs took a different shape to that of Madame Tussaud's, as they were executed in public, attracting large masses of spectators, among whom was Dickens himself.[34]

The 'curious colony of mountaineers' in Soho, which Dickens mentions in *No Thoroughfare*, draws on a historically accurate situation:

> Swiss watchmakers, Swiss silver-chasers, Swiss jewellers, Swiss importers of Swiss musical boxes and Swiss toys of various kinds, draw close together here. Swiss professors of music, painting, and languages; Swiss artificers in steady work; Swiss couriers, and other Swiss servants chronically out of place; industrious Swiss laundresses and clear-starchers; mysteriously existing Swiss of both sexes; Swiss creditable and Swiss discreditable; Swiss to be trusted by all means, and Swiss to be trusted by no means; these diverse Swiss particles are attracted to a centre in the district of Soho. Shabby Swiss eating-houses, coffee-houses, and lodging-houses, Swiss drinks and dishes, Swiss service for Sundays, and Swiss schools for week-days, are all to be found there. Even the native-born English taverns drive a sort of broken-English trade; announcing in their windows Swiss whets and drams, and sheltering in their bars Swiss skirmishes of love an animosity on most nights in the year.[35]

Many Swiss immigrants worked as maids, waiters or in other – usually serving – positions, a fact which is echoed in the wide collection of references to Swiss employees in nineteenth-century literature. However, Dickens also describes what he himself saw, when he visited his uncle, Thomas Barrow. When Dickens was still a child, Barrow

---

[33] Ibid., 322.
[34] Also see Chapter 3, 123ff.
[35] Collins and Dickens, *No Thoroughfare*, 136.

24   *Dickens and Switzerland*

had broken his leg in a fall; and, while laid up with this illness, his lodging was in Gerrard Street, Soho, in the upper part of the house of a worthy gentleman then recently deceased, a bookseller named Manson, [whose widow] lent [Dickens] books to amuse him; among them Miss Porter's *Scottish Chiefs*, Holbein's *Dance of Death*, and George Colman's *Broad Grins*.[36]

Soho often figures in Dickens's fiction, and Jaggers's office in *Great Expectations*, for example, is in Gerrard Street. The great number of Swiss expats living in Victorian Soho is evidenced by the establishment of the Swiss Church in 1775 near Moor Street, before it was relocated to its current location on Endell Street in 1855. There had also been a 'sign of The Thirteen Cantons' in King Street, Golden Square, which 'was adopted in compliment to the thirteen Protestant cantons of Switzerland, and to the numerous natives of that country who at one time took up their residence in the parish of Soho'.[37] Incidentally, one of the books Dickens was given to read, and which turned into one of his favourites, also bears a connection to Switzerland: Francis Douce's edition of the *Dance of Death*, the version which Dickens read and owned, mentions Holbein's stay and work in Basel and outlines the Swiss city's importance for the publication and circulation of Holbein's images.[38] It is unlikely to be a coincidence that the protagonist in *The Frozen Deep*, one of the plays which Dickens and Wilkie Collins wrote collaboratively, is called Richard Wardour, as there was a North Pole pub in Wardour Street, Soho.[39]

Yet, as a young editor, Dickens also dealt with texts written in Switzerland which were adapted and translated for a British audience. On at least two occasions, he refers to stories originally composed by the German-Swiss author Johann Heinrich Zschokke.[40] Even though Zschokke has fallen mostly into oblivion now, he was one of the most-read and renowned historians and writers of his time. Originally from Germany, he took Swiss citizenship and, after travelling the country, moved to Aarau, a small town with a rich history between Basel and Zurich, which has vanished from the stage of public attention almost as entirely as Zschokke himself.

---

[36] Forster, *Life of Dickens*, 17.
[37] Leopold Wagner, *Names and Their Meanings: A Book for the Curious* (London: T. Fisher Unwin, 1897), 190.
[38] Hans Holbein, *The Dance of Death*, ed. Francis Douce (London: William Pickering, 1833).
[39] Wagner, *Names and Their Meanings*, 191.
[40] To Cruikshank, ?24 April 1837, *Letters*, vol. 1, 252 and to E. W. P. Sinnett, ?late May 1837, vol. 1, 265.

Nonetheless, it was none other than Goethe himself who adapted Zschokke's novel *Aballino* into a successful play. While Zschokke's *Blue Wonder*, the first text Dickens refers to, was published in *Bentley's Miscellany*, the second was not. Dickens's motivation to publish these stories seems to have been first and foremost to feed his readership with new and original material.

Switzerland itself appeared relatively frequently in Victorian texts. The examples given here are by no means conclusive: in Wilkie Collins's *Woman in White*, Frederick Fairlie has a Swiss valet; there is a Swiss confectioner in Florence in *Little Dorrit*; in *Middlemarch*, Dorothea and Celia Brooke's early education takes place in a Swiss family in Lausanne. Switzerland and the Swiss appear in all sizes and shapes throughout nineteenth-century literature: in *Oliver Twist*, Nancy reeks of 'a wholesale perfume of Geneva' – a euphemism for the smell of gin.[41] In *Martin Chuzzlewit*, the proofs of the family's 'noble' heritage 'might be heaped upon each other until they formed an Alps of testimony', and Tom Pinch discovers some watches in Salisbury that are 'smaller than Geneva ware'.[42] In *Dombey and Son*, Mrs Skewton remarks that what she has always sighed for 'has been to retreat to a Swiss farm, and live entirely surrounded by cows – and china'.[43] Trollope's *Can You Forgive Her?* features Switzerland as the location of a love plot. In Charlotte Brontë's first novel, *The Professor*, Frances Evans Henri is an orphan whose mother was English, but her father, a pastor, was Swiss.[44] There is a Swiss boat-house in Mary Braddon's *Lady Audley's Secret* and a Swiss soubrette, a lady's maid, in Benjamin Disraeli's *Young Duke*.

These references are for the most part insignificant for the main plot and are rather passing allusions, but this is precisely the point. Despite their marginality, they serve as class denominators, reflect on aspects of the picturesque or serve comedy. Like Dickens, these authors understood the adjective 'Swiss' to be meaningful to their readers so that they did not need to elaborate on it.

There is, however, one novel, which may have had a late, but nonetheless direct influence on Dickens's writing that can be directly traced. Sir Walter Scott was 'an important influence on Dickens's early career', even though his name 'does not appear on the famous childhood

---

[41] Dickens, *Oliver Twist*, ed. Kathleen Tillotson (Oxford: Oxford University Press, 1982), 161.

[42] Dickens, *Martin Chuzzlewit*, ed. Margaret Cardwell (Oxford: Clarendon Press, 1982), 5; 70.

[43] Dickens, *Dombey and Son*, ed. Alan Horsman (Oxford: Clarendon Press, 1974), 284.

[44] Charlotte Brontë, *The Professor*, ed. Heather Glen (London: Penguin, 1989), 167.

reading list in *David Copperfield*'.[45] In the 1830s, Dickens was still rather proud of the fact that George Hogarth, his future wife's father, had been an intimate friend of Scott's and freely boasted of it during the period of his engagement to Catherine. Scott wrote more than just one text about Switzerland. Among them, for example, was the poem *The Battle of Sempach*. Despite the development of Dickens's relationship with Catherine, his reading of Scott may have found a direct echo in his writing as late as in 1867: *No Thoroughfare*'s Marguerite is most likely based on the Swiss heroine in Scott's eponymous *Anne of Geierstein or, The Maiden of the Mist*. Published in 1829, the novel is one of the lesser known works of the Waverley series. Dickens probably read these volumes 'in the early 1830s'.[46]

In a reversal of the 'damsel in distress' plot, both Scott's and Dickens's Swiss heroine save a young Englishman they will later marry. Disguised as merchants, Arthur Philipson, the English hero of Scott's story, and his father, travel through Switzerland at the beginning of the story. Just as in *No Thoroughfare*, the Swiss maiden saves the young Englishman – who, in reality, is of noble descent – from certain death in the mountains after an accident. But whereas Arthur Philipson's fall is self-induced and opens Scott's plot, George Vendale is melodramatically pushed over the cliff by Obenreizer towards the end of *No Thoroughfare*. Both are tales of disguised or unknown identities. Their resolution enables an international marriage between the Englishman and the Swiss maid.

Both women are their uncles' wards when they meet their future husbands. But whereas Arnold Biedermann, Anne's uncle, is a noble ruler, Obenreizer is abusive and treacherous. He shares the physical strength and vigorous appearance of Anne's cousin, Rudolph von Donnerhugel, who is the Englishman's rival in Scott's story. Anne is a picture of virtue:

> Her long fair hair fell down in a profusion of curls, on each side of a face, whose blue eyes, lovely features, and dignified simplicity of expression, implied at once a character of gentleness, and of the self-relying resolution of a mind too virtuous to suspect evil and too noble to fear it. [...]
>
> I have only to add, that the stature of the young person was something above the common size, and that the whole contour of her form, without being in the slightest degree masculine, resembled that

[45] Andrews in Schlicke, *Oxford Reader's Companion to Dickens*, 518; 519.
[46] Walter Scott, *Anne of Geierstein*, ed. J. H. Alexander (Edinburgh: Edinburgh University Press, 2000); Andrews in Schlicke, *Oxford Reader's Companion to Dickens*, 518.

of Minerva, rather than the proud beauties of Juno or the yielding graces of Venus. The noble brow, the well-formed and active limbs, the firm and yet light step – above all, the total absence of anything resembling the consciousness of personal beauty, and the open and candid look, which seemed desirous of knowing nothing that was hidden, and conscious that she herself had nothing to hide, were traits not unworthy of the goddess of wisdom and of chastity.[47]

Note the striking similarity in the description of Marguerite in *No Thoroughfare*, who is a picture of modesty, cleanliness and propriety:

The young lady wore an unusual quantity of fair bright hair, very prettily braided about a rather rounder white forehead than the average English type, and so her face might have been a shade – or say a light – rounder than the average English face, and her figure slightly rounder than the figure of the average English girl at nineteen. A remarkable indication of freedom and grace of limb, in her quiet attitude, and a wonderful purity and freshness of colour in her dimpled face and bright grey eyes, seemed fraught with mountain air. Switzerland too, though the general fashion of her dress was English, peeped out of the fanciful bodice she wore, and lurked in the curious clocked red stocking, and in its little silver-buckled shoe.[48]

Marguerite's Swissness is not only displayed through her expression, but also through her clothing. The differences between her and an 'average English girl at nineteen' seem slight but present, and the blending of this Swiss appearance in an English dress (albeit with a Swiss twist) are understood to be a good match and create the picture of a desirable young woman. In combination with the close attention to detail and the sensual alliteration in the description of the stocking, the verbs 'peeped' and 'lurked' occupy a space of meaning between detailed observation and erotic voyeurism.

Like Marguerite, Anne is described as physically strong and active. Despite this, the two women are not, like Marian Halcombe in Collins's *Woman in White*, 'dark and ugly' creatures, 'crabbed and odd', with 'a large, firm, masculine mouth and jaw; prominent, piercing, resolute brown eyes; and thick, coal-black hair, growing unusually low down on her forehead'.[49] Whereas Marian's physical strength, initiative and free will make her unattractive, the same is not true for Anne and Marguerite.

[47] Scott, *Anne of Geierstein*, 27.
[48] Collins and Dickens, *No Thoroughfare*, 140.
[49] Collins, *The Woman in White*, ed. Matthew Sweet (London: Penguin Classics, 2003), 35.

The Key-Note, or, Swiss Singing and Songs

Switzerland became a small, yet undeniable, part of nineteenth-century British art and entertainment culture, positioned in the space of homely domesticity rather than exotic foreignness. This is reflected in Leman Thomas Rede's *Road to the Stage*, published in 1827 and containing 'an encyclopaedic wealth of information about the provincial theatre and detailed advice for the aspiring stroller'. His list of costumes of 'General Utility' advises the purchase of a 'Peasant's dress, Swiss, French, Spanish, Old English, &c. – for Savoyards of all nations'.[50] These 'Savoyards' were songs performed as interludes either between or within plays, usually presented in appropriate costumes:[51]

> In the theatre as Dickens knew it, a play was virtually never presented on its own. [...] It was customary for an evening's programme to include two, or more, usually three, principal attractions and the performance of dramatic works constituted only a portion of the interest. Between the pieces, the actress who had represented the witch in *Macbeth* would step forward to sing the ballad of Rory O'More; the actor who had portrayed a murderous henchman in the melodrama would perform his celebrated jockey dance.[52]

The performance of folklore – English and foreign – was popular throughout the nineteenth century. One of the best-known Swiss songs was 'The Merry Swiss Boy', often performed as an interlude on stage. Dickens was very familiar with the tune and, as late as 1860, humorously referred to a friend visiting him from Switzerland as his 'merry Swiss boy'.[53]

Charles Mathews (1776–1835), one of the most famous comedians of his day and among Dickens's favourite actors, used to give performances that came to be known as 'At Homes', which consisted

---

[50] Thomas Rede Leman, *The Road to the Stage* (London: Joseph Smith, 1827), 31.

[51] The *OED* links 'Savoyard' to either performers or admirers of Gilbert and Sullivan operas, but the source mentioned above is older than that. The Savoyard being described as 'French, Spanish, Old English, &c.' also excludes the definition of the word describing a 'native or inhabitant' of Savoy. Here it is therefore assumed that 'Savoyard' means the traditional peasant songs performed on stage before the era of Gilbert and Sullivan.

[52] Schlicke, *Dickens and Popular Entertainment*, 52; also see Jane Moody, *Illegitimate Theatre in London, 1770–1840* (Cambridge: Cambridge University Press, 2000).

[53] To David Roberts, 19 June 1860, *Letters*, vol. 9, 265; 265n3.

of 'a mixture of narrative, impersonation and song'.[54] In *Charles Dickens and His Performing Selves*, Malcolm Andrews speaks of Mathews's 'famous virtuoso performance' and calls him 'Dickens's model, if not inspiration for the art of impersonation, and a prototype for the public Readings'.[55] Yet Mathews was also another source for episodic representations of Switzerland and the experience of 'Swissness' through popular English culture. His 'At Homes' appear in some ways as an extension of the Savoyards described above. Among Mathews's songs were

> Comic Songs of The Humours of a Country Fair, and Street Melodies (a medley), including Welsh, French, Scotch, Irish, African, Italian, Swiss, and English aires, [*sic*] with embellishments.[56]

In this list, Swiss songs are only one category among others, but this only highlights its episodic nature. Charles Mathews's *Mémoirs*, written by his wife, give a more detailed description of his performances, including the type of songs that he showcased *entre-acte*:

> After this water-scene we have one of those extraordinary medleys, for which Mr. Mathews is so celebrated. In an attempt to convey an idea of street music he gives us specimens, with accompaniments on the harp, flageolet, violin, and bagpipe, of the national music of Italy, France, Switzerland, Ireland, England, and Scotland, with appropriate dresses and imitations.[57]

In contrast to the range outlined above which also includes exotic 'African' songs, in this quote the 'Swiss' ones appear in a collection limited to European productions. With the exception of Italy and Switzerland, all nations mentioned have close-knit and long-standing cultural, historical and political ties to England. Italy and Switzerland became two of the most popular travel destinations for British travellers when the idea of the Grand Tour was born in the middle of the eighteenth century. Yet Switzerland stands out because, as Sir John Wraight points out in *The Swiss and the British*:

> Indeed Switzerland is the only European nation which Britain has never fought against as an enemy nor alongside as an ally. Both

---

[54] Schlicke, *Dickens and Popular Entertainment*, 234.

[55] Malcolm Andrews, *Charles Dickens and His Performing Selves: Dickens and the Public Readings* (Oxford: Oxford University Press, 2006), 259.

[56] Mrs Mathews, *The Life and Correspondence of Charles Mathews, the Elder. Comedian*, ed. Edmund Yates (London: Routledge, Warne and Routledge, 1860), 449.

[57] Mrs Mathews, *Mémoirs of Charles Mathews, Comedian* (London: Richard Bentley, 1839), vol. 4, 177.

30   *Dickens and Switzerland*

nations have, by and large, been able to choose the degree of their
relations with each other based on a reasoned assessment of each
other's qualities, faults, achievements and place in the world.
Moreover, the Swiss have never posed a threat to Britain's interests
as each of Switzerland's neighbours has at one time or another. Nor
has Britain posed a serious threat to Switzerland.[58]

With a few exceptions, Mathews's selection of songs therefore represented mostly familiar, 'domestic' cultures, which in some cases
had almost come to be understood to be part of Britain's own. It was
not just probable but likely that the wealthier individuals among his
audience, able and keen to travel, had heard some authentic version
of his 'At Homes' in their countries of origin. This was precisely the
experience Dickens would have in Switzerland. However, in his case,
which certainly was no exception, he heard the songs on the British
stage before encountering them in Switzerland.

In June 1846, after having visited Switzerland alone twice, on his
way to and from Italy, Dickens moved his family to Lausanne. In a
letter to Forster he describes a festival the family had attended. The
language Dickens uses here reveals how his earliest associations with
Switzerland were closely tied to the stage:

> There were various booths for eating and drinking, and the selling of
> trinkets and sweetmeats; [...] It was very pretty. In some of the drink-
> ing booths there were parties of German peasants, twenty together
> perhaps, singing national drinking-songs, and making a most exhila-
> rating and musical chorus by rattling their cups and glasses on the
> table and clinking them against each other, to a regular tune. You
> know it as a stage dodge, but the real thing is splendid.[59]

The 'German peasants' are probably Swiss-German-speaking individuals rather than German nationals. Most likely, they were visiting from neighbouring cantons on occasion of the festivities. Both
Dickens and Forster knew Swiss 'national drinking-songs' as what,
according to the *OED*, was a 'clever or adroit expedient or contriv-
ance' in the slang of Victorian England. Experienced in Switzerland
and not in an English theatre, this 'stage dodge' becomes a splendid
'real thing'.

Switzerland's representation in both fiction and singing is episodic
and often incidental. On stage, singing is often used to express a

---

[58] John Wraight, *The Swiss and the British* (Wilton, Salisbury: Michael Russell Ltd.,
1987), 1.
[59] To Forster, 5 July 1846, *Letters*, vol. 4, 580.

Performing Switzerland   31

particular state of mind or a transition, for which Switzerland and its dramatic landscape offer a suitable background. Singing is also associated with childhood memories and reminiscences of 'home' or one's own nation. Following Ian Watt's readings in 'Oral Dickens', singing may also be a socially acceptable version of 'oral patterns of the distant past', and like 'sucking, eating, and speaking [singing] employ[s] the same organs and reflexes – the lips, the tongue, the jaws, the throat, the breathing apparatus'.[60] It has the same 'oral-erotic character' as sucking and eating, and also offers a direct link back to the maternal.

Nostalgia or homesickness in connection with singing was particularly strongly linked to Switzerland. In 1866, George Augustus Sala, one of Dickens's friends, a regular contributor to his magazines and also one of the men who accompanied him to Switzerland in 1853, wrote an article in *All the Year Round*, which he introduced with a discussion of

> a mysterious disease which the doctors find difficult of diagnosis, and from which foreign conscripts are said to suffer. They call it nostalgia, or le mal du pays – in plainer English, home-sickness. We have all read how the bandmasters of the Swiss regiments in the French service were forbidden to play the Ranz des Vaches, lest the melancholy children of the mountains, inspired by the national melody, should run home too quickly to their cows – that is to say, desert.[61]

Unflatteringly, the next examples are dogs, who will 'pine and fret to death for love of the masters they have lost' and the llama, who 'if you beat, or overload, or even insult him, he will, after one glance of tearful reproach from his fine eyes, and one meek wail of expostulation, literally lie himself down and die'.[62]

In Switzerland, David Copperfield experiences a reversal of what the 'foreign conscripts' from Sala's article experience abroad. After the death of his wife, Dora, Copperfield leaves England, and travels 'restlessly from place to place' having 'no purpose, no sustaining soul within me, anywhere'.[63] But one evening, when he wanders into an unnamed valley:

> In the quiet air, there was a sound of distant singing – shepherd voices; but, as one bright evening cloud floated midway along the

[60] Ian Watts, 'Oral Dickens', *Dickens Studies Annual* 3 (1979): 174.
[61] George Augustus Sala, 'Form-Sickness', *All the Year Round*, 20 January 1866, 41.
[62] Ibid., 41.
[63] Dickens, *David Copperfield*, 697.

> mountain's side, I could almost have believed it came from there, and was not earthly music. All at once, in this serenity, great Nature spoke to me; and soothed me to lay down my weary head upon the grass and weep as I had not wept yet, since Dora died![64]

The singing is a sort of nostalgia, but also offers comfort. It triggers earlier memories, both of Copperfield's own mother through the metaphorical invocation of 'great Nature' as well as his dead wife, whom he finally manages to mourn. The fact that it almost seemed as if it came from a 'bright evening cloud' and 'was not earthly music' accentuates the link with the two deceased female figures. The 'sound of distant singing – shepherd voices' and 'great Nature' which speaks to Copperfield not only suggests a return to the long-lost mother herself, but also to the feminine and motherly which Agnes, his future wife, represents. The effect which 'speaking' Nature has on Copperfield is remarkable: it 'soothed me to lay down my weary head upon the grass, and weep as I had not wept yet, since Dora died!' Copperfield experiences a cathartic moment, regaining a childlike state in which 'great Nature' substitutes for his mother. Tears, even though not formed by the mouth, also originate from the head. The dynamics between giving and receiving are worth another thought: speaking and singing are actions of motherly giving, very much in line with Agnes' own 'calm, good, self-denying influence' on Copperfield.[65]

Copperfield's mother is repeatedly described in moments when she sings. In consequence, the protagonist seems to be particularly attracted to characters who sing. Agnes, Dora and Steerforth as well as the Micawbers all sing, and whenever they do, Copperfield experiences a state of bliss. In the first part of the novel, when he returns home from school, his nostalgia for a happier childhood overwhelms him:

> God knows how infantine the memory may have been, that was awakened within me by the sound of my mother's voice in the old parlour, when I set foot in the hall. She was singing in a low tone. I think I must have lain in her arms, and heard her singing so to me when I was but a baby. The strain was new to me, and yet it was so old that it filled my heart brim-full; like a friend come back from a long absence.[66]

---

[64] Ibid., 698.
[65] Ibid., 262.
[66] Ibid., 94.

Copperfield would relive the same sensation in Switzerland. Even though he relates his feelings there to Dora's death, this much earlier passage shows that there is even more at stake. In Switzerland, Copperfield not only bemoans the death of his wife and his problematic marriage, but is also reminded of his happy early childhood and the sudden loss of it. Incidentally, this is also caused by a marriage – his mother's unfortunate union with the Murdstone family. Switzerland is the place which allows Copperfield to remember, to re-engage with the maternal, but also to overcome past experiences. It is not just a place for remembrance, but also for development. In Switzerland, Copperfield also finds Agnes' letters, which allow for a new beginning. The experience of rethinking one's own biography is one the protagonist shares with his creator. Dickens too underwent a crisis during his time in Lausanne, and we will return to this in more detail in Chapter 2.

Switzerland not only allows Copperfield to start anew, but also to imagine – and eventually live – an alternative story. Dora's death becomes a blessing in disguise, as it ends the rather ill-suited match between Copperfield and his 'child wife'. In Switzerland, he 'tried to get a better understanding of myself and be a better man', but also 'did glance, through some indefinite probation, to a period when I might possibly hope to cancel the mistaken past, and to be so blessed as to marry her'.[67] Even though he loses his hope a little later, his wish is eventually fulfilled and the story comes to a happy ending. On the surface, Copperfield's stay in Switzerland does not seem to bear any similarities with the popular entertainment Dickens saw as a young man. Yet the significance of singing, the feeling it triggers and the episodic nature of Copperfield's stay show how subtly Dickens revises and adapts his own observations.

Singing, or rather 'chaunting' made Dickens's trip to the St Bernard Pass in 1846 a very memorable one. A letter Dickens writes to Forster about the 'most distinct and individual place I have seen, even in this transcendent country', features a sentence which is of such significance that it will figure again in this discussion:

> At five o'clock in the morning the chapel bell rang in the dismallest way for matins: and I, lying in bed close to the chapel, and being awakened by the solemn organ and the chaunting, thought for a moment I had died in the night and passed into the unknown world.[68]

---

[67] Ibid., 700.
[68] To Forster, ?6 September 1846, *Letters*, vol. 4, 618.

34 *Dickens and Switzerland*

The 'chaunting' is a significant part of Dickens's experience and certainly is another example of his associations of singing with Switzerland. This one, however, is much more sombre and instead of expressing patriotism and merriment, it is connected with death. This representation of Switzerland is in the same vein as the Dorrits's experience of the St Bernard in *Little Dorrit*, where a disconnected narrator – unnoticed by his characters – discovers the frozen bodies of dead travellers in the morgue on the mountain pass. Though there is no mention of singing here, there is strong emphasis on the oral:

> While all this noise and hurry were rife among the living travellers, there, too, silently assembled in a grated house half a dozen paces removed, with the same cloud enfolding them and the same snow flakes drifting in upon them, were the dead travellers found upon the mountain. The mother, storm-belated many winters ago, still standing in the corner with her baby at her breast; the man who had frozen with his arm raised to his mouth in fear or hunger, still pressing it with his dry lips after years and years. An awful company, mysteriously come together! A wild destiny for that mother to have foreseen! 'Surrounded by so many and such companions upon whom I never looked, and never shall look, I and my child will dwell together inseparable, on the Great Saint Bernard, outlasting generations who will come to see us, and will never know our name, or one word of our story but the end.'[69]

Each of the three dead bodies, despite being dead, performs an act with their mouth. The child is still at the mother's breast, the man has 'his arm raised to his mouth in fear or hunger', while the mother seems to speak to the narrator. She is probably the most uncanny and mysterious of the three, as she tells and does not tell. She speaks and does not speak to the narrator, as her words are but what the narrator imagines her to say. Nor does she disclose her story, but only hints at it and the fact that it will never be known.

On a side note, this is the second baby on a mother's body that we encounter in this chapter – out of three in the whole book. Another reference, also in this chapter, is to a child 'carried in a sling by the laden peasant-woman toiling home'. The child is 'quieted with picked-up grapes' in the course of a grotesque vintage scene set on the borders of Lake Geneva.[70] The first mention of a child on its mother's body in the novel is only a metaphor, rather

---

[69] Dickens, *Little Dorrit*, ed. Harvey Peter Sucksmith (Oxford: Clarendon Press, 1979), 421.
[70] Ibid., 419.

than an actual scene. Arthur Clennam's mother uses the image to threaten her son:

> In the days of old, Arthur, treated of in this commentary, there were pious men, beloved of the Lord, who would have cursed their sons for less than this: who would have sent them forth, and sent whole nations forth, if such had supported them, to be avoided of God and man, and perish, down to the baby at the breast.[71]

This is a very telling thing for her to say, given what we learn later about Arthur's true mother. The baby at a mother's breast – or body – is a recurring theme in Dickens's representation of Switzerland.[72] Yet the example above, unrelated to Switzerland, confirms that it is one of the images through which Dickens represents his rather negative views of Catholicism. Both in Italy and in the Catholic Swiss cantons he visited, he attributed some of the poverty and misery of the people to their Catholic faith. The idealised depictions of the Madonna and Child which he found there stand in stark contrast to the women Dickens saw in real life.

Sleary's Horsemanship, or Astley's

'There is no place', Dickens writes, 'which recalls so strongly our recollections of childhood as Astley's.'[73] Astley's Amphitheatre opened in 1784 and specialised in 'hippodrama', melodramatic and pantomimic performances mostly acted out on horseback.[74] Philip Astley, the venue's founder, was a retired cavalryman and is credited with inventing the modern circus.[75] Dickens dedicated a whole piece to Astley's to convey an experience at the circus, but the venue appears in other texts as well, for example in 'Private Theatres' and 'The Boarding House'. The circus turned into a veritable institution in nineteenth-century London until it closed in 1893, but its heyday was between the 1820s and 1840s. Even though when writing 'Astley's' Dickens claims that his 'histrionic taste is gone', there is

---

[71] Ibid., 48.

[72] See Chapter 2, 113.

[73] Dickens, 'Astley's', in *Sketches by Boz*, ed. Dennis Walder (London: Penguin, 1995), 129.

[74] Frederick Burwick et al., eds., *The Encyclopedia of Romantic Literature* (Oxford: Blackwell Publishing, 2012), 431.

[75] Michael R. Booth, 'Astley's Amphitheatre', in *The Oxford Companion to Theatre and Performance*, ed. Dennis Kennedy (Oxford: Oxford University Press, 2010), 33.

36   *Dickens and Switzerland*

a pleasure in going there still, as 'with shame we confess, that we are far more delighted and amused with the audience, than with the pageantry we once so highly appreciated'.[76] But what would Dickens have seen at Astley's as a child and young man?

'Patriotic military spectacle' was what Astley's did most successfully.[77] Some of its most popular equestrian dramas included *Timour the Tartar*, *The Battle of Waterloo* and *Mazeppa*, but there had also been a selection of shows with a 'Swiss' subject: during the 1820s, Astley's performed *The Sisters; or The Heroines of Switzerland*, probably written by William Barrymore. Although the 1822 issue of the *Rambler's Magazine* did not praise the actors, the play was later restaged in an equine-free environment under the new title of *The Amazon Sisters* at the Royal Cobourg Theatre.[78] In 1829, Astley's also produced a piece called *Bonaparte's Passage of the Great St. Bernard*.[79] Yet, probably the most successful 'Swiss' hippodrama was *The Swiss Maid and her Tyrolean Lover*, sometimes also referred to as *The Tyrolean Sheppard* [*sic*; but also 'Shepherd'] *and Swiss Milkmaid*. It was so popular that it quickly made its way to the colonies: the *Sydney Morning Herald* of 1851 features an advertisement for a performance of the show.[80] In May 1830, shortly after the piece's premiere in London, the *Athenaeum* published a review:

> The Circus, on Tuesday evening presented a very agreeable novelty, 'the Shepherd of the Tyrol and the Swiss Milkmaid', performed by those accomplished equestrians Messrs. Ducrow and Miss Woolford. The lady first appears in very picturesque attire having under her arm her milk pail which in the course of a round or two she transfers to her back. The swain comes cantering along after the maiden, and as he beckons to her from the opposite side of the arena, Mr. Ducrow managed to give so much effect to his gesticulations, and like a skilful artist, threw so much space into his picture, that we could almost fancy him on the summit of the Brenner saluting his fair mistress, as she was enjoying the prospect from the heights of the Righi. [...] This equestrian ballet was very delightfully

---

[76] Dickens, 'Astley's', 129.

[77] Booth in Kennedy, *The Oxford Companion to Theatre and Performance*, 274.

[78] 'Theatricals', *The Rambler's Magazine*, 1 September 1822, 417: 'Mrs. Makeen and Miss Price play the SISTERS pretty well; Mr. G. Raymond is too rough for WERNER; Mr. Slader is too fat for ERIC, and Mr. Villiers is too bad an actor to be fit for any thing.'

[79] A. H. Saxon, *Enter Foot and Horse. A History of Hippodrama in England and France* (New Haven, CT: Yale University Press, 1968), 134.

[80] 'Advertising', *The Sydney Morning Herald*, 3 March 1851.

executed by both performers; Mr. Ducrow's pantomimic was as excellent as his horsemanship.[81]

The piece focuses on a melodramatic love plot and presents a picturesque peasant scene. As illustrated above, the 'Swiss maid' had already become a type by this time and the major novelty of Astley's piece was probably its performance on horseback. The visual appeal of such performances was undoubtedly their endless 'reinvention' of picturesque landscapes and shepherd idylls. Combined with melodramatic love plots, these performances created seemingly irresistible entertainment for their nineteenth-century audience. The appeal of these performances has gone and tastes have changed in modern audiences. For the most part, this was also the general consensus among contemporary drama critics. Until relatively recently, Victorian drama was seen as 'crude, embarrassing, primitive' and 'comparatively insignificant, even unworthy of attention'.[82] Only a few years ago, some scholars 'rediscovered' Victorian melodrama as a point of interest, but until now and only with very few exceptions, it has not found its way back to the stage.

The 'Messrs. Ducrow' mentioned in the quote above are Andrew and John, two brothers of whom the first became the manager after Astley's death. It is he whom Dickens presents in *Sketches by Boz* as the 'riding master:'

> Every body knows the man, and every body remembers his polished boots, his graceful demeanour, stiff, as some misjudging persons have in their jealousy considered it, and the splendid head of black hair, parted high on the forehead, to impart to the countenance an appearance of deep thought and poetic melancholy.[83]

Andrew Ducrow 'roamed the Continent', and performed in 'Holland, Belgium, Switzerland, Italy, and Spain, but', according to Arthur Saxon, 'it was in Paris and the provincial cities of France that provided the more usual and most congenial settings for his performances'.[84] Louisa Woolford, more than twenty years Ducrow's junior, married him in 1838 and 'was second only to Ducrow in popularity with

---

[81] 'Astley's Amphitheatre', *Athenaeum*, 15 May 1830, 302.

[82] Kerry Powell, ed., *The Cambridge Companion to Victorian and Edwardian Theatre* (Cambridge: Cambridge University Press, 2004), xiii; 3; on melodrama, see Peter Brooks, *The Melodramatic Imagination: Balzac, Henry James, Melodrama, and the Mode of Excess* (New Haven, CT: Yale University Press, 1976).

[83] Dickens, 'Astley's', 132.

[84] Saxon, *Life and Art of Ducrow and the Romantic Age of the English Circus* (Hamden, CT: Archon Books, 1979), 81.

38   *Dickens and Switzerland*

audiences at Astley's'.[85] Dickens's references to her in 'Astley's' and *Hard Times* certainly reflect this opinion.

Sketches by Boz features one of the first mentions of Switzerland in Dickens's fiction. It is no coincidence that it appears in connection with popular entertainment, and Astley's in particular. In a piece called 'The Last Cab-Driver, and the First Omnibus Cad', Dickens describes a 'gorgeously painted' cabriolet:

> Our fondness for that red cab was unbounded. How we should have liked to see it in the circle at Astley's! Our life upon it, that it should have performed such evolutions as would have put the whole company to shame – Indians, chiefs, knights, Swiss peasants, and all.[86]

In contrast to Mathews's 'At Homes', where the Swiss song figured in a range of songs from related, or at least 'familiar' cultures, here, the 'Swiss peasants' appear in a context of exotic, but popular, theatrical types. Dickens's text implicitly assumes that his London audience, well acquainted with Astley's and its performances, shares the author's familiarity with the theatrical types outlined. No further description is needed as Dickens draws on a shared cultural knowledge. The reference towards Switzerland is typical of Dickens's writing, but also of many other Victorian texts. The allusions are quick, often embedded in a larger, implicit context, fleeting, seemingly unimportant and therefore easily missed. This reference once more confirms Switzerland's episodic nature both in travel and in art. Not only in Dickens, Swiss scenes often appear at moments in which the main plot is not developed further, but where we find sub-plots, detours and excursions.

Switzerland had not always been a travel destination. At first, journeys through Switzerland were 'merely passages through the country'.[87] John Wraight confirms that 'In the days of the European Grand Tour, most travellers still used Switzerland as only a staging post on the way to or from Italy', where the actual point of interest was.[88]

> It was not until near the end of the eighteenth century that wider British interest began to awaken in Switzerland for its own sake. Descriptions of the country in the works of Wordsworth, Shelley and Byron and later of Ruskin, among others, caused more of their

---

[85] Ibid., 213, 155.
[86] Dickens, 'The Last Cab-Driver, and the First Omnibus Cad', in *Sketches by Boz*, 171.
[87] Gavin de Beer, *Travellers in Switzerland* (Oxford: Oxford University Press, 1949), xiii.
[88] Wraight, *The Swiss and the British*, 34.

countrymen to come and see for themselves, among them the politicians Fox, Disraeli and Cobden.[89]

Goethe and some of the early German Romantics had slightly earlier reinvented the passage through Switzerland as a lesson in the natural sublime before they crossed to Italy, which since the beginning of the Enlightenment era had become the 'go-to' place for an experience of the cultural sublime. It took the British, and the Victorians in particular, to turn travel to Switzerland into a mass phenomenon.

The Milkmaid and her Tyrolean Lover 'execute an exquisite *pas de deux*', in the piece, but are 'interrupted by the entrance of the angry father, who separates the lovers, and pursues his daughter with fury'.[90] With its two lovers, a clown and the irate father, the play is unmistakably pantomimic in form and the term itself figures twice in a review which appeared in the *Athenaeum* in May 1830: the Tyrolean 'goes through all the pantomimic range of the jealousy-stricken lover' and Ducrow's 'pantomimic' is pointed out as 'as excellent as his horsemanship'.[91] There have been some excellent studies of Dickens and the theatre: Paul Schlicke's *Dickens and Popular Entertainment* and Edwin Eigner's *The Dickens Pantomime* are two of the works on which the following reading is based.

Dickens renders an unexpected homage to the *Tyrolean Lover* in *Hard Times*, where Louisa and Thomas Gradgrind secretly watch the announcement of Miss Josephine Sleary's 'graceful equestrian Tyrolean flower-act'.[92] As Kate Flint notes, this 'seems to be an imaginative compilation of several circus acts', probably a conflation of *The Swiss Maid* and another act, *The Italian Flower Girl*, or as Margaret Simpson suggests, *La Rosière*.[93] It is no coincidence, then, that in *Hard Times*, where the circus plays such an important role, 'the pattern of pantomime characters reconstitutes itself to some extent'.[94] In *The Dickens Pantomime*, Edwin Eigner observes:

> James Harthouse comes back from the melodrama to try his dandy wiles at seducing the Columbine, and Bounderby is another unsuitable lover, a veritable Squire Bugle from the Regency pantomime.

---

[89] Ibid., 34.

[90] *Sheffield Iris*, 22 November 1836, qtd. in Saxon, *Life and Art of Ducrow*, 220.

[91] 'Astley's Amphitheatre', *Athenaeum*, 302.

[92] Dickens, *Hard Times*, 18.

[93] Ibid., 305n9; Margaret Simpson, *The Companion to* Hard Times, *The Dickens Companions* (Westport, CT: Greenwood Press, 1997), 60.

[94] Edwin Eigner, *The Dickens Pantomime* (Berkeley, CA: University of California Press, 1989), 172.

40   *Dickens and Switzerland*

Gradgrind, moreover, who puts Bounderby forth as a candidate for his daughter's hand, is one of the better and more meaningful Pantaloons in Dickens. But how disappointing a Clown is Sissy Jupe! And where is Louisa Gradgrind's Harlequin?[95]

There is – and will be – no Harlequin for Louisa. In the novel she inhabits, her father assumes a similar role to that of the Swiss maid's father in the performance she watches: the Pantaloon.

> All the characters in the harlequinade give mixed signals, but none is more confusing than this mischievous old lecher, who represents patriarchal authority and corrupt hierarchy. [...] In the opening Pantaloon is the blocking figure of New Comedy who tries to force his daughter into a loveless marriage and whom Northrop Frye characterizes as 'generally cruel or foolish.' After his harlequinade transformation, moreover, Pantaloon's standard business in the plot is a prolonged attempt to capture the young lovers and frustrate their desires.[96]

Certainly, Gradgrind is no old lecher and he is not intentionally mischievous. Dickens would not be Dickens if he simply copied types without animating his characters with 'the common experience of an Englishman' and the 'violent transitions and abrupt impulses of passion or feeling' that life brings with itself.[97] Nonetheless, Gradgrind does stand for 'patriarchal authority and corrupt hierarchy'. Even though he does not force his daughter into a loveless marriage, he 'advises' her 'to consider this question', as she has been 'accustomed to consider every other question, simply as one of tangible Fact'.[98] It becomes clear, however, that he would like her to consent to the union. Unlike in the pantomime, Pantaloon gets his way in *Hard Times*. The short novel is therefore an experiment and offers an alternative story to that of the regular pantomime.

The storyline of traditional Victorian pantomime, foreign to us nowadays, typically worked towards a moment of climax in which the Good Fairy appeared, triggered a transformation and began anew with the so-called harlequinade where the lovers turn 'into *Harlequin* and *Columbine*, the old curmudgeon into *Pantaloon*, and the body servant into *Clown*', thus enabling a fortunate resolution of the plot.[99] But in *Hard Times*, even the remotest glimpse at romance is

---

[95] Ibid., 172.
[96] Ibid., 70.
[97] Dickens, Preface to *Little Dorrit*, lix; Dickens, *Oliver Twist*, 102.
[98] Dickens, *Hard Times*, 97.
[99] James Robinson Planché, *Recollections and Reflections*, qtd. in Eigner, *Dickens Pantomime*, 2.

interrupted from the beginning when Thomas and Louisa Gradgrind watch the 'graceful Tyrolean flower-act'. It is a secret interlude, a glimpse into another world, as the chapter's title, 'A Loophole', suggests. As the children's watching is interrupted prematurely by their father, they will never know that, at last, in the story they are watching, 'reconciliation takes place, the mounted mountaineers embrace, and make their bow and exit'.[100] Happy endings are an outcome the Gradgrind children are not familiar with and their experience at Sleary's almost seems to foreshadow their own unhappy fate.

The script of pantomime does not foresee a victorious Pantaloon and therefore, in *Hard Times*, the progression of the plot with a potentially happy outcome remains in uncertain limbo. Neither of the stories – that which Thomas and Louisa Gradgrind watch at the circus and that of *Hard Times* itself – find a positive conclusion. The novel ends thus:

> Dear reader! It rests with you and me, whether, in our two fields of action, similar things shall be or not. Let them be! We shall sit with lighter bosoms on the heart, to see the ashes of our fires turn grey and cold.[101]

But does it really rest 'with you and me' if the narrator in the next sentence urges us to 'Let them be!'? Kate Flint's rightly concludes that this utterance

> reads two ways: both as a call of action, and paradoxically and more troublingly, as a plea for passivity, the realities of industrial life providing the basis on which both didactic and imaginative writing are built.[102]

Hard Times leaves an open end, as open as the outcome of the play which Louisa and Thomas watch, but also, perhaps even more ironically, as open as Astley's *Tyrolean Lover* remains for us today, since understandably the reviews of the play do not give a full account in order not to 'spoil their pleasure by revealing the end of the piece'.[103]

Only Mrs Gradgrind, small as her role in the novel may be, senses in the moment of her death that something has gone wrong:

> But there is something [...] that your father has missed, or forgotten, Louisa. I don't know what it is. I have often sat with Sissy near me,

[100] 'Astley's Amphitheatre', *Athenaeum*, 302.
[101] Dickens, *Hard Times*, 288.
[102] Flint, 'Introduction', in Dickens, *Hard Times*, xxx.
[103] *Sheffield Iris*, 22 November 1836, qtd. in Saxon, *Life and Art of Ducrow*, 220.

and thought about it. I shall never get its name now. But your father may. It makes me restless. I want to write to him, to find out for God's sake, what it is. Give me a pen.[104]

The 'something' that Mr Gradgrind has 'missed, or forgotten' remains unmentioned. Mrs Gradgrind, like her husband, is unable to fill the gap. Sissy, familiar with the pantomimic mode due to her early life at the circus, has triggered the thought of this 'something'. The act which may bring the missing 'something' back, is writing. It is, however, too late and Mrs Gradgrind's futile attempt at rewriting the plot only expresses itself in 'figures of wonderful no-meaning'.[105] From this perspective, *Hard Times* is a highly experimental novel, in that it explores a pantomime gone wrong. Dickens's novel asks: what happens if Pantaloon succeeds?

Men and Masters, or William Tell

In 1802, Astley's climbed aboard the bandwagon and staged a version of probably the best-known Swiss plot in early nineteenth-century popular entertainment culture: William Tell. The legend was first recorded in the White Book of Sarnen, an archive of ancient contracts and other legal documents.[106] Although there had been doubts about the legend's authenticity and its Swiss origin for centuries, it experienced several revivals in which its historic accuracy only played a minor role.[107] Among others, Johann Kaspar Lavater, the physiognomist, whose influence is 'ubiquitous' throughout Dickens's works, significantly contributed to a new wave of Tell enthusiasm towards the end of the eighteenth century with his own writings.[108] It was during this time that Tell started to become a symbol for freedom and the abolition of tyrannical regimes.

The cult of Tell also had its effects in Switzerland: during the short-lived Helvetian Republic, a regime which Napoleon had

---

[104] Dickens, *Hard Times*, 194.

[105] Ibid.

[106] *Historisches Lexikon der Schweiz*, s.v. 'Tell, Wilhelm', accessed 31 January 2024, www.hls-dhs-dss.ch/textes/d/D17475.php.

[107] In 1760 Uriel Freudenberger and Gottlieb Emanuel von Haller published their anonymous pamphlet entitled 'Der Wilhelm Tell, ein dän. Mährgen' ['William Tell, a Danish Legend'], which caused uproar among those who defended not only Tell's Swiss origins but also his historic existence.

[108] Hollington in Schlicke, *Oxford Reader's Companion to Dickens*, 559; *Historisches Lexikon der Schweiz*, s.v. 'Tell, Wilhelm'. See Conclusion, 178 for more on Lavater's influence on Dickens.

installed, the Swiss felt the need for patriotic symbols and embraced what was believed to be a rediscovered heritage in many surprising ways. The French General Guillaume Brune, for example, suggested naming one of the three territories into which he intended to split the country, Tellgau, that is 'Tell's county', or, 'the county of Tell'.[109] When in 1803, the newly founded canton of Vaud, where Dickens would later live, was in need of a flag, the proposed draft consisted of two joint hands upholding a sword which featured William Tell's hat on its point. The idea was only abandoned because it was seen as too complicated to reproduce.[110]

England adopted its fancy for the William Tell material from France, where the 'heroic acts [of Tell] had been on the stage since Antoine-Marin Le Mierre's tragedy opened in 1766'.[111] The French Revolution helped to promote the myth across Europe, as it was widely used among revolutionary circles to legitimise political upheavals. '[B]y far the most popular tale of William Tell was that told by Jean-Pierre Claris de Florian in his fables for children', which were translated into English around the turn of the century.[112] Florian's fable is the basis for Astley's play, which was called *William Tell, The Hero of Switzerland*.[113] The material,

> with its drama of a wicked tyrant, abused peasants, and an imperiled father and son, [was] well suited for presentation in song and pantomime, and afforded a splendid occasion for the display of horsemanship and archery. For better or worse, the 'William Tell' of fable and melodrama held sway through the first two decades of the nineteenth century. It was the nature of melodrama to give emphasis to action and special effects over dialogue.[114]

The Tell legend saw an abundance of adaptations, both in England and on the Continent. Between 1800 and 1870, more than twenty different operas, plays, extravaganzas, burlesques and other forms of entertainment were staged in London with *William Tell* appearing in their title.[115]

---

[109] *Historisches Lexikon der Schweiz*, s.v. 'Tell, Wilhelm'.

[110] Julien Magnollay, '1803: le drapeau vaudois est recalé', *24 Heures*, 28 February 2012.

[111] Frederick Burwick, *Playing to the Crowd: London Popular Theatre, 1789–1830* (Basingstoke: Palgrave Macmillan, 2011), 110.

[112] Ibid., 111.

[113] Gustav Schirmer, 'Über James Sheridan Knowles' William Tell', *Anglia* 12 (1889): 1–12; and Burwick, *Playing to the Crowd*, 111.

[114] Burwick, *Playing to the Crowd*, 112.

[115] See Nicoll, *A History of English Drama 1660–1900*, vol. 4.

44   *Dickens and Switzerland*

One of the first and most successful adaptations of the material in early nineteenth-century Europe was Schiller's, which premiered in Weimar in 1804. Rossini's opera, an adaptation of Schiller's play, was first performed in Paris in 1829. Schiller's play and Rossini's opera remain two of the best-known versions today. Yet in England, the earliest performances were based on French sources, and Schiller's and Rossini's pieces underwent some interesting modifications before being shown in their original versions.

The first of many adaptations of Rossini's opera was brought to the London stage by James Robinson Planché and Henry Rowley Bishop. Since Planché, the son of a Huguenot watchmaker who had learned his trade in Geneva, felt that 'the story of William Tell had already been dramatized in so many shapes and forms', he selected 'a portion of the history of Hofer, the celebrated Tyrolean chieftain, who, like the immortal Tell, endeavoured to free his country from foreign thraldom'.[116] In other words, Planché feared that, at least in England, the story of Tell had already been overused. Rather unceremoniously, he therefore replaced the Swiss hero with an Austrian one, Andreas Hofer, all the while retaining Rossini's music. Hofer was attractive for an English audience because his rebellion was more recent than that of Tell, and he was also a historical rather than a legendary figure. Furthermore, Hofer had fought against Napoleon, a common enemy. In consequence, London saw the first adaptation of Rossini's opera as *Hofer; or, The Tell of the Tyrol* in 1830.[117]

There is no evidence for Dickens having attended any of the Hofer productions, but since he claims to have gone to the theatre frequently during these years, it is not unlikely that he did. There are no references to the Austrian hero in his letters, but he is mentioned four times in Dickens's magazines.[118] Three of these articles were written or co-written by Henry Morley, who was the only 'in-house graduate' at *Household Words*, and later became a Professor of English at the University College in London.[119] If Dickens had not seen *Hofer*, at least some of the people he worked with certainly had, and Dickens would have been aware of the performance.

---

[116] Quoted in Theodore Fenner, *Opera in London. Views of the Press, 1785–1830* (Carbondale, IL: Southern Illinois University Press, 1994), 491.

[117] Nicoll, *A History of English Drama 1660–1900*, vol. 4, 379.

[118] 'A Roving Englishman: Benighted; Out Shooting', *Household Words*, 29 November 1851, 217; 'The Enemy', *Household Words*, 4 September 1852, 573; 'Little Commissions', *Household Words*, 14 March 1857, 241; 'Starting for Siberia', *All the Year Round*, 28 November 1863, 329.

[119] Philip Collins in Schlicke, *Oxford Reader's Companion to Dickens*, 393.

More importantly, however, we know that Dickens was indeed familiar with the Tell legend itself. The most famous and influential English adaptation of it was probably that of James Sheridan Knowles, whose *William Tell* opened at Drury Lane in 1825.[120] The leading role was performed by William Charles Macready, to whom Dickens was introduced by Forster in 1837. Between Dickens and Macready, a 'relationship of great warmth and trust developed, and continued unbroken until [Dickens's] death'.[121] According to the editors of the *Pilgrim* edition of his letters, Dickens had probably seen Macready first as William Tell in 1838, when he was twenty-six.[122] By this point, Macready had been playing Tell for a full thirteen years. No wonder then, that at least among his friends, Macready came to be associated with the role so closely that it became a running joke to address him in the form of his stage character. To Daniel Maclise, painter and another of Dickens's close friends, he was 'William Macready Tell'.[123] When Macready wanted to visit Dickens in Switzerland in 1846, the author greets him in the following way: 'Why, Lord love your heart, William Tell, times are changed since you lived at Altdorf.'[124] Altdorf in Central Switzerland is, of course, 'William Tell's town', as Dickens noted in a letter to Forster in 1845.[125] Dickens's close and early association of Switzerland with Tell is also visible in a letter to a friend, written shortly before moving there in 1846: 'Is there anything I can do for you in Switzerland – any apple or other fruit I can shoot off any friend's or relation's head – in return?'[126] The actor's association with him in this role and the general public's appreciation of it went so far that a review in the *Theatrical Journal* even claimed that 'not to see Macready in William Tell would be like seeing *Hamlet* without Hamlet'.[127] The reviewer in the *Monthly Chronicle* in 1838, however, was rather less impressed with the piece, although he did put the blame on Knowles rather than Macready's performance of the role:

> [Knowles] has not treated 'William Tell' with the success which might be expected where the subject was so congenial to him. [...] Mr. Knowles has made William Tell a rude, brave, honest, and patriot mountaineer. Certainly refinement would have been out of

[120] Nicoll, *A History of English Drama 1660–1900*, vol. 4, 339.
[121] To Richard Bentley, ?27 June 1837, *Letters*, vol. 1, 279n1.
[122] To Macready, 24 October 1846, *Letters*, vol. 4, 646n2.
[123] To Maclise, ?16 August 1841, *Letters*, vol. 2, 360n4.
[124] To Macready, 24 October 1846, *Letters*, vol. 4, 646.
[125] To Forster, 15 June 1845, *Letters*, vol. 4, 321.
[126] To Thomas Powell, 19 May 1846, *Letters*, vol. 4, 549.
[127] To Macready, 24 October 1846, *Letters*, vol. 4, 645n2.

place, – but William Tell should have the elevation of a deliverer. Emotion, too, is excited, not so much by the sympathy of passions and affections, as by the apprehension of physical pain. The peril of Tell in the hands of Gessler is analogous to the preliminaries of a Newgate execution – the horrible alternative of shooting at the apple placed on the head of the child, is a mere agony; both are melodramatic, and the comedy is no better than that of Virginius and Gracchus; it is, perhaps, even worse. The loves and humours of a sort of rustic Mercutio, and the daughter of the Castellan are but a mere *réchauffé* [*sic*] of the trite conventions of English comedy.[128]

Compared to Schiller's grave drama reminiscent of 'gothic tragedy', Knowles's version, according to Frederick Burwick, transforms Tell 'from a shrewd, quiet, honest man of action into a swaggering hero out of the pantomimes' and 'sought no complexity beyond the simple fare of melodrama: a cruel villain, innocence threatened, and a brave hero'.[129] This is a stern comment for a play which was quite successful in its time. Michael R. Booth's entry in the *Oxford Companion to Theatre and Performance* is similarly unflattering when he says that 'Knowles was fortunate in having the best actors of the day in his principal characters, but his work, now unplayable, represents the last twilight of the legitimate Elizabethan-influenced verse tragedy and comedy'.[130] Knowles's adaptation certainly brought a powerful shift towards the domestic, which is linked to the strong melodramatic tradition in which it stands, and which is probably Booth's reason to qualify it as 'now unplayable'. In Knowles's version it is Tell's home – rather than his country, as in Schiller's – which is threatened, facilitating the identification with the hero for an international audience. In Knowles we meet the personalities of a village community rather than a whole people. We have already noticed a strong 'domestic' dimension in the discussion of Charles Mathews's 'At Homes', and it was the same staged domesticity which significantly contributed to the appeal of Knowles's *Tell* for a Victorian audience.

The apple-shooting scene, clearly the much-anticipated climax of the play, was met with particular criticism due to its comedy: 'Tell

---

[128] 'The Theatres', *The Monthly Chronicle*, March–June 1838, 174; *Virginius* and *Caius Gracchus* are two earlier tragedies by Knowles, both with a Roman theme. *Caius Gracchus* was first performed in Belfast in 1815, while *Virginius* opened in Glasgow in 1820. The 'loves and humours' of the 'rustic Mercutio' and 'the daughter of the Castellan' refer to the love plot in Knowles's *William Tell*: Jagheli, a young Swiss, falls in love with the Austrian Castellan's step-daughter, Anneli.

[129] Burwick, *Playing to the Crowd*, 113; 114; 115.

[130] Kennedy, *The Oxford Companion to Theatre and Performance*, 322.

Performing Switzerland   **47**

at first refuses to shoot unless he is placed so that the sun may shine on the apple; then he accuses Gesler of having chosen the smallest apple.'[131] But borrowing from the pantomimic mode, the delays do not end there. When Tell finally aims at his son's head, a man faints and has to be removed. Tell aims again – and this time a woman faints. Once she has been transported from the stage, Tell finally shoots. Even contemporary critics could not refrain from considering it a 'lapse of judgement' in Knowles to have 'imported the ridiculous delaying strategies from the comic pantomime versions'.[132] Yet this is the tone Dickens draws on when he mentions Tell or Gesler. Dickens remembers the comedy associated with William Tell on English stages when writing about Switzerland. The emphasis on the domestic and the pantomimic descriptions are all condensed into his writing on Switzerland and tend to reappear in the most unexpected of situations, just as those in Knowles's play do. The much criticised melodrama, the winks to pantomime and the comedy were intended. Knowles's *Tell* was so successful precisely because it built on pre-established conventions of late eighteenth- and early nineteenth-century English comedy. Consequently, when Tell appears in Dickens's writing, it is not in the shape of a 'deliverer', but as the 'rude, brave, honest, patriot' – and comic, melodramatic – mountaineer whom Knowles presents. With its excited emotion and emphasis on physical pain, it is not difficult to see both where Dickens's appreciation for the piece comes from and where he found inspiration for his style.

The abundance of William Tell stories which Planché mentioned is reflected in Dickens's fictional references to the legend: they are as incidental in their appearance as his other allusions to Switzerland. Most importantly though, they are implicit and address themselves to a reader who is familiar with the theatrical plots outlined here. Considering the popularity of the plot and the many points of contact Dickens had with the material both through his own experience and his social circle, the number of references is very small, similar to the relation between the number of Dickens's journeys to Switzerland and its – at least apparently – small influence on his literary output. Yet, mentions of Tell appear in some of Dickens's shorter pieces, in *Bleak House*, *No Thoroughfare* as well as *The Uncommercial Traveller*. There he figures, like the Swiss chalet at the beginning of the chapter, as the familiar point of reference in a comparison, to

---

[131] Burwick, *Playing to the Crowd*, 114.
[132] Ibid.

48   *Dickens and Switzerland*

evoke skill, dedication and 'masculinity'.[133] He is also an occasional presence in Dickens's magazines, *Household Words* and *All the Year Round*, receiving significantly more mentions than Robin Hood. The references to Tell often trigger a quick but fleeting association, creating an atmosphere of mild nostalgia or a memory of a pompous drama once seen, and often have soft comic undertones, borrowed from the 'Swiss' plays on stage.

In Dickens's novels, Tell is only explicitly mentioned in *Bleak House*. When Inspector Bucket discovers Mr George, the owner of George's Shooting Gallery, to be hiding his friend Gridley, Mr George tells him that 'it wasn't handsome' in Bucket to have found him out, and Bucket retorts:

> Gammon, George! Not handsome? [...] I don't say it wasn't handsome in you to keep my man so close, do I? Be equally good-tempered to me, old boy! Old Willam Tell! Old Shaw, the Life Guardsman! Why, he's a model of the whole British army in himself, ladies and gentlemen.[134]

Bucket tries to lift Mr George's mood with a joke and pays him a compliment by comparing his shooting skills with those of Tell and John 'Jack' Shaw, a particularly brave member of the 2nd Life Guards during the Battle of Waterloo. Once more we see Tell appear in the context of British popular culture. The war hero, Shaw, was given a prominent place in *The Battle of Waterloo*, which was 'one of the greatest, and next to *Mazeppa*, most frequently performed dramas in the entire history of Astley's'.[135] Shaw's 'story outlived the play as a whole in its ring popularity'.[136] Mr George, whom Bucket jokingly calls the 'model of the whole British army in himself', is compared to two good fighters for the freedom of their country. Interestingly, Dickens here prefers to mention Tell rather than his English equivalent, Robin Hood, an equally good shot. The reason for this is undoubtedly the popularity of the Tell plot at the time, a fact that is also reflected in the less frequent mentions of the English hero in Dickens's magazines.

---

[133] Charles Dickens, *Bleak House*, ed. Nicola Bradbury (London: Penguin, 2003), 402; Collins and Dickens, *No Thoroughfare*, 213; Dickens, 'Travelling Abroad' in *The Uncommercial Traveller*, *The Dent Uniform Edition of Dickens' Journalism, Vol. 4: 'The Uncommercial Traveller' and Other Papers, 1859–70*, ed. Michael Slater and John Drew (London: J. M. Dent, 2000), 85.

[134] Dickens, *Bleak House*, 402.

[135] Saxon, *Enter Foot and Horse*, 137.

[136] Tracy C. Davis and Peter Holland, *The Performing Century. Nineteenth-Century Theatre's History* (Basingstoke: Palgrave Macmillan, 2007), 257.

There is also a curious connection between Knowles's piece and the Ternan family who would play such an important role later in Dickens's life. On 27 January 1847, Dublin's *Freeman's Journal and Daily Commercial Advertiser* announced a performance of Knowles's *William Tell, The Hero of Switzerland* at the Theatre Royal in Dublin. Albert, Tell's son, was played by Frances Ternan, Ellen Ternan's sister, and Emma, Tell's wife, by Mrs Ternan, her mother.[137] A playbill held in the University of Kent's Theatre Collections advertises Mrs Ternan 'and her talented daughters' again in William Tell and two more plays for a performance at the Theatre Royal in Hull on 16 August the same year.[138] This time, both Fanny and Maria, the latter called Mary on the bill, appear alongside their mother on the advertisement, but Ellen, who was only twelve, remains unmentioned.

As with any popular plot, the William Tell legend was prone to parody. Comic versions of the story appeared until the end of the 1860s, among others *William Tell or, the Arrow; the Apple and the Agony; William Tell with a Vengeance or, the Pet, the Patriot and the Pippin; William Tell or, A Telling Version of an Old Tell-Tale; William Tell or, the Strike of the Cantons*. One of the most successful comic adaptations of the myth, however, was John Maddison Morton's *Harlequin and William Tell; or, the Genius of the Ribstone Pippin*. This play is particularly relevant to Dickens studies because he wrote a little-noted review of it for the *Examiner* in 1842. 'We forbear', Dickens begins,

> our annual lament over the departed spirit of legitimate pantomime. After lamenting for several years, we do not find that anything better comes of it. It will be wiser to confess the altered time, and discover amusement, if we can, in the substitutes provided.[139]

With his comment on the 'departed spirit of legitimate pantomime', Dickens participates in and resists the perennial complaint that the pantomimes of yore had been much better.[140] His comment

---

[137] 'Advertisements & Notices', *Freeman's Journal and Daily Commercial Advertiser*, 23 January 1847.

[138] Theatre Collections at the University of Kent. Description available online, accessed 31 January 2024: www.kent.ac.uk/library/specialcollections/theatre/r.php/37115/show.html

[139] Dickens, 'Theatrical Examiner, Drury Lane', *The Examiner*, 31 December 1842; also mentioned in Dickens, *The Dent Uniform Edition of Dickens's Journalism, Vol. 2: The Amusements of the People and Other Papers: Reports, Essays and Reviews, 1834–51*, ed. Michael Slater (London: J. M. Dent, 1996), 376.

[140] Jill A. Sullivan, *The Politics of the Pantomime: Regional Identity in the Theatre, 1860–1900* (Hatfield: University of Hertfordshire Press, 2001), 3.

50 *Dickens and Switzerland*

corresponds to the nostalgic tone he adopts when speaking about Astley's in *Sketches by Boz*, which we discussed above. We soon understand that the review's initial statement is actually ironic and that the 'spirit of legitimate pantomime' has, in fact, not departed at all. Immediately after this seemingly negative initial opening, Dickens qualifies it: 'There is', he writes, 'certainly a vast deal of merriment and fun in the burlesque introduction to *William Tell*. It is the best we have had for years.'[141]

Dickens did indeed spend a cheerful evening at Drury Lane:

> The starting encounter of Liberty and Slavery took the holiday folks by storm. The scene opens in the regions of the latter demon, where 'tyrant's orders' are beheld in the course of execution on a large and prompt scale, when suddenly a British cruiser heaves in sight, chasing a pirate slaver, and a small figure-head Britannia descends from her prow, and her decks and rigging swarm with Lilliputian sailors, and her sides disgorge miniature marines, and after an encounter with hordes of full-grown lubberly slave-drivers, in which a marvellously small boatswain, with enormous whiskers, and a whistle as big as himself, behaves with unparalleled bravery, Liberty wins the day and goes off in her triumph to 'Rule the waves'.[142]

The pleasure Dickens took in watching this fast-paced, colourful, rich spectacle is displayed in the language he uses to describe the scene: the last sentence covers more than two-thirds of the entire paragraph and is interspersed with grotesque contrasts. Dickens's fascination with the interplay of disproportions in the boatswain's short body as well as the gargantuan dimension of his moustache and whistle are unmistakeable. The same is true for his interest in the uncertainty of something being animate or inanimate: the figurehead in the shape of a Britannia becomes alive and 'descends from her prow', while the sides of the British cruiser which carried her, 'disgorge miniature marines'. It is a moment of carnivalesque exuberance which Dickens evidently enjoyed and, as we will see in Chapter 2, a style used in other moments in which he wrote about Switzerland.[143]

Other reviewers judged *Harlequin and William Tell* very differently. The *Satirist* called it 'a wretched failure' and the reviewer felt 'little disposed to relish the pantomime, even if it had been twenty times than it is'.[144] The *Morning Post* found the 'practical part'

---

[141] Dickens, 'Theatrical Examiner, Drury Lane', 837.
[142] Ibid.
[143] See Chapter 2, 107–9.
[144] 'Theatres', *The Satirist; or, the Censor of the Times*, 1 January 1843.

'eminently prosy', but the introductory drama 'supereminently prosy'. After an account is given of the story, the review concludes: 'The rest of the entertainment may be well imagined, when we pronounce it the "slowest" thing of the sort ever placed upon the stage of the patent theatres.'[145] The *Penny Satirist* held an equally negative view of the play, and only the *Era* was a little softer in its criticism.[146] It stated that the play was 'certainly not the best of its class' and that it produced 'a strange compound of the domestic-tragico-burlesque' by throwing 'demons and democrats, Britannia and Tell, journeymen, imps, and British tars, realms of slavery, the "open sea", valley, lakes and snowy peaks' all into one 'comic cauldron'.[147] In fact, out of the reviews I consulted, only Dickens's is full of praise. Even though he does not mention Macready, the actor who had gained considerable fame in the role of Tell from 1825 onwards, it was he who managed the stage at Drury Lane when Dickens wrote this review. Whereas it is of course possible that Dickens truly enjoyed the pantomime, he might not have wanted to anger his friend.

There certainly is no indication of foreignness or 'otherness' in *Harlequin and William Tell*. Even though Dickens points out the 'diverging points of the burlesque from the old Swiss legend', he remains uninterested in debates of nationhood and focuses on the characters instead.

> Thus *Albert* is an obstinate, gluttonous, mischief-making, incorrigible young vagabond, who lodges arrows in his father's rear instead of the target, and can only with the greatest difficulty be made to stand still when the apple is to be shot from his head. So *Melchtal* has been obliged to pay *Gesler's* tax with his ears instead of his eyes, while *Tell* in the market place, as submission to *Gesler's* cap goes on, with calm contempt plays 'All round my Hat' on the Hurdy-gurdy, and when asked to bow to the symbol of tyranny, contents himself with taking a double sight at it. *Gesler*, upon the whole, may be pronounced true to history. When disturbed by his toilet by what he supposes the too flattering evidence outside his window of a somewhat inconvenient popularity, and, presenting himself at the casement with fond and gratified reluctance, receives a sudden shower of turnips, cabbages, and other vegetable decomposition; there is nothing in the incident that offends historic propriety.[148]

---

[145] 'The Theatres', *Morning Post*, 27 December 1842.
[146] 'Theatricals', *Penny Satirist*, 14 January 1843.
[147] 'Music and Drama', *Era*, 1 January 1843.
[148] Dickens, 'Theatrical Examiner, Drury Lane', 837.

Dickens takes quite an interest in Albert, Tell's son, who in Knowles's play is worthy of his dignified father. In the pantomime, he becomes an 'obstinate, gluttonous, mischief-making, incorrigible young vagabond'. Dickens's experience with the narration of the William Tell plot, both in Knowles's and Morton's version, have left their mark in his own writings on Switzerland. There are often moments in which the tone and style of a scene changes and turns from a picturesque into a comic, exuberant and grotesque episode. Switzerland and pantomime go well together for Dickens, not only because of his fondness for popular culture, but also because both allow him to experiment, to reimagine a plot, add a detour or a dead end. Many of Dickens's references to Switzerland are such detours. The most prominent is certainly *Little Dorrit*, in which the Dorrit family travel to the top of the St Bernard Pass, but do not cross into Italy from there and return to Martigny instead. The opening of the second book of *Little Dorrit* is an interlude, which also allows Dickens to discuss the character of Mrs General, the lady who 'might have been taken – had been taken – to the top of the Alps and the bottom of Herculaneum, without disarranging a fold in her dress, or displacing a pin'.[149] David Copperfield's journey is similarly episodic in that it gives him a space to come to terms with his lost childhood, mourn his dead wife and realise that he loves Agnes. In 'A Message from the Sea', a collaborative piece Dickens wrote with Wilkie Collins in 1860, Switzerland appears in a story told within the main story. The same is true for *The Holly-Tree Inn*, where Switzerland figures in another series of stories about inns. As mentioned earlier, Mrs Skewton in *Dombey and Son* brings matters to a head when she claims to have always wanted to 'retreat to a Swiss farm, and live entirely surrounded by cows – and china'.[150] Mrs Skewton's is possibly the shortest of all Swiss interludes in Dickens, and yet, there is a double irony behind her utterance, as Dickens had, in fact, begun to write the novel in Switzerland.

In Dickens's review, Gesler, the villain, becomes a more interesting and prominent figure than Tell himself. This underlines Eigner's point that in the course of the Victorian age, the villain, that is Clown or Pantaloon, became a more interesting character than the hero.[151] That Tell goes unmentioned in his summary however, cannot be blamed on the actor, as Dickens makes clear. He states:

[149] Dickens, *Little Dorrit*, 438.
[150] Dickens, *Dombey and Son*, 284.
[151] Eigner, *Dickens Pantomime*, 105; 130.

'We ought not to close this notice without a mention of the exqusite [*sic*] burlesque acting of Mr C. J. Smith in *Tell*.' In contrast to this, the Gesler was only 'also good'. Dickens's interest therefore does not originate from the convincing performance of the relevant actor, but his interest in the role of the villain.

Once more Switzerland is an interlude. In *Harlequin and William Tell*, the Swiss episode is placed between two moments which are distinctly 'English': before the Tell plot, there is a patriotic fight between Liberty, Britannia – described as Liberty's right hand – and the Demon of Slavery. After the apple is shot, the stage transforms again and the harlequinade follows with typically 'English' items such as kettles, 'singing lustily [...] their English song'. Switzerland is so closely embraced that, to Dickens, it is not even worth mentioning. Once more, the scene is not exotic, but outspokenly domestic. There is some heavy irony in the domesticity, of course, as the printed version advertises the play as the 'grand, romantic, domestic, tragi-comic' Christmas Pantomime.[152]

The Great Manufacturer, or Dickens, William Tell and Fiction

In April 1860, Dickens published the sixth instalment of his *Uncommercial Traveller* series. It was called 'Travelling Abroad' and appeared in his magazine *All the Year Round*. The text is particularly restless at the beginning, constantly driving forward. It is written in generally short, syntactically clear and chronologically unambiguous sentences, reflecting the images seen from the moving coach. And yet, despite the fact that the text creates an impression of continuous progression both in form and plot, the movement is, in effect, backwards. The journey described is a trip back in time, a memory so vivid that the sudden end of the story almost appears as an anti-climax at first. The narrator is not actually travelling abroad, but sitting in a coach he intends to buy for a friend. However, consolation lies in the fact that despite the distorted chronology, all the events described have once been 'real', that the experience has truly been lived, the journey performed.

'Travelling Abroad' takes us back to continental travel in Europe before the establishment of linking railway networks. It is a relived

---

[152] *Dialogue, & c. in the Grand, Romantic, Domestic, Tragi-Comic Christmas Pantomime, Entitled Harlequin and William Tell* (London: S. G. Fairbrother, 1842), 1.

journey, a memory, a reverie, as we become acutely aware at the end of the text when we understand that the narrator has been stationary in a carriage throughout. The reality presented at the beginning of the plot is not the same as that at the end. The memory of the journey which spans several days in the narrative and fills more than four pages in the magazine only lasts 'half a minute' in reality, as we are told at the end of the story. As the narrator leaves England in his daydream, he is prepared to metamorphose into new characters, just as he is in fact imagining himself as a traveller. At the very beginning, he states his desire to adopt new roles, having 'no idea where I was going (which was delightful), except that I was going abroad'.[153] The 'where' in this sentence is not limited to space, but includes the dimensions of identity and time as well. Truth and reality become irrelevant in the face of the creative opportunities the narrator's objective observations offer when linked to the subjective interpretations of his mind.

His memory of Paris is filled with constant reminders of a dead man's body he had seen at the morgue, but in Strasbourg it is the 'vaudeville [...] played for me at the opposite house' which keeps him busy.[154] The scene, like the one in Switzerland, is 'real' insofar as it is based on a close observation of a real event, but it inspires the narrator to find his own story for it. In France, he turns into a puzzling hybrid between playwright and audience. He passes 'a wet Sunday evening' not at the purpose-built theatre, but his window, where he finds a plot for himself.

Once the 'uncommercial traveller' reaches Switzerland, he is fully immersed in his daydream:

> And now I came into the land of wooden houses, innocent cakes, thin butter soup, and spotless little inn bedrooms with a family likeness to Dairies. And now the Swiss marksmen were for ever rifle-shooting at marks across gorges, so exceedingly near my ear, that I felt like a new Gesler in a Canton of Tells, and went in highly-deserved danger of my tyrannical life.[155]

The first sentence sets the scene: the 'wooden houses' and 'spotless little inn bedrooms' suggest domestic warmth and comfort, embracing the simplicity but sufficiency of the food with its 'innocent cakes' and 'thin butter soup'. Now the narrative is ready for the story.

---

[153] Dickens, 'Travelling Abroad', 85.
[154] Ibid., 92.
[155] Ibid., 95.

Performing Switzerland   **55**

The rebellious spirit of William Tell seems to have produced a multitude of marksmen in Switzerland, some of them even of English descent. While in 'Travelling Abroad' the 'more than usually accomplished and amiable countryman of my own, who had shot himself deaf in whole years of competition' remains anonymous, a letter discloses that this is a portrait of the fourth Baron Vernon:

> a very good-humoured gentleman, but who has fallen into the strange infatuation of attending every rifle-match that takes place in Switzerland [...] He wins all kinds of prizes; gold watches, flags, teaspoons, teaboards, and so forth; and is constantly travelling about with them from place to place.[156]

Lord Vernon's son also recalled his father's 'singular appearance on such occasions, with spoons and soup-ladle in his button-holes'.[157] In 'Travelling Abroad', Dickens refers to a man he had met fourteen years earlier and who died seven years previously. The rifle-shooting scene is rooted in an event which Dickens witnessed in 1846, but in the process of transforming the real-life event into his fantasy, he adds an irresistibly comic and unmistakeably theatrical dimension to it. Consider the passage in the letter to Forster in which Dickens relates the event:

> Farther down the hill, other peasants were rifle-shooting for prizes, at targets set on the other side of a deep ravine, from two to three hundred yards off. It was quite fearful to see the astonishing accuracy of their aim, and how, every time a rifle awakened the ten thousand echoes of the green glen, some men crouching behind a little wall immediately in front of the targets, sprung up with large numbers in their hands denoting where the ball had struck the bull's eye – and then in a moment disappeared again.[158]

In his letter, Dickens appears as a mere observer who does not relate whether and how he is taking part in the festivities. Once Dickens turns personal experience into fiction in 'Travelling Abroad', the description is much shorter, but richer, funnier and undoubtedly more suggestive than the letter. The scene becomes hyperbolic with the marksmen 'for ever rifle-shooting'. In 'Travelling Abroad', Dickens is no longer the bystander and observer he was in the letter to Forster, but assumes an active part and reimagines himself as the

---

[156] To Forster, ?15–17 August 1846, *Letters*, vol. 4, 605.
[157] Ibid., 605n7.
[158] To Forster, 5 July 1846, *Letters*, vol. 4, 580.

56 Dickens and Switzerland

villain of the story. Dickens's identification with Gesler also adds a comic dimension, of course, particularly his statement that he 'went in highly-deserved danger of my tyrannical life'. This association seems to spring from a fancy for reading the world in theatrical plots and thereby assuming various different roles: we understand from the start that he leads no more of a tyrannical life than the actor impersonating Gesler on stage. Tyrannical impulses or guilt might, however, have their source in Dickens's life at the time of writing. It was a time when, as Claire Tomalin puts it, 'Secrets and lies threaded through the family's social arrangements', and Dickens 'was leading three distinct lives'.[159] He had split from his wife, was probably entangled in a secretive love affair with Ellen Ternan, was struggling to find occupations for his sons and also trying to bring his daughters into society.

Before developing her own argument in *Dickens's Villains*, Juliet John notes that the 'extreme imbalance between Dickens's ability to render the "bad" psyche and his inability to animate the "good" psyche' has often been pointed out by his critics.[160] Whereas I agree with her that Dickens does not fail to 'animate the "good" psyche', it is undeniable that he also 'had a particular weakness for villains whose express intention it is to smash up happy homes', as John Carey jokingly puts it.[161] Gesler, too, intends to 'smash up' William Tell's happy home. Much emphasis is put on the domestic bliss of the Tell household in Knowles's play: the second act opens with a view of Tell's Cottage, surrounded by a lush Alpine landscape with Emma, Tell's wife, exclaiming:

> O, the fresh morning! Heaven's kind messenger.
> That never empty-handed comes to those
> Who know to use its gifts.[162]

Little wonder, then, that Gesler should be more insistent in Dickens's literary imagination than Tell himself.

The Tell plot is mentioned on a few occasions in *Household Words*, but Dickens only appears twice as the author: once as the author of 'The Best Authority' and as the coauthor of 'My Mahogany

---

[159] Claire Tomalin, *Charles Dickens. A Life* (London: Penguin, 2012), 306; Michael Slater, *Charles Dickens* (New Haven, CT: Yale University Press, 2009), 471.

[160] Juliet John, *Dickens's Villains: Melodrama, Character, Popular Culture* (Oxford: Oxford University Press, 2001), 3.

[161] John Carey, *The Violent Effigy* (London: Faber, 1973), 17.

[162] James Sheridan Knowles, *William Tell. A Play in Five Acts* (London: Thomas Dolby, 1825), 19.

Friend' with Mary Louisa Boyle.[163] Michael Slater calls 'The Best Authority' 'a distracted search for a frequently named but always elusive figure'.[164] In a paragraph about halfway through the text, the narrator, resentful of this 'Best Authority' which fails to present itself to him, slips into the role of an anglicised Tell:

> Why am I, a free-born Briton, who never, never will – or rather who never, never would, if I could help it – why am I to truckle to this tyrant all the days of my life? Why is the Best Authority Gesler-like, to set his hat upon a pole in the épergne of every dinner table, in the hall of every club-house, in the stones of every street, and, violating the Charter proclaimed by the Guardian Angels who sang that strain, to demand me for his slave?[165]

Slater only mentions Dickens's literary allusion to James Thomson's 'Rule Britannia!' for this passage, but Dickens also draws on Knowles's play here. Thomson's lines do not feature the word 'free-born', but it appears twice in Knowles's text and is spoken by Tell on both occasions. In fact, the rhetoric of freedom in 'Rule Britannia!' and Knowles's *Tell* are so similar that it is hard to discern how much Dickens owes to each of these sources. The almost identical rhetoric, however, reflects the surprisingly close association of the Tell plot with British patriotism. In Dickens's text, both are comically distorted. While the anthem breaks off in its most important moment and we fill in for ourselves what it is that the 'free-born Briton' 'never, never' will be or do, the William Tell story is incessantly re-enacted in every corner of society where 'the Best Authority' appears, from dinner tables to 'the stones of every street'. The Tell in this story is quarrelsome and argumentative, fighting his Gesler with the quill rather than a set of arrows.

The second text which explicitly refers to William Tell and in which Dickens figures as a coauthor, is 'My Mahogany Friend', which appeared in *Household Words* in March 1851. Originally written by Mary Louisa Boyle (1810–1890), the text was heavily edited and rewritten by Dickens himself. In a letter to Boyle, he apologises for the changes he made: 'I hope, when you see it in print, you will not be alarmed by my use of the pruning-knife. I have tried to exercise

---

[163] Mary Louisa Boyle and Charles Dickens, 'My Mahogany Friend', *Household Words*, 8 March 1851, 560; 'The Best Authority', *Household Words*, 20 June 1857, 578.

[164] Dickens, *The Dent Uniform Edition of Dickens's Journalism, Vol. 3: 'Gone Astray' and other Papers from* Household Words *1851–59*, ed. Michael Slater (London: J. M. Dent, 1998), 407.

[165] 'The Best Authority', *Household Words*, 20 June 1857, 578.

58   *Dickens and Switzerland*

it with the utmost delicacy and discretion.'[166] Nonetheless, to Harry Stone, Dickens's revisions 'seem ubiquitous and transforming – a contribution acknowledged in the Contributors' Book by his designation as a joint author'.[167] Mary Boyle, the cousin of Mrs Lavinia Watson, whom Dickens had met in Switzerland, was an amateur actress and one of the women Dickens was close friends with. Michael Slater comments that Dickens made her 'the object of one of the longest lasting of his comic epistolary mock-flirtations', and Claire Tomalin states that if their friendship 'meant more to her than to him there was real warmth on both sides, and they enjoyed mock-flirtatious exchanges'.[168] Ada Nisbet, however, clearly believes that their exchange was less mocking and more actual flirtation – if not more than that.[169] Whatever their relationship, Dickens told his friend Edward Bulwer Lytton that she was 'the very best actress I ever saw, off the stage – and immeasurably better than a great many I have seen on it'.[170]

If Knowles's 'Tell' was domestic, Boyles and Dickens's is so in the extreme. Here, Tell's battles are fought in the home. The little tale takes domesticity as far as it can be taken, as the outside world is shut out and inaccessible. The story's focus, the family's mahogany hatstand, is entirely stationary and capable of telling a story precisely because it never moves. Even though some of the events seem to be taking place outside the family home, they manifest themselves most visibly inside it. Yet the characters, including the narrator, are ever out and about: they travel by the sea, to Italy and Switzerland, but what truly matters are the people in the house, or more precisely their hats, whose type and location on the hatstand determine the wearer's status in the family. It is through the presence and absence of these various forms of hats that the story is told. The overly loquacious hatstand, the 'Mahogany Friend', enters into imagined dialogues with the narrator. Whenever he returns to the house, sometimes after several years, he is presented with the next episode of the family fortunes by sitting in the 'picturesque old hall' and observing his 'Mahogany Friend'. Thereby he performs a physiognomy of objects,

---

[166] To Mary Boyle, 21 February 1851, in Harry Stone, *Charles Dickens's Uncollected Writings from* Household Words, *1850–1859* (Bloomington, IN: Indiana University Press, 1968), vol. 1, 217.

[167] Ibid.

[168] Slater, *Charles Dickens*, 300; Tomalin, *Charles Dickens*, 231.

[169] Ada Nisbet, *Dickens and Ellen Ternan* (Berkeley, CA: University of California Press, 1952), 81n36.

[170] To Bulwer Lytton, 3 September 1850, *Letters*, vol. 6, 162.

as the narrator is able to deduct a wearer's personality from their hat. The text openly alludes to some of its sources, most prominently William Tell, Walpole's *Castle of Otranto*, and perhaps surprisingly for a coauthored text, also Dickens's own biography. Stone notes that 'Some of the names, personalities and interrelationships in this piece bear a curious resemblance to those in the Dickens household'.[171] The children of the house are called Katie, Harry, Minnie, Tom and George, and with the exception of the last two boys' names, they are remarkably close to Dickens's own Katey, Harry and Mamie. In the narrative, George attends Eton, like Charley Dickens, and, as Harry Stone points out, 'the children's aunt (Georgina Hogarth) – like the aunt who appears a little later in the story – was living in the home and increasingly dominating the household'.[172] However, whereas there is no indication that Dickens's children did not welcome the presence of their mother's sister in the family household, the children in the story perceive their aunt as an illegitimate intruder. The aunt's hat, an exceptionally heavy beaver bonnet under which even the 'Mahogany Friend' suffers, is a trigger for an explicit reference to the Tell plot. The 'Mahogany Friend' asks the narrator:

> 'What do you think Harry did one day?' [...] 'He stuck [the beaver bonnet] up at the top of all (where, between ourselves, I have no doubt it will establish itself some day) and then he called Katie and Minnie to come and bow down before Gesler's hat. Minnie looked terrified, and kept watching "Aunt's" door – it opens on the staircase, that she may come out at odd times and glare at us, to see what we are all about. Katie tossed her black locks and said she did not care who came out, for she supposed Harry might put the things where he pleased, in his own mother's hall. There they stood, such a pretty group of rebels on a small scale, looking up at me!'[173]

The children link their situation to a plot they know, and by adapting it to their own situation they reimagine their aunt's hat as that of Gesler's, putting themselves into the position of the oppressed Swiss. Katie, very much in the mindset of the rebellious hero, defends her next of kin, reaffirms their family ties and supports his view of a foreign tyrant having invaded their home.

According to his son, Dickens's own children regularly acted out plays at Tavistock House 'on or about the 6th of January' and 'in a scratch sort of manner, and with no special assistance from the

---

[171] Dickens, *Uncollected Writings*, vol. 1, 220n.
[172] Ibid.
[173] Ibid., 221.

60   *Dickens and Switzerland*

authorities'.[174] These plays included Albert Smith's *Guy Fawkes* and Robert Barnabas Brough's extravaganza *William Tell*.[175] Like Dickens's children, those in the story act out their own play with 'no special assistance from the authorities' and cover the offending bonnet with a 'scarlet fez' pinched 'into a Cap of Liberty'.[176] In the story, however, the children's father disapproves of their deed. Revealingly, his name is William.

The beaver bonnet is the only hat which 'towers'; all other hats 'hang'. The order of the hats on the stand establishes a family hierarchy. William's hat, in his unquestioned role as the head of the house, hangs topmost, and yet, with the noble humility of his Swiss namesake, his hat is 'rather lower in the crown than the generality of hats, but, quite conventional enough to pass muster'.[177] It has a 'stern look as it inclined downwards; but it was neat and well-brushed, and had a very respectable appearance altogether'.[178] Just in case the reader may not quite have grasped the noble but modest manliness of the father, the 'Mahogany Friend' points out: 'That is William's, old William, or Sweet William, as we call him; see how manly it looks.'[179]

The mother's hat hangs 'On the left side, far lower down'.[180] Her physical and mental condition are expressed in her hat's position, but after being absent for a while, William's hat returns with 'a rather different look about it' and brings with him a 'strange straw hat, a Swiss hat'.[181] The narrator – or the hatstand? – points out, however, that strange as it may be, this hat was 'such as ladies (not peasants) wear in their excursions through Switzerland'. William's present companion stands on more equal terms with her partner, since her hat 'always hung next to William's – very close indeed – and the two hats always went out and came in at the same time'. When the couple depart on foreign travels again, the beaver bonnet 'established itself

---

[174] Charles Dickens Jr., 'Glimpses of Charles Dickens', *The North American Review*, 1 May 1895, 531.

[175] Ibid. Charles Dickens Jr.'s claim that he and his friend performed Brough's and Smith's plays in 'the years 1852 and 1853' must be a mistake either in date or in play, as Brough's extravaganza only came out in 1852 and Smith's pantomime in 1855. Robert Hanna claims that Brough's play was only performed in 1864. See Robert Hanna, 'Selection Guide to Dickens's Amateur Theatricals – Part 2', *Dickensian* 108, no. 486 (2012): 44.

[176] Dickens, *Uncollected Writings*, vol. 1, 221.

[177] Ibid., 219.

[178] Ibid.

[179] Ibid.

[180] Ibid.

[181] Ibid., 222.

Performing Switzerland **61**

much higher, immediately over the Cottage [hat]'.[182] The aunt's positioning herself 'immediately over' the dead wife's hat expresses forceful dominance of one female over another, but also creates a physical image of the pseudo-triangular relationship between the man of the house and the two women.

We do not learn whose sister the aunt is, but it is no matter, as she follows the footsteps of other problematic aunts. Mrs Chick in *Dombey and Son*, the novel which Dickens began in Switzerland, equally seizes power over the Dombey household, but does so even before Florence's mother dies. In *David Copperfield*, another novel with Swiss references, we meet two intimidating portraits of aunts at the beginning of the novel, that of Betsey Trotwood, his father's sister, and Copperfield's step-aunt, Miss Murdstone. David's fear of Betsey Trotwood turns out to be unjustified, and yet her displeasure with her brother and his wife originate in the fact that she seems unable to exert this kind of control.

The role of the children's mother is also fraught with problems, and is connected to the appearance of the domineering aunts. The blame for these invading aunts is exclusively put on absent or weak mothers rather than the fathers who seem to mean well by inviting them. The weakness and subordination of the lady of the house in 'My Mahogany Friend' is expressed in her plain straw cottage bonnet with its 'simple pale blue ribbon', contrasting with the 'manly' master's hat 'looking downwards' towards that of his wife's. William's wife follows the long line of absent or weak mothers we find almost everywhere in Dickens's writing. The plot of the absent mother also drives the narrative of *No Thoroughfare*, where first Wilding and later Vendale search for their origins.[183] The fact that the children's mother was wearing a straw hat does not seem to have been the issue, however, as William's new wife also wears a straw hat, albeit a Swiss one. Whereas the straw hat simply seems to indicate a modest but attractive female, the new wife's hat is 'strange', and 'made for more sun than she will get here'.[184] 'A Swiss hat, such as ladies (not peasants) wear' must suffice as a description not only for the hat but also for the character wearing it. If straw hats express femininity in this text, the aunt's 'grim' beaver bonnet's heaviness equals that of Miss Murdstone's 'heavy eyebrows' and the 'heavy

---

[182] Ibid.

[183] On absent mothers in Victorian fiction, see Carolyn Dever, *Death and the Mother from Dickens to Freud: Victorian Fiction and the Anxiety of Origins* (Cambridge: Cambridge University Press, 1998).

[184] Boyle and Dickens, 'My Mahogany Friend', 225.

chains' with which her bag hangs from her arm when David sees her for the first time.[185]

A particularly comic moment in 'My Mahogany Friend' is the description of young Harry's collection of hats, prompted by his friends who keep presenting him with them; as he 'spends almost all his time out of doors, what can be a more appropriate present than a covering for that wild head of his, eh, sir?'[186] Ironically, he also owns the 'green Tyrolese hat, with the peacock's feathers', probably a similar model to the Tyrolean Lover's in Astley's hippodrama. Harry's concern with what he puts on top of his head might reflect the vanity of an ordinary youth, but since it is he who invokes the parallel with Gesler and is also the son of a William, it might not be too daring to read this moment as a sort of filial compulsion to look for the right object, the one apple, through which his father may free the household from family tyrants.

Dickens's references to Switzerland were heavily influenced by the performances he saw on stage. Particularly before his first trip in 1844, his references to the country drew on a general cultural knowledge, which Dickens shared with his readers. This means that his mention of Switzerland and the Swiss often imply a knowledge of nineteenth-century theatre which is inaccessible to many readers today. Allusions to this culture are therefore often missed or considered irrelevant by contemporary critics. Until the end of his life, Dickens never quite forgot his first encounters with Switzerland and the Swiss on stage, which are visible in the frequently comic undertone and the fancy for pantomimic distortion that many of his references bear. Switzerland in Dickens is often comic and domestic in the extreme, and its representations borrow from pantomime and the circus. It is often episodic and incidental, offering a retreat or a moment for comic relief, but is rarely the subject or location where Dickens's characters remain for a longer time. There is, however, also another side to Dickens in Switzerland. It is more serious and personal than the one outlined above. This different form of involvement is the subject of Chapter 2.

---

[185] Dickens, *David Copperfield*, 41.
[186] Boyle and Dickens, 'My Mahogany Friend', 220.

Chapter 2

Narrating Switzerland

'Mrs Pipchin, my dear Paul,' returned his sister, 'is an elderly lady – Miss Tox knows her whole history – who has for some time devoted all the energies of her mind, with the greatest success, to the study and treatment of infancy, and who has been extremely well connected. Her husband broke his heart in – how did you say her husband broke his heart, my dear? I forget the precise circumstances.'

Dombey and Son, Chapter 8

Recognizant and Reflective, Dickens and the 'Need for Streets'

On the rather rare occasions Switzerland appears in Dickens scholarship, it is most often in connection with the author's complaint about Lausanne's 'absence of streets' and the resulting difficulties with writing. From Lausanne, Dickens complained to Forster:

For a week or a fortnight I can write prodigiously in a retired place (as at Broadstairs), and a day in London sets me up again and starts me. But the toil and labour of writing, day after day, without that magic lantern, is IMMENSE!! I don't say this, at all in low spirits, for we are perfectly comfortable here, and I like the place very much indeed, and the people are even more friendly and fond of me than they were in Genoa. I only mention it as a curious fact, which I have never had an opportunity of finding out before. *My* figures seem disposed to stagnate without crowds about them. I wrote very little in Genoa (only the *Chimes*), and fancied myself conscious of some

64   *Dickens and Switzerland*

such influence there – but Lord! I had two miles of streets at least, lighted at night, to walk about in; and a great theatre to repair to, every night.[1]

This has led critics to conclude that in Switzerland, the 'particular elasticity of imagination' which had allowed Dickens to write *Pickwick* and *Oliver Twist* at the same time 'appears to have deserted' him and that he was 'obviously in a creative crisis'.[2] Michael Slater agrees and notes that the author may have struggled with the fact that he had to

> begin his [Christmas] book when he had just got started on *Dombey*. [...] He had in earlier days managed to write two stories simultaneously but the first one had always been well under way before he had begun the second.[3]

At the same time, Slater also notes that 'The plot of *Dombey* was planned out in much greater detail previous to the actual writing than had been the case with any of its predecessors, with the possible exception of *Barnaby Rudge*'.[4] John Butt and Kathleen Tillotson equally claim that 'With *Dombey and Son*, in fact, Dickens begins a new chapter in his work', and that Dickens now 'found it desirable for the first time to plan each instalment on paper before he began writing'. These plans 'present valuable evidence both of the degree of consistency with which Dickens maintained his initial purpose, and of the changes in plan made during the course of the writing'.[5] If *Dombey* had been so well planned and structured before Dickens started with the actual process of writing, why was he struggling?

This chapter explores Dickens's various ways of narrating Switzerland. It is as much a chapter of Dickens's writing *in* Switzerland, as of Dickens writing *about* Switzerland, as the two are linked. The challenge here is that his representation of the country is fractured and incoherent. Its only consistency is its surprising appearance in unexpected moments: David Copperfield wakes from the trauma of his wife's death in Switzerland; the Dorrit family find themselves on top of the St Bernard after leaving the Marshalsea; in

---

[1] To Forster, 30 August 1846, *Letters*, vol. 4, 613.

[2] Peter Ackroyd, *Dickens* (London: Sinclair-Stevenson, 1990), 512; Neil Forsyth and Martine Hennard Dutheil de la Rochère, 'The Need for Streets', in *Charles Dickens and Europe*, ed. Maxime Leroy (Newcastle: Cambridge Scholars: 2013), 110.

[3] Slater, *Charles Dickens*, 260.

[4] Ibid., 257.

[5] John Butt and Kathleen Tillotson, *Dickens at Work on 'Dombey and Son'* (London: Methuen, 1951), 71.

'Lying Awake', a sleepless narrator's mind wanders back to experiences made in Switzerland; in 'Travelling Abroad', a daydream takes the uncommercial traveller back to the Alps; and finally, in 'Shy Neighbourhoods', an English walker dissociates from his environs and reimagines himself in the Swiss mountains. Dickens's writing goes far beyond travel writing and truly did become a 'means of worldmaking and of self-fashioning'.[6]

'Switzerland' is therefore not a coherent narrative in Dickens's fictional and factual writing and any attempt to make it so will inevitably come short of the plurality that Switzerland was to Dickens. In his writing, it keeps resurfacing like a spectre, and there is certainly an uncanny, ghostly and haunting dimension to it. Through a Freudian lens, its appearance can, on occasion, even bear parallels with the consistent but arrhythmical recurrence, the '*compulsion* to repeat', of a trauma. As we will see below, there is reason to believe that this comparison may not be too far-fetched. Yet, Switzerland is a theatre of emotions in Dickens's writing: it can also be the place of comic and carnivalesque release, of wonder and astonishment, introspection and self-discovery, flight and escape, of peace and revolution. Switzerland's fragmentary nature urges a multitude of approaches, making it difficult to contain it in a single critical narrative. In this chapter, I consequently discuss Dickens's narratives of Switzerland in linked but interdependent sections.

Switzerland's plurality manifests itself in different plots, motifs, themes and narrative modes in Dickens's writing. The variety of lenses which Dickens employs have certain regularities, and many of these tropes and modes can be found in his other writings as well. They include, but are by no means limited to, juxtapositions of the picturesque and the sublime, a fascination with grotesque bodies, mental and physical deformity, supernatural experiences, identity, change and death. As with many of Dickens's texts, trying to determine the genre of his Swiss writings is redundant. His texts are not a single dish but a meal with carefully chosen courses – just like those his wife would describe in the cooking manual she published under a pen name.[7] 'In nothing', it has rightly been claimed, for example, 'is *Dombey* more characteristically Dickensian than in its complex orchestration of a variety of literary modes'.[8]

---

[6] Judith Adler, 'Travel as Performed Art', *American Journal of Sociology* 94, no. 6 (1989), 1368.

[7] See Introduction, 7 and 7n24.

[8] Schlicke in Schlicke, *Oxford Reader's Companion to Dickens*, 187.

66 *Dickens and Switzerland*

The formats he chooses for his narratives are similarly varied. Switzerland appears in virtually every medium Dickens decided to put his pen to: it figures in novels (explicitly in *David Copperfield*, *Little Dorrit* and *Our Mutual Friend*; implicitly or very marginally in *Dombey and Son*, *Hard Times* and *Martin Chuzzlewit*), shorter pieces and short stories (*Sketches by Boz*, *Pictures from Italy*, 'To Be Read at Dusk', 'Lying Awake', 'Travelling Abroad', to name but a few), a play (*No Thoroughfare*), numerous fictional and non-fictional articles ('Our Bore', 'Idiots', 'A Few Conventionalities' and many more), several collaborations (including *The Holly-Tree Inn*, 'A Message from the Sea' and 'My Mahogany Friend') and, of course, his letters.

The first part of this chapter is mainly biographical, an indispensable context for gaining an insight into Dickens's challenges during his first attempt at starting a new novel in a foreign country. It is, in essence, a reassessment of Dickens's writing difficulties during his stay in Lausanne in 1846. It mentions one of his earliest known encounters with factual travel writing about Switzerland, offers a brief discussion of the texts he wrote when in the country and provides a review of the surprising number of stories he seems to have conceived during his stay in Lausanne. The second part is a survey and explores two aesthetic forms, the grotesque and the sublime, as well as the theme of the oral, all of which appear and reappear in an ever-changing manner in Dickens's texts connected to Switzerland.

A *Separation*, or Moving to Switzerland

A combination of factors seems to have made Dickens 'full of disquietude and anxiety' during his stay in Lausanne. The resulting restlessness made him 'sick, giddy and capriciously despondent', and he eventually developed 'a bloodshot eye' paired with a severe headache which caused him 'a pain across the brow, that I thought I must have got cupped'.[9] Most biographers point to Dickens's trouble in Switzerland, and many attribute it to the strain of writing two texts at the same time. Forster remains strangely elusive about the reasons, though he too seems to have blamed his friend's condition on the simultaneous composition of *Dombey* and *The Battle of Life*.[10]

---

[9] To Forster, 26 September 1846, *Letters*, vol. 4, 625; to Forster, 30 September and 1 October 1846, *Letters*, vol. 4, 626.

[10] Forster, *Life of Dickens*, 450.

There are a great number of unanswered questions surrounding Dickens's move, life and work in Switzerland. It is unclear when and why he decided to go to Switzerland, why he chose Lausanne and what it was that triggered his 'restless' state. Some of the most frequently quoted reasons, all of them present in the extract of a letter to Forster below, clarify why he wanted to leave London:

> I don't think I *could* shut out the paper sufficiently here, to write well. No ... I will write my book in Lausanne and Genoa, and forget everything else if I can; and by living in Switzerland for the summer, and in Italy or France for the winter, I shall be saving money while I write.[11]

In spring 1846, Dickens was trying to come to terms with the relative failure of his short-lived editorship at the *Daily News*. After the debacle at the newspaper, Dickens may have wanted to 'leave the scene of the crime', as Peter Ackroyd put it.[12] The reasons Dickens provides here are all very convincing arguments to leave England, but they do not explain why he decided to move to Switzerland. Dickens's explanation that he would be saving money by moving abroad has been accepted as another reason. The *Pilgrim* editors claim that 'his expenses would be lower', but they do not provide any evidence whether this was, in fact, the case.[13] Michael Slater supports this view, adding that Dickens wanted 'to give himself some respite from the pressures he was always under in London', and that 'financial considerations were also important' since living abroad would be cheaper.[14] At any rate, judging from his surviving letters, money did not seem to be of particular concern in his decision, as he never mentioned it again. But Forster was opposed to the idea that Dickens should go abroad again and there seems to have been 'much discussion' about the subject.[15] The surviving extract of Dickens's letter above does indeed look like a part of a longer and more elaborate attempt to convince Forster of his need to leave London. The explicit desire to remove himself from the city also puts the popular and self-perpetuating vision of Dickens as an essentially urban writer in perspective. It is in this extract that Dickens first mentions his intention of going to Switzerland in 1846. Considering that it was written in April and he was there in June, leaving London may have been a spontaneous decision. Another explanation may have been

---

[11] To Forster, ?17–20 April 1846, *Letters*, vol. 4, 537.
[12] Ackroyd, *Dickens*, 274.
[13] To Forster, ?17–20 April 1846, *Letters*, vol. 4, 538n1.
[14] Slater, *Charles Dickens*, 252.
[15] Forster, *Life of Dickens*, 408.

68   *Dickens and Switzerland*

his wife: many critics – with the notable exception of Forster – point out Catherine's objection to moving back to Genoa, where Dickens had lived before, thus further promoting the idea of Switzerland as a second-rate escape rather than the result of a deliberate choice.

Only days later, when he had definitely decided that it was not going to be Genoa again, Dickens began to announce his absence to other friends, providing other, albeit no more convincing, explanations as to why he had chosen Switzerland. Angela Burdett Coutts, the rich, unmarried heiress and philanthropist, was a close friend and took great interest in Charley, Dickens's youngest son:

> Until within a fortnight or three weeks ago, I have retained the intention of entering Charley [for Eton] in May. But since then, I have conceived the idea of going to Switzerland for a year. Firstly, because I am most desirous to separate myself in a marked way from the Daily News (with which I have long since ceased to have any connexion, and in connecting myself with which at all, I have no doubt I made a mistake). Secondly, because I have a long book to write, which I could write better in retirement. Thirdly, because I want to get up some Mountain knowledge in all the four seasons of the year, for purposes of fiction. Now I think that if I go to Lausanne or some such place, where there are English Clergymen who take pupils, and keep Charley in good training under such auspices, he will enter King's College at greater advantage and with a better prestige about him, than if he began as I originally designed.[16]

Even though Dickens's explanation for going to Switzerland is more structured in this letter, it is only slightly more convincing. He could have separated and removed himself from the newspaper – and from London – in many other places, but the seclusion he must have been hoping for was to be found, in his mind at least, in Switzerland. David Copperfield would later experience the country in a way that Dickens here outlined for himself. The only argument in favour of Switzerland rather than London is the idea to 'get up some Mountain knowledge'. The *Pilgrim* editors quite rightly point out, however, that Dickens did not include Switzerland in his fiction until his later works.[17] The 'Mountain knowledge' Dickens acquired in Lausanne was important, but cannot be measured in the number of its fictional representations in his works. Dickens's reflections, associations and references to Switzerland are often tacit, personal and random. Nor do all of his Swiss associations, reminiscences and experiences

---

[16] To Miss Burdett Coutts, 22 April 1846, *Letters*, vol. 4, 539.
[17] Ibid., 539n3.

manifest themselves as such. Those that do are only the tip of the iceberg, as it were.

Whereas his decision to leave London may have been impulsive and spontaneous, going to Switzerland was not a new idea but something Dickens had been contemplating for a while. In 1845, he had already hoped to 'linger for a month or so, in France or Switzerland, on our way home'.[18] However, the desire to visit the country was even older than that. In 1843, a year before travelling to Switzerland for the first time, he told Forster:

> I shall take all the family, and two servants – three at most – to some place which I know beforehand to be CHEAP and in a delightful climate, in Normandy or Brittany, to which I shall go over, first, and where I shall rent some house for six or eight months. During that time, I shall walk through Switzerland, cross the Alps, travel through France and Italy; take Kate perhaps to Rome and Venice, but not elsewhere; and in short see everything that is to be seen. I shall write my descriptions to you from time to time, exactly as I did in America; and you will be able to judge whether or not a new and attractive book may not be made on such ground. At the same time I shall be able to turn over the story I have in my mind, and which I have a strong notion might be published with great advantage, *first in Paris* – but that's another matter to be talked over.[19]

The travel 'descriptions' were of course the first ideas for his *Pictures from Italy*. Switzerland does feature in the *Pictures*, but much more marginally than Dickens seems to outline here. According to the *Pilgrim* editors, the story Dickens was thinking about may have been 'for a novel with a continental setting' which 'never matured, though it persisted for some years'; 'alternatively', they suggest, 'the first notion of *Dombey and Son* may already have been in his mind'.[20] Despite their claim that Dickens's idea for a continental novel 'never matured', significant parts of *A Tale of Two Cities*, *Little Dorrit* and *No Thoroughfare* are set on the Continent. Whereas Switzerland appears in *Little Dorrit* and *No Thoroughfare*, *A Tale of Two Cities* has more implicit links to Dickens's stay in Lausanne.[21]

The books Dickens read as a young boy and the numerous representations on stage discussed in the last chapter were not the only

---

[18] To Miss Coutts, 18 March 1845, *Letters*, vol. 4, 281; to Count D'Orsay, 18 March 1845, *Letters*, vol. 4, 284.

[19] To Forster, 1 November 1843, *Letters*, vol. 3, 587.

[20] Ibid., 588n2.

[21] See Chapter 2, 82ff.

70 *Dickens and Switzerland*

sources to familiarise him with popular images and narratives of the country. *Murray's Handbook for Travellers in Switzerland* is often the first source scholars refer to when discussing Dickens's travels, probably because he had ordered books from this publisher in March 1844 before he went to Italy.[22] However, William Thomson's *Two Journeys through Italy and Switzerland*, a travelogue written by Catherine Dickens's uncle, is an earlier, and probably the first, travel book on Switzerland that Dickens read when he was correcting its proofs in 1835.[23] Thomson's book introduced or at least reminded Dickens of another particular and popular kind of narrative about Switzerland. Just like Dickens's *Pictures*, Thomson's account was based on letters he wrote while travelling. While Thomson's book is organised in 'Letters' rather than chapters, Dickens reorganised the *Pictures* in a way which no longer tells of their original format as 'Travelling Letters' in the *Daily News*. *Two Journeys* is a rather straightforward travel diary, so much so that Thomson begins his preface on an apologetic note:

> Another volume of Travels may appear an unnecessary addition to the mass, already accumulated, of this description of literature – more especially as the path along which the reader of the following pages will be conducted is by no means an unbeaten one. I have visited no unknown regions, met with no surprising adventures, and discovered no remarkable objects which have not already been described by abler pens. Yet I publish this volume, believing, notwithstanding these disadvantages, that its contents may be found not altogether destitute of interest.[24]

Thomson does not elaborate on what this interest is, but provides another example of the concern that his audience's interest in accounts and depictions of Italy and Switzerland may already have been satisfied. Apart from *Pictures*, perhaps, Thomson does not seem to have been a significant influence for Dickens's representation of Switzerland.

Rather than giving general information in his travel accounts, Dickens – like Thomson – put great emphasis on individual experience.[25] His two travel books, *Pictures from Italy* and *American*

---

[22] To John Murray, 5 March 1844, *Letters*, vol. 4, 36. Also see footnote n9 and Kathleen Tillotson, in the Preface to *Letters*, vol. 4, viii.

[23] William Thomson, *Two Journeys through Italy and Switzerland* (London: John Macrone, 1835).

[24] Ibid., iii.

[25] Ibid., v.

Notes, are determinedly 'records of the writer's personal experiences and responses, rather than guidebooks'.[26] Yet Dickens's own Swiss texts are more innovative and multifaceted than Thomson's account. Even though they borrow some of their rhetoric and their play with the picturesque and sublime from Victorian travel literature and popular entertainment, they are essentially 'Dickensian' in style. Dickens makes the unfamiliar familiar, but can reverse the process too. He often follows his impulse to 'dwell upon the romantic side of familiar things', refusing to draw a clear line between 'self' and 'other', 'domestic' and 'foreign'.[27] Dickens narrates Switzerland both through and beyond the country's stereotypes.

These new and innovative effects introduce an aspect of fluidity and transcendence to his Swiss writings and make it nigh impossible to attribute a single genre to them. Even in *Pictures from Italy*, Dickens's earliest extended writing on Switzerland and still a broadly 'traditional' travel narrative, the narrator seems unable to control his memories and consequently his writing. Despite his awareness of the text's geographical and cultural limitations, personal impulse overcomes intention. Dickens admits that 'The business of these recollections being with Italy, and my business, consequently, being to scamper back thither as fast as possible, I will not recall (though I am sorely tempted)'. What follows is a tour de force of apophasis or paralipsis on Switzerland and France, each beginning with 'Or how ...', of what the narrator is 'not' recalling. Writing about 'the other' suddenly becomes a playful contemplation of the 'self' and about what 'I will not recall'. It turns into a teasing intermediary between telling and not telling, between consciousness and unconsciousness, as well as the unsuccessful attempt of controlling memory and the moment it resurfaces. The narrative is told in a multi-rhetorical trope, a kind of irony, which seems to keep triggering more and more of the pleasurable but not-to-be-told Swiss material until, after a journey on the Mediterranean from Marseille to Genoa, the story reaches the literal and figural safety of Italian soil once again. Nathalie Vanfasse has called it an act of preterition and confirms what we have seen in Chapter 1, namely that, for Dickens, Switzerland had a homely and familiar quality to it even before he visited the country for the first time. In *Pictures*, she claims, due to the country's orderliness and cleanliness Switzerland prepares the traveller

---

[26] Leonee Ormond in Schlicke, *Oxford Reader's Companion to Dickens*, 456.
[27] Charles Dickens, *Bleak House*, 7.

72 *Dickens and Switzerland*

for his return to England, whereas the parts of France he sees on his journey back to his home country are more reminiscent of Italy in its state of developmental delay.[28]

It may not be quite clear why Dickens decided to move to Switzerland in 1846, but it is even less evident why he chose Lausanne. Thomson does not mention it in his book and at first, it appears, Genoa was also an option. He did not seem to know anyone in Lausanne – one of the town's attractions, perhaps – nor did he have any other visible connection to it. It does not figure in his known writing before April 1846. In a letter to Augusta de la Rue, a very special friend he had made during his time in Genoa, he claimed that his wife was opposed to returning to Italy and that he would, by 'coming as near you as I could, pitch my tent somewhere on the Lake of Geneva – say at Lausanne, whence I should run over to Genoa immediately'.[29] How truthful this explanation was is difficult to ascertain. Other places – Geneva, Milan and Nice, for example – would have been closer and more convenient. Despite his claim, Dickens only met his Genoan friends once in 1846.[30] Judging from Dickens's letters, Lausanne was the family's intended destination when they left England. Yet Forster reports that

> having been tempted as they came along to rest somewhat short of it, by a delightful glimpse of Neuchâtel [Dickens] thought it best to come on here [to Lausanne], in case I should find, when I begin to write, that I want streets sometimes. In which case, Geneva (which I hope would answer the purpose) is only four and twenty miles away.[31]

From the start therefore, Dickens had had his 'need for streets' in mind and planned accordingly. Once he had decided that he was definitely going abroad again around 20 April, he initially contemplated staying in Switzerland for the whole year, but by the end of June he had settled for moving 'to Paris before Christmas'.[32] If Lausanne was indeed too much of a 'mighty dull little [t]own' for Dickens, he hid it well.[33] He praised it in his letters and of *Rosemont*, the house he had

---

[28] Nathalie Vanfasse, *La Plume et la route. Charles Dickens, écrivain-voyageur* (Aix-en-Provence: Provence University Press, 2017), 42.

[29] To Augusta de la Rue, 17 April 1846, *Letters*, vol. 4, 534. See the Conclusion, 181 for more on Dickens's relationship with the de la Rues.

[30] To Emile de la Rue, 20 August 1846, *Letters*, vol. 4, 608.

[31] To Forster, ?13 or 14 June 1846, *Letters*, vol. 4, 560.

[32] To Thomas Mitton, 20 April 1846, *Letters*, vol. 4, 537; to Augusta de la Rue, 17 April 1846, *Letters*, vol. 4, 534; to H. P. Smith, 22 April 1846, *Letters*, vol. 4, 540; to Joseph Valckenberg, 25 June 1846, *Letters*, vol. 4, 572.

[33] To Frederick Dickens, 16 June 1846, *Letters*, vol. 4, 562.

rented, he said that it was placed in 'the most lovely and delicious situation imaginable'.[34]

Confidential and Accidental, or Trouble in Lausanne

We have already seen that Dickens had trouble writing in Lausanne. According to Peter Ackroyd, he even experienced 'some kind of nervous collapse'.[35] Yet, this difficult period by no means extended over the full five months which he spent in Switzerland. In fact, his nervousness reached a peak whenever he was thinking of or trying to work on his Christmas book, *The Battle of Life*. Due to the significant amount of critical attention paid to his distress, it is easy to forget that during most of his time in Switzerland, Dickens travelled, entertained, visited the Asylum for the Blind that his new friend William Haldimand had founded, took an interest in educational matters, the prison and criminal system, walked, got to know the area and its people and seemed to be at his ease.

He began *Dombey* about a month after arriving in Switzerland, 'writing slowly at first, of course', but hoping to finish 'the first number in the course of a fortnight at farthest'.[36] In July, he reported an 'extraordinary nervousness it would hardly be possible to describe', and which Forster claims '*came upon him after he had been writing all day*'.[37] Understandable, though, that after a good day's work even Dickens underestimated his achievements and needed a break. It was only by the end of August that Dickens's rhetoric turned to hyperbole, the mode becoming tragic and the mood desperate. Much critical emphasis has been put on Dickens's description of the 'infinite pains I take, or what extraordinary difficulty I find in getting on FAST'.[38] Forster remarks, however, that in 'less than a week from this date his second number [of *Dombey*] was finished, his first slip of the little book done, and his confidence greater'.[39]

But the confidence did not last. Dickens still believed that he was writing slowly with 'infinite pains' and 'extraordinary difficulty'. This coincides with Forster's description of him 'burning to get to

---

[34] To Douglas Jerrold, 16 June 1846, *Letters*, vol. 4, 565.

[35] Ackroyd, *Dickens*, 513.

[36] To Forster, 5 July 1846, *Letters*, vol. 4, 579.

[37] Ibid., 579. Emphasis in original.

[38] To Forster, 20 August 1846, *Letters*, vol. 4, 612.

[39] Forster, *Life of Dickens*, 449.

74   *Dickens and Switzerland*

work' on the Christmas Book of which the 'general idea' seemed 'pretty well matured'.[40] *Dombey* was

> the first of Dickens's novels for which a complete set of working notes survives, planning every number in detail. Dickens was two full months ahead of the publisher at the outset [...] but his lead was gradually eroded until he was barely a week ahead by the end.[41]

Contrary to his own assessment of his progress, Dickens was never truly late with *Dombey*. He had only taken about a week longer to complete the first number than he had planned. True, just after his arrival he had told Forster that he intended 'to get Four Numbers of the monthly book done here, and the Christmas book', but nowhere does he express any concern regarding the quality of the novel.[42] In August, he even told his friend about the composition of *Dombey*: 'My troubles are not greater, thank God, than they usually are, when I am plunging neck and heels into a new Book. It is always an anxious and worrying time. Mais il faut manger.'[43] Initially, then, *Dombey* was not the problem. Yet by the time he was working on the longer novel, he could not help but constantly think about the Christmas book. It interfered and haunted him, would not let go of him and eventually became his *idée fixe*. 'If you knew how it hangs about me', he complained to Forster in July, confessing that it would be 'an immense relief to have it done'.[44] He was losing himself in the hope that the 'shapeless visions' he had of it would eventually materialise into a more tangible form. He could not 'but think there may turn out to be something good in them when I see them more plainly' and yet he never did. The *Battle* would remain an 'odd shadowy undefined' and 'foggy' idea – if not to its author, who concluded that 'it may be pretty and affecting, and comfortable too', then certainly to its readers.[45]

The main cause of Dickens's restlessness in Switzerland therefore seems to have been more closely related to the composition of the *Battle* than any of the other possible causes outlined above, that is the lack of streets and the attempt to write two texts at the same time. The most acute period of his discomfort was limited to about two months, which corresponds fairly closely to the composition of

---

[40] To Forster, 30 August 1846, *Letters*, vol. 4, 612; 614.
[41] Schlicke in Schlicke, *Oxford Reader's Companion to Dickens*, 184.
[42] To Forster, ?22 June 1846, *Letters*, vol. 4, 569.
[43] To Emile de la Rue, 20 August 1846, *Letters*, vol. 4, 608.
[44] To Forster, 18 July 1846, *Letters*, vol. 4, 586.
[45] To Forster, 25 June 1846, *Letters*, vol. 4, 569; to Forster, 18 July 1846, *Letters*, vol. 4, 586; to Forster, 31 October 1846, *Letters*, vol. 4, 650.

the Christmas Story. Among other critics, René Rapin has claimed that Dickens's uneasiness was 'largely caused, as he had begun to realise after some two and a half months' happy stay at *Rosemont*, by a deep, unsatisfied craving in his nature for the bustle and excitement of city life' and its streets.[46] It was not, however, his 'need for streets' that caused Dickens's problems with the *Battle*. It was the other way round.

The creation of the *Battle* went hand in hand with a growing preoccupation with life, death, the past, memory, (auto)biography and his own childhood. Inevitably, this also affected the process of writing *Dombey* and culminated in his idea to write an autobiography. The only visible link between the *Battle* and its composition in Switzerland is Dickens's dedication of it 'to my English Friends in Switzerland'. That at least the beginning of *Dombey* was strongly linked with Dickens's stay in Switzerland becomes apparent in a perhaps surprising place. In 1858, on occasion of the publication of the Cheap Edition, Dickens wrote a new preface for the novel:

> I began this book by the lake of Geneva, and went on with it for some months in France. The association between the writing and the place of writing is so curiously strong in my mind, that at this day, although I know every stair in the little Midshipman's house, and could swear to every pew in the church in which Florence was married, or to every young gentleman's bedstead in Doctor Blimber's establishment, I yet confusedly imagine Captain Cuttle as secluding himself from Mrs Mac Stinger among the mountains of Switzerland.[47]

With the exception of Mrs Skewton's exclamation about cows, Switzerland only seems to have been present in Dickens's mind when he thought about *Dombey*. It was a deeply personal and implicit association which, in this case, is only visible in the novel's paratext and context.

Towards the end of his stay in Lausanne, Dickens's reflections about life were besieged by relentless thoughts about death. This period of excessive inspiration is coupled with intense mental and physical discomfort expressed as but not necessarily due to a 'lack of streets'.[48] His plans for stabilising his financial situation and further professional development ('a great deal of money might possibly be made [...] by one's having Readings of one's own books') are shot

---

[46] René Rapin, 'Lausanne and some English Writers', *Etudes de Lettres* 2, no. 3 (1959): 111.

[47] Dickens, *Dombey and Son*, Appendix A, 834.

[48] To Forster, 30 August 1846, *Letters*, vol. 4, 612.

76 *Dickens and Switzerland*

through with memories of childhood.[49] These dichotomies are also visible in his Swiss texts: moments of the picturesque and the sublime abruptly turn into tableaux of the grotesque; landscapes of peacefulness and serenity are threatened by potential outbreaks of violence. The Swiss, with their admirable Protestantism, their 'wonderful education', 'splendid schools' and 'noble independence of character' occasionally morph into manipulative villains such as Obenreizer in *No Thoroughfare* and Rigaud in *Little Dorrit*, or become degenerate 'idiots' inhabiting destitute Catholic regions such as the one 'lying on the wood-pile who sunned himself and nursed his goitre' and his mother, 'throwing her child over one of her shoulders and her goitre over the other' in *The Uncommercial Traveller*.[50] Dickens's Switzerland triggers a storytelling of and in extremes which creates irresistible tensions and seemingly irreconcilable contrasts.

The tension thus created often releases itself in hints at the supernatural. The ghostly, the haunted and the uncanny which fluctuate between the world of the living and the dead while belonging to neither of them, are Dickens's strategies to express these contrasts. From the start, the Switzerland that Dickens describes has an otherworldly quality to it: in 1844, shortly before his first experience of the country, he imagines himself 'cutting through the Snow in the Valleys of Switzerland: and plunging through the Mountains in the Dead of Winter'.[51] In Lausanne he is struck by its 'haunted-looking old towers' and the 'eternally changing range of prodigious mountains [...] sometimes very ghosts in the clouds and mist'.[52] While thinking about his alleged need for streets, he fancied being haunted by spectres himself:

> The absence of any accessible streets continues to worry me, now that I have so much to do, in a most singular manner. It is quite a little mental phenomenon. I should not walk in them in the day time, if they were here, I dare say: but at night I want them beyond description. I don't seem able to get rid of my spectres unless I can lose them in crowds.[53]

'The possessor', Rosemarie Bodenheimer notes, 'is again possessed'.[54] As this passage suggests, transitions between day and night, states

---

[49] To Forster, 11 October 1846, *Letters*, vol. 4, 631.

[50] To Douglas Jerrold, 24 October 1846, *Letters*, vol. 4, 644.

[51] To Thomas Mitton, 5 November 1844, *Letters*, vol. 4, 212.

[52] To Forster, 5 July 1846, *Letters*, vol. 4, 581; to Forster, ?22 June 1846, *Letters*, vol. 4, 598.

[53] To Forster, ?20 September 1846, *Letters*, vol. 4, 622.

[54] Rosemarie Bodenheimer, *Knowing Dickens* (Ithaca, NY: Cornell University Press, 2007), 182; Dickens, 'Travelling Abroad', 95.

of wakefulness and sleep, and of consciousness and unconsciousness play another important role in Dickens's portrayal of Switzerland. In *No Thoroughfare*, Obenreizer poisons Vendale at night in Basel. 'To Be Read at Dusk' already suggests the ideal time of reading in its title. 'Lying Awake' already features a direct connection with sleep through its title, of course, and Dickens's own experience of waking up on top of the St Bernard, not knowing where he was, and reporting to Forster that he 'thought for a moment I had died in the night and passed into the unknown world' may be one of the sources for this frequent image.[55] After Dora's death, David Copperfield's travelling abroad resembles a dream, the exact steps of which he cannot retrace until he is in Switzerland: 'There are some dreams that can only be imperfectly and vaguely described; and when I oblige myself to look back on this time of my life, I seem to be recalling such a dream.'[56] Amy Dorrit's own experience of Switzerland is not dissimilar:

> It was from this position that all she saw appeared unreal; the more surprising the scenes, the more they resembled the unreality of her own inner life as she went through its vacant places all day long. The gorges of the Simplon, its enormous depths and thundering waterfalls, the wonderful road, the points of danger where a loose wheel or a faltering horse would have been destruction, the descent into Italy, the opening of that beautiful land as the rugged mountain-chasm widened and let them out from a gloomy and dark imprisonment – all a dream – only the old mean Marshalsea a reality.[57]

Amy's dreamlike state continues in Italy, but Peter Orford is only partly correct when he claims that 'in this quest for unreality, Dickens relocates the action to that place in which he himself was personally overwhelmed by fancy, Venice'.[58] Amy is already feeling the same way when she is in Switzerland.

In 'Shy Neighbourhoods', the narrator falls 'asleep to the monotonous sound of my own feet' and 'as the day broke mistily (it was autumn time)', he cannot 'disembarrass myself of the idea' that he is in Switzerland. This 'sleepy notion' is stronger than reality and the narrator describes how it is a 'curiosity of broken sleep' that he 'made immense quantities of verses on that pedestrian occasion' and that

---

[55] To Forster, ?6 September 1846, *Letters*, vol. 4, 618.
[56] Dickens, *David Copperfield*, 697.
[57] Dickens, *Little Dorrit*, 451.
[58] Peter Orford, 'An Italian Dream and a Castle in the Air: The Significance of Venice in *Little Dorrit*', *Dickensian* 103, no. 472 (2007): 159.

he 'spoke a certain language once familiar to me, but which I have nearly forgotten from disuse, with fluency'.[59] He further explains:

> Of both these phenomena I have such frequent experience in the state between sleeping and waking, that I sometimes argue with myself that I know I cannot be awake, for, if I were, I should not be half so ready. The readiness is not imaginary, because I often recall long strings of the verses, and many turns of the fluent speech, after I am broad awake.[60]

Other characters experience such a 'state between sleeping and waking' in Switzerland as well. In 'A Message from the Sea', the narrator's brother decides 'to yield no longer to this dreaming apathy' which befalls him in an inn on a Swiss mountain. We find out later that it is the foreshadowing of a death.[61] He falls asleep in a chair, but in the morning, he finds himself 'lying on the bed, without being able to remember in the least how or when he reached it'.[62] The next morning, 'he almost doubted the events of the night, and, but for the evidence of his watch, which still pointed to twenty minutes before twelve, would have been disposed to treat the whole matter as a dream'.[63] Here, the broken sleep, dreams and watch stand for a friend's death, similar to Vendale's perturbed nights in *No Thoroughfare*, which announce Obenreizer's attempt to kill him. In *No Thoroughfare*, when Vendale falls into 'the strangest confusion of dreams', this is less figurative, and caused by Obenreizer's poison instead. Vendale, too, is in a semi-conscious state between sleeping and waking, as Obenreizer's 'creeping hand' trying to rob him calls him 'out of that dream, though he could not wake from it'.[64]

To Dickens, Forster tells us, Lausanne 'had its natural dullness increased by its streets going up and down hill abruptly and steeply, like the streets in a dream; and the consequent difficulty of getting about it'.[65] Yet there were other reasons for Dickens to think about memory and dreaming during his stay in Switzerland. After visiting the Asylum for the Blind, he reported a remarkable meeting with one of the inmates to Forster:

[59] Charles Dickens, 'Shy Neighbourhoods', in *The Uncommercial Traveller, Dent Uniform Edition of Dickens' Journalism*, vol. 4, 118.
[60] Ibid.
[61] Dickens, 'The Club-Night' in 'A Message from the Sea', *Household Words*, 25 December 1860, 600.
[62] Ibid., 601.
[63] Ibid.
[64] Collins and Dickens, *No Thoroughfare*, 196.
[65] To Forster, ?22 June 1846, *Letters*, vol. 4, 568.

Soon after this, [the patient] had a dream of being bitten in the shoulder by some strange animal. As it left a great impression on his mind, he told M. the Director that he had told another lie in the night. In proof of it he related his dream, and added, 'it must be a lie you know, because there is no strange animal here, and I never was bitten'. Being informed that this sort of lie was a harmless one, and was called a dream, he asked whether dead people ever dreamed while they were lying in the ground. He is one of the most curious and interesting studies possible.[66]

Dreams, memory and death occur within the same moment. The blind patient at the institution is remembering his dream so vividly that he takes it to be a lie. Having been punished for lying before, he now confesses this new 'lie' about being bitten as well. Dickens himself expressed his anxiety about *The Battle of Life* in a metaphor of dreaming: 'At all other times since I began, I have been brooding and brooding over the idea that it was a wild thing to dream of, ever: and that I ought to be at rest for the *Dombey*.'[67]

There are some indications as to what triggered the moments of Dickens's intense re-examination in Switzerland. One of the most memorable nights must have been that spent on the St Bernard when Dickens, after seeing the morgue and its frozen travellers near the monastery, 'thought for a moment I had died in the night and passed into the unknown world'.[68] The morgue had clearly left a mark, which would keep haunting Dickens:

Beside the convent, in a little outhouse with a grated iron door which you may unbolt for yourself, are the bodies of people found in the snow who have never been claimed and are withering away – not laid down, or stretched out, but standing up, in corners and against walls; some erect and horribly human, with distinct expressions on the faces; some sunk down on their knees; some dropping over on one side; some tumbled down altogether, and presenting a heap of skulls and fibrous dust. There is no other decay in that atmosphere; and there they remain during the short days and the long nights, the only human company out of doors, withering away by grains, and holding ghastly possession of the mountain where they died. It is the most distinct and individual place I have seen, even in this transcendent country.[69]

---

[66] To Forster, ?12 July 1846, *Letters*, vol. 4, 585.
[67] To Forster, 26 September 1846, *Letters*, vol. 4, 626.
[68] To Forster, ?6 September 1846, *Letters*, vol. 4, 618.
[69] Ibid., 619.

The mountain reappears in *Little Dorrit*, 'Lying Awake' and, most unexpectedly, in *Our Mutual Friend*. In the stage version of *No Thoroughfare*, Vendale and Obenreizer ascend the St Bernard, rather than the Simplon as in the novel. During his stay in Lausanne, 'one of the prettiest girls in Lausanne was drowned in the lake – in the most peaceful water, reflecting the steep mountains, and crimson with the setting sun'.[70] The two different kinds of beauty – that of the girl and that of the lake – meet in death. The 'crimson' points forward to several moments in Dickens's Swiss texts where he draws attention to the colour of the setting sun and sets it up as a metaphor for blood and death. Mountains in combination with water or the sea were inextricably linked in Dickens's mind and were irresistibly attractive to him. While working on the last few chapters of *David Copperfield*, including the passages set in Switzerland, he explains to de Cerjat: 'I am finishing Copperfield here – writing to the Music of the sea', during a stay in Broadstairs.[71]

In Switzerland, Dickens's most efficient coping mechanism for suppressing, overwriting and displacing unwanted thoughts, but also for transforming precisely these thoughts into fiction and generating new ideas out of this material by wandering the bustling city streets, was unavailable to him. By walking the streets, Dickens was trying to both chase after and escape from his ghosts. The period of pain and discomfort he consequently suffered therefore unveils the fixations and anxieties of an author unprotected by one of his ordinary strategies of controlling his psyche. Dickens as the 'urban *flâneur*' who cannot live and work without his streets is at least partly a well-nourished myth, and one he may have wanted to believe himself.[72] His walking may have been as much of a displacement behaviour for getting rid of unwanted thoughts as the compulsive attempt at chasing them up. Dickens always remained a great walker, but when he moved to Gad's Hill, his walks were no longer primarily urban ones. Instead, they took place in the Kentish countryside and yet Dickens never complained of his 'need for streets' there.

Even though he had spent some difficult days in Switzerland, after his return to England Dickens never again blamed his trouble on the 'need for streets' when speaking of his time in Lausanne. Instead, he was full of nostalgia and praise for it, and desperate to

---

[70] To Forster, 18 July 1846, *Letters*, vol. 4, 587.
[71] To W. F. de Cerjat, 1 October 1850, *Letters*, vol. 4, 183.
[72] On Dickens and the concept of the flâneur, see Michael Hollington, 'Dickens the Flâneur', *Dickensian* 77, no. 394 (1981): 71–87.

return to it whenever times became difficult.[73] As soon as he had left Switzerland, he wrote to Forster:

> I may tell you, now it is all over. I don't know whether it was the hot summer, or the anxiety of the two new books coupled with D. N. [*Daily News*] remembrances and reminders, but I was in that state in Switzerland, when my spirits sunk so, I felt myself in serious danger.[74]

In his biography, Forster too gives mixed signals. He speaks of Dickens's suffering on the one hand, but his chapters on Dickens's stay in Lausanne suggest the same domesticity and focus on the personal that Dickens would often reproduce in later references to the country. His first chapter is called 'A Home in Switzerland' (he renamed it 'Retreat to Switzerland' in later versions) and the *Pilgrim* editors note that Dickens found more of a home in Switzerland than in Genoa.[75] Forster's second chapter on Dickens in Switzerland discusses 'Sketches Chiefly Personal', and only a third looks at 'Literary Labour in Lausanne', as if the domesticity and introspection had been rather disconnected from what had been going on in terms of Dickens's writing. The chapter divisions and titles seem to suggest a split between the personal and the professional which, however, is not only unnecessary but might even be misleading.

Shadows of the Past and Future, or Inspiration

Dickens's stay in Lausanne was not as unproductive as his surviving letters might suggest. Quite the opposite is the case: it might be difficult to find another period in Dickens's life as rich in inspiring such a large amount of material for future works as the one in Switzerland. In *My Father as I Recall Him*, his daughter Mamie even uses one of his early letters from Lausanne to give an example of the 'almost incredible' amount of work he could accomplish at times.[76] I would therefore like to argue that Dickens's unsettledness in Switzerland was, in fact, part of an important creative process which he himself may not have fully understood at the time. His 'restlessness', which occasionally turned into sheer despair ('I fear there may be NO

---

[73] See Chapter 3, 132ff.

[74] To Forster, ?30 November 1846, *Letters*, vol. 4, 670.

[75] Tillotson, Preface to *Letters*, vol. 4, xiv.

[76] Mamie Dickens, *My Father As I Recall Him* (Westminster: Roxburghe Press, 1902), 62.

82 *Dickens and Switzerland*

CHRISTMAS BOOK!'), was also a sign of a tremendous activation process in Dickens's imagination.[77] This experience came at a high price though, and left him scarred but also fascinated for the rest of his life. Just as the *Battle* kept interfering with *Dombey* and haunted its author in nightmares, Switzerland manifests itself in Dickens's writing randomly, in the most awkward of places and the most unexpected of times. Its effect is often abrupt, disorientating and surprising.

Yet, at some point, Dickens may have understood that his time in Switzerland was more dynamic than he thought at the time. In 1852, more than a year before he would travel to Switzerland again, he complains to Forster of his inability to 'grind sparks out of this dull blade' and plans to go to Paris, probably to get some inspiration. But this, as we find out, is only because 'I could not get to Switzerland very well at this time of year. The Jura would be covered with snow. And if I went to Geneva I don't know where I might *not* go to'.[78] What Dickens was struggling with in Lausanne was not so much keeping up with the progress of his stories as keeping track of the wealth of material his imagination was generating at the time. 'Invention, thank God, seems the easiest thing in the world', Dickens wrote to Forster, 'and I seem to have such a preposterous sense of the ridiculous, after this long rest, as to be constantly requiring to restrain myself from launching into extravagances in the height of my enjoyment'.[79] On the one hand, Dickens blamed this on his 'two years' ease' and on the other, on the 'absence of streets and numbers of figures'.[80] Could the 'absence of streets and numbers of figures' suggest that Dickens felt he had a lack of options? Even though he firmly believed that his unsettledness was making him unproductive, the ideas for future works he conceived in Switzerland clearly contradict this. I agree with John Carey, who points out that Dickens recognised the 'bond between imagination and inconsistency' himself when he spoke of the 'wayward and unsettled feeling which is part (I suppose) of the tenure on which one holds an imaginative life'.[81]

There was certainly inconsistency in 1846 – some accidental, some self-induced. This came at a dangerous price, though, as Forster makes quite clear in his assessment of Dickens in Switzerland,

---

[77] To Forster, 26 September 1846, *Letters*, vol. 4, 625.
[78] To Forster, ?10–16 March 1852, *Letters*, vol. 4, 627.
[79] To Forster, 30 August 1846, *Letters*, vol. 4, 612.
[80] Ibid.
[81] To Forster, 5 September 1857, *Letters*, vol. 8, 434; Carey, *The Violent Effigy*, 9.

probably foreshadowing the circumstances under which Dickens would eventually work himself to death:

> He had restless fancies and misgivings before he settled to his first notion. 'I have been thinking this last day or two,' he wrote on the 25th of July, 'that good Christmas characters might be grown out of the idea of a man imprisoned for ten or fifteen years; his imprisonment being the gap between the people and circumstances of the first part and the altered people and circumstances of the second, and his own changed mind. Though I shall probably proceed with the Battle idea, I should like to know what you think of this one?' It was afterwards used in a modified shape for the *Tale of Two Cities*. 'I shall begin the little story straightway,' he wrote a few weeks later; 'but I have been dimly conceiving a very ghostly and wild idea, which I suppose I must now reserve for the *next* Christmas book. *Nous verrons*. It will mature in the streets of Paris by night, as well as in London.' This took ultimately the form of the *Haunted Man*, which was not written until the winter of 1848.[82]

Even though Dickens certainly reused the idea of 'a man imprisoned for ten or fifteen years' in *A Tale of Two Cities*, he first explored the idea in *Little Dorrit*, which abounds in prisons and prisoners of all shapes and sizes, and has two sharply contrasting halves.

Ironically, the piece which also seemed to trigger these other writings, *The Battle of Life*, is generally regarded as the least successful of them all and is, despite its haunting nature, also the only Christmas book not to feature supernatural elements.[83] Dickens felt that a Christmas book was too short for the plot he had in mind, and despite thinking that it promised 'to be pretty' and to have 'quite a new idea in the story' he found 'a difficulty so perplexing' to 'manage it without the supernatural agency now impossible of introduction, and yet to move it naturally within the required space'.[84]

Dickens's interest in biography and identity would also become an important if challenging employment during his time in Switzerland. New in Dickens at this point was a more open and visible occupation with the self, and a remarkable number of writings drafted and composed in Switzerland are concerned with life, containing the word in the title. He called his 1846 Christmas Story *The Battle of Life*, writes at least half of *The Life of our Lord* in Lausanne

---

[82] Forster, *Life of Dickens*, 448. Forster confirms this later, at 551.
[83] To Forster, 26 September 1846, *Letters*, vol. 4, 625n2. For reviews of the *Battle*, see Michael Slater in Schlicke, *Oxford Reader's Companion to Dickens*, 34.
[84] To Forster, 26 September 1846, *Letters*, vol. 4, 625.

84 *Dickens and Switzerland*

and started thinking about writing an autobiography there. *The Life of Our Lord*, or *The Children's New Testament*, as Dickens called it, was never intended for publication and only appeared in 1934.[85] Due to a dating mistake in the preface by Marie Dickens, wife of Henry Fielding Dickens, who probably followed Mamie Dickens's claim that it had been written in 1849, critics did not and occasionally still do not connect the *Life* with Dickens's stay in Switzerland; this is the case with the edition published by Collins in 1970, which claims that Dickens wrote the text in 1849. The 1934 Simon & Schuster edition, however, gives the correct time frame, which is 1846–49.[86] Yet Dickens mentioned the *Testament* in a letter to Forster in 1846 when he wrote: 'Half of the children's New Testament to write, or pretty nearly. I set to work and did *that*'.[87] If he managed to write half of the *Testament*, 'or pretty nearly' within a few days, the 'reference suggests that he completed it in June'.[88] Kathleen Tillotson calls the *Testament* a 'piece of "private" writing', connected 'with his growing concern over his own children's education; and this in turn may be associated with his reflections on his own childhood'. She links Dickens's 'writing to Forster about Paul Dombey at Mrs Pipchin's ... with what is probably the first of his reminiscent confidences, the seed from which grew the "autobiography" and the childhood chapters of *David Copperfield*'.[89] The novel narrates the story of an alternative self, Dickens's 'favourite child', and he believed he had done it 'ingeniously, with a very complicated interweaving of truth and fiction'.[90] The writing Dickens did in Switzerland, as well as this comment on *David Copperfield* highlight the difficulty for both a reader or critic and perhaps Dickens himself of distinguishing between 'truth and fiction' in his texts. In the case of Dickens – and Dickens and Switzerland in particular – it sometimes becomes impossible to tell. Nothing could be more accurate in this respect concerning Dickens than what Judith Adler points out about the connection between travel and identity:

> Travel lends itself to dramatic play with the boundaries of selfhood, and the character ideals of the performers and their audiences are as various as the performances. But no description of travel style can be

---

[85] Tillotson, Preface to *Letters*, vol. 4, xii.

[86] Dickens, *The Life of Our Lord* (London: Collins, 1970), 7.

[87] To Forster, ?28 June 1846, *Letters*, vol. 4, 573; also see 573n2.

[88] Ibid., 573n2.

[89] Tillotson, Preface to *Letters*, vol. 4, xii.

[90] Dickens, *David Copperfield*, Appendix A, 752; to Forster, 10 July 1849, *Letters*, vol. 4, 569.

complete without attention to the kind of character, as well as the form of reality, that it is designed to test and confirm. Enduring identities are often narratively constructed on the basis of brief adventures.[91]

This also applies to the novel Dickens began to write in Switzerland. Considered 'the first novel of [Dickens's] artistic maturity', *Dombey* has been claimed to be 'inextricably tied to his own life, as no previous novel had been' and that its title 'indicated an increased concern with contemporary life'.[92] One of the 'lives' Dickens created in Switzerland, that of little Paul Dombey, was only 'born, to die' and Dickens ended up, in his own words, 'slaughtering' the boy.[93]

From Switzerland Dickens wrote to Forster:

> I hope you will like Mrs Pipchin's establishment. It is from the life, and I was there – I don't suppose I was eight years old; but I remember it all as well, and certainly understood it as well, as I do now. We should be devilish sharp in what we do to children. I thought of that passage in my small life, at Geneva. Shall I leave you my life in MS. when I die?[94]

As 'dating evidence is confusing' for this letter, we cannot know for certain when Dickens started writing his autobiography, or versions of it, and there was probably more than one draft.[95] This letter, however, is special. Not only does Dickens connect his writing of *Dombey* with an event in his own childhood, but he also links the memory to his stay in Geneva. Seemingly out of the blue, he then also asks Forster whether he should leave him his autobiography when he dies. The request exposes a touching vulnerability as fiction ('I hope you will like Mrs Pipchin's establishment') turns into fact ('It is from the life') and a memory ('I remember it … well') which suddenly affects the present ('I thought of that passage in my small life, at Geneva'), the future ('Shall I leave you my life') and the ultimate end ('when I die'). After Dickens's death, the memory, but more so the actual fact – on which he does not elaborate   will live on in the manuscript. The suggestion Dickens made in this letter of writing an autobiography, under the implicit title 'my life', also belongs to and is perhaps the most important of the series of life-writings which Dickens conceived in Switzerland.

---

[91] Adler, 'Travel as Performed Art', 1385.

[92] Schlicke in Schlicke, *Oxford Reader's Companion to Dickens*, 185; Butt and Tillotson, *Dickens at Work on 'Dombey and Son'*, 73.

[93] Schlicke in Schlicke, *Oxford Reader's Companion to Dickens*, 184.

[94] To Forster, 4 November 1846, *Letters*, vol. 4, 653.

[95] Collins in Schlicke, *Oxford Reader's Companion to Dickens*, 158.

86 *Dickens and Switzerland*

Dickens wanted to leave Forster his 'life' at the time of his death, but the context in which he placed the question and his warning that 'we should be devilish sharp in what we do to children' suggest that he intended to stress the events in his 'small life' rather than those of his adulthood. Accordingly, the autobiography remained a fragment and never reached the stage of maturity – neither in its own form, nor with the subject it treated. In the 1850s, a time of reconsideration and change in Dickens's life, he told Maria Beadnell, his first love with whom he briefly got back in touch in 1855, that:

> A few years ago (just before Copperfield) I began to write my life, intending the Manuscript to be found among my papers when its subject should be concluded. But as I began to approach within sight of that part of it, I lost courage and burned the rest.[96]

In her excellent *Knowing Dickens*, Rosemary Bodenheimer explains the 'dangers' that autobiography bore for Dickens. She notes that from the 1840s onwards, 'Dickens spoke of autobiography only in connection with his own death'.[97] Although Forster was born the same year as himself, for some reason Dickens must have imagined that he would die prior to his friend. The passage nicely illustrates the problematic nature of autobiography: rather than elucidating what it is that he remembers 'well', Dickens surrounds 'that passage in my small life' with mystery. He does not reveal what it was in Geneva that made him think of 'that passage', as if he was running the risk of giving away too much if he elaborated on it.

Whatever happened in Geneva, it left a mark, and his wife Catherine was aware of it. In 1850 he wrote to her from Broadstairs:

> Forster was in a tip top state of amiability, but I think I never heard him *half so loud*. (!) He really, after the heat of the walk, so disordered me that by no process I could possibly try, could I get to sleep afterwards. At last, I gave it up as a bad job, and walked about the house 'till 5 – paying Georgina a visit, and getting her up for company. I was just as I was that night at Geneva. But I tumbled out again at half past 7 this morning, and tumbled into the sea.[98]

It is Forster, his designated biographer, who 'disordered' Dickens to such an extent that he could not sleep and needed Georgina's company. In this letter also, he refused to elaborate on what it was

---

[96] To Mrs Winter, 22 February 1855, *Letters*, vol. 4, 543.
[97] Bodenheimer, *Knowing Dickens*, 61.
[98] To Catherine Dickens, 3 September 1850, *Letters*, vol. 4, 161.

that upset him. All we learn is that 'I was just as I was' in Geneva. Had Forster triggered a childhood memory by being loud and boisterous? The fact that Dickens could not get to sleep, gave it up as a bad job and walked about the house seems to have found an echo in 'Lying Awake', in which the narrator is 'lying: not with my eyes half closed, but with my eyes wide open; [...] not just falling asleep by any means, but glaringly, persistently, and obstinately, broad awake'.[99] His thoughts begin to wander and

> up I go, for no reason on earth that I can find out, and drawn by no links that are visible to me, up the Great Saint Bernard! I have lived in Switzerland, and rambled among the mountains; but why I should go there now, and why up the Great Saint Bernard in preference to any other mountain, I have no idea.[100]

In September 1850, Dickens was working on the second-last number of *David Copperfield*, just before the protagonist escapes to Switzerland. The country brings back childhood memories for Copperfield as well. Remembering Agnes, he confesses: 'I had accustomed myself to think of her, when we were both mere children, as one who was far removed from my wild fancies.'[101] Copperfield's memories include a strong sensation of nostalgia and repentance. He even goes so far as to wish to 'cancel the mistaken past' with Dora and contemplates 'how the things that never happen, are often as much realities to us, in their effects, as those that are accomplished'.[102]

Dickens did not feel restless and unsettled for the first time in Switzerland, nor was the episode unique. Forster notes:

> It was not fully revealed until later on what difficult terms, physical as well as mental, Dickens held the tenure of his imaginative life; [...] In all intellectual labour, his will prevailed so strongly when he fixed it on any object of desire, that what else its attainment might exact was never duly measured; and this led to frequent strain and unconscious waste of what no man could less afford to spare. To the world gladdened by his work, its production might always have seemed quite as easy as its enjoyment; but it may be doubted if ever any man's mental effort cost him more. His habits were robust, but not his health; that secret had been disclosed to me before he went to America; and to the last he refused steadily to admit the enormous price he had paid for his triumphs and successes.[103]

---

[99] Dickens, 'Lying Awake', in *Dent Uniform Edition of Dickens' Journalism*, vol. 3, 89.
[100] Ibid., 91.
[101] Dickens, *David Copperfield*, 700.
[102] Ibid., 700; 701.
[103] Forster, *Life of Dickens*, 405.

88 *Dickens and Switzerland*

This is not to say that Dickens did not suffer when he was in Switzerland: he did, and greatly. Forster's insistence on the constant difficulty of intellectual labour to Dickens should, however, help us to put this episode into perspective and allow us, at the same time, to understand that Dickens was generating and processing material for many years to come. Dickens's biographer once more emphasises the impact Switzerland had on Dickens's mind and writing a little later in his book:

> At his heart there was a genuine love of nature at all times; and strange as it may seem to connect this with such forms of humorous delineation as are most identified with his genius, it is yet the literal truth that the impressions of this noble Swiss scenery were with him during the work of many subsequent years: a present and actual, though it might be seldom a directly conscious, influence.[104]

Forster's strong claim supports my own observation that references to Switzerland in Dickens's writing are widespread, but seem to appear fractured. In this light, Dickens's complaint about Lausanne's lack of streets is not only a comment on the geographical situation of Lausanne, but also an image of his mental state at the time. Harry Stone goes even further in his *Night Side of Dickens*. His explanation for Dickens's want for streets, this 'curious fact', as Dickens called it himself, is this:

> Dickens does not connect this 'curious fact' with a striking counter-part fact, a fact which no one but Dickens (and a few mute members of his family) knew at the time he made these statements about his need for busy city streets to walk in. That counterpart fact is very simple, and it is this: that Dickens's induction into walking alone through miles and miles of dark, crowded city streets, walking those miles of streets six dark winter mornings and six dark winter nights each week, had taken place during his servitude at the blacking warehouse; indeed; those somber street journeys were the solitary beginning and the solitary conclusion of each day's servitude, a concomitant and inseparable part of that humiliating bondage. This intense boyhood experience of tramping alone through dark crowded city streets – on the one hand, an engaged and life-thronged experience (looking out entrancedly, at times also fearfully, at the astonishing street-world all about him); on the other hand, a removed and solitary experience (looking inward, alone and hopeless – alone though surrounded by crowds – at the dark, secret, Cainlike desolation filling his being and corroding his soul); and, finally, a

---

[104] Ibid., 446.

humiliating and shame-filled experience (being stared at and pointed to – so he felt – like a freakish curiosity or a repulsive beast) – this emotion-laden and unexpungeable experience of dark, crowded city streets, an experience so diverse, even contradictory, yet so intricately interfused and intertwined even in its contradictions, was to shape Dickens' vision and his art in innumerable ways.[105]

Stone's argument may explain Dickens's obsessive walking, but it does not explain why Dickens was reminded of Warren's blacking factory in Geneva. Catherine Dickens and Forster may have known, but it is unlikely that we ever will. His work at Warren's, which brought great suffering to him and which he found profoundly humiliating, 'was kept a dark secret from everyone except his wife and John Forster until revealed in the latter's biography'.[106]

Dickens may have come to think 'of that passage' of his life in Geneva because he found an environment that triggered conscious or subconscious associations with experiences in his childhood. In his biography, Forster does not elaborate on what happened in Geneva, though he may have known more than he was willing to share. The material Dickens conceived in Switzerland reflects this new understanding, namely that his 'spectres' could not be destroyed.

The Happy Pair, or Switzerland and the Sublime

Ever since Romantic poets and painters described the experience of Switzerland's landscape as sublime, the country has been closely associated with this term, described by Philip Shaw: 'whenever experience slips out of conventional understanding, whenever the power of an object or event is such that words fail and points of comparison disappear, *then* we resort to the feeling of the sublime'.[107] Dickens's 'sublime', however, is popular and proudly anti-intellectual. A statement he once made about his sub-editor William Henry Wills tells as much about the audience Dickens was writing for and the experience of working for him, as about Wills himself: 'Wills has no genius, and is, in literary matters, sufficiently commonplace to represent a very large proportion of our readers.'[108] It is certainly not a

---

[105] Harry Stone, *The Night Side of Dickens. Cannibalism, Passion, Necessity* (Columbus, OH: Ohio State University Press, 1994), 456.

[106] Schlicke in Schlicke, *Oxford Reader's Companion to Dickens*, 596.

[107] Philip Shaw, *The Sublime* (London: Routledge, 2006), 2.

[108] To Bulwer Lytton, 15 May 1861, *Letters*, vol. 9, 415.

90   *Dickens and Switzerland*

very complimentary statement, and yet even Forster claimed him to be Dickens's most intimate friend towards the end of his life.[109] Even if Dickens himself had read Edmund Burke's *Philosophical Enquiry into the Origin of our Ideas of the Sublime and Beautiful*, he did not expect his readers to be familiar with Burke's ideas in detail. He did, however, expect them to understand the word 'sublime' itself, as he uses it more than thirty times, evenly distributed and appearing in most of his fictional texts once and up to three times. The 'sublime' is almost exclusively ironic in his fiction. His use is frequently that which the *OED* defines as 'Chiefly *colloq*. In ironic use, with references to undesirable qualities: downright, utter, "out-and-out"'. Dickens applies it to human behaviour, feelings, characters or abstract concepts, such as 'truth' in *The Old Curiosity Shop*, 'morality' in *Barnaby Rudge*, 'address' in *Martin Chuzzlewit*, 'satisfaction' in *Bleak House*, 'principle', 'idea' and 'discovery' in *Little Dorrit*, 'compassion' in *Great Expectations*, 'history', 'attention' and the name 'Snigsworth' in *Our Mutual Friend*. It appears slightly less frequently in his letters, still often in a mocking tone but not always as sharp, and on occasion it is meant sincerely and expresses genuine admiration. Dickens's 'ability to perceive and fix visual values oscillating between realism and caricature or grotesque effect' not only applies to his treatment of the picturesque, but also that of the sublime.[110]

The term first appears in *Mudfog Papers* where it describes in typical hyperbolic fashion some 'gigantic researches and sublime and noble triumphs'.[111] In 1841, Dickens shares his impressions of the Scottish Highlands in a letter to Forster:

> I don't bore you with accounts of Ben this and that, and Lochs of all sorts of names, but this is a wonderful region. The way the mists were stalking about to-day, and the clouds lying down upon the hills; the deep glens, the high rocks, the rushing waterfalls, and the roaring rivers down in deep gulfs below; were all stupendous. This house is wedged round by great heights that are lost in the clouds; and the loch, twelve miles long, stretches out its dreary length before the windows. In my next, I shall soar to the sublime, perhaps; in this here present writing I confine myself to the ridiculous.[112]

---

[109] Forster, *Life of Dickens*, 558.
[110] Francesca Orestano, 'Charles Dickens and Italy: The "New Picturesque"' in Hollington and Orestano, eds., *Dickens and Italy*, 55.
[111] Dickens, *Mudfog Papers* (Gloucester: Alan Sutton, 1987), 72.
[112] To Forster, 5 July 1841, *Letters*, vol. 2, 322.

Once more, Dickens is poking fun at ideas of the sublime – or simply being modest. His hint to 'soar' to it in a next letter is another instance of his partiality to creating comic effect by hyperbole. Nevertheless, the description is genuine, his appreciation truthful.

There are few occasions in which Dickens applies the term to express genuine awe towards a particular landscape. In his fiction, Dickens prefers to invoke sublime images rather than use the word itself, but there are moments in which it appears without a mocking undertone. One of them is his account of travelling to the Simplon in *Pictures from Italy*, where he describes how 'the serenity of the night, and the grandeur of the road, with its impenetrable shadows, and deep glooms, and its sudden turns into the shining of the moon and its incessant roar of falling water, rendered the journey more and more sublime at every step'.[113] In 'To Be Read at Dusk', the 'mountain in the sunset had stopped the five couriers in a conversation. It is a sublime sight, likely to stop conversation'.[114] In 1845, Dickens wrote to Forster from Switzerland:

> We came over the St. Gothard [*sic*], which has been open only eight days. The road is cut through the snow, and the carriage winds along a narrow path between two massive snow walls, twenty feet high or more. Vast plains of snow range up the mountain-sides above the road, itself seven thousand feet above the sea; and tremendous waterfalls, hewing out arches for themselves in the vast drifts, go thundering down from precipices into deep chasms, here and there and everywhere: the blue water tearing through the white snow with an awful beauty that is most sublime.[115]

On Dickens's second brief visit to Switzerland he uses the word 'sublime' for one of his first times to describe the country's scenery. In its series of violent verbs (cut, hew, thunder, tear), its emphasis on the terrible ('open *only* eight days', 'tremendous waterfalls', 'deep chasms', 'awful beauty', 'here, there and everywhere') and the outline of the gigantic ('massive snow walls, twenty feet high or more', 'vast plains', 'seven thousand feet above the sea', 'vast drifts'), Dickens's passage would be very much in line with Burke's definition of the sublime in the *Philosophical Enquiry* – were it not for the word 'beauty' with which the water is 'tearing through the white snow': according to Burke, 'objects of great dimensions are incompatible

---

[113] Dickens, *Pictures from Italy*, ed. Kate Flint (London: Penguin, 1998), 97.
[114] Dickens, 'To Be Read at Dusk', in *Selected Short Fiction*, ed. Deborah A. Thomas (London: Penguin, 1985), 66.
[115] To Forster, 15 June 1845, *Letters*, vol. 4, 320.

with beauty, the more incompatible as they are greater; whereas the small, if ever they fail of beauty, this failure is not to be attributed to their size'.[116] The sublime, for both 'Burke and Kant [...] a way of thinking about excess as the key to a new kind of subjectivity', and as an idea interested in violence and the terrible, takes into account much of what strongly attracted Dickens himself.[117]

Dickens may have read Burke, but neither of the two existent catalogues of his library feature an entry for the philosopher. However, among the imitation book covers Dickens had made for his study at Tavistock House we find 'Burke (of Edinburgh) *On the Sublime and Beautiful*, 2 vols'.[118] Edmund Burke was Irish, as was William Burke, to whom Dickens's title is a comical reference. William Burke (1791–1829) and his partner, William Hare, had emigrated to Edinburgh where they committed a series of murders, making 'theirs perhaps the best-known pair of names in Scottish history'.[119] It did not take long for their actions to be defined in a new term: 'burking' spread quickly across the country, meaning, according to the *OED*, 'to murder, in the same manner or for the same purpose as Burke did; to kill secretly by suffocation or strangulation, or for the purpose of selling the victim's body for dissection'. Dickens uses the verb in *The Pickwick Papers* – anachronistically, as Owen Dudley Edwards reminds us.[120] Forty years later, Dickens used the word again in a letter, where he discusses whether a particular story 'is Burked or is to appear' in *All the Year Round*.[121]

Dickens's 'earliest known published writing had been for John Fairburn, a London bookseller who would have sold plenty of Burkeana in 1829' and, as a young shorthand writer, Dickens had attended a very similar trial which resurrected memories of William Burke's.[122] The same Burke also appears in a 'slightly malicious' joke Douglas Jerrold shared with Dickens about Forster:[123] 'Madame Tussaud intends to do Forster next, as Kitely [...] and that he is

---

[116] Edmund Burke, *A Philosophical Enquiry into the Origin of our Ideas of the Sublime and Beautiful* (Oxford: Oxford University Press, 1998), 144.

[117] Adam Phillips, introduction to ibid., ix.

[118] *Letters*, vol. 4, Endmatter, appendix C: 'List of Imitation Book-Backs Sent to T. R. Eeles on 22 October 1851', 851.

[119] *Oxford Dictionary of National Biography*, s.v. 'Burke, William'.

[120] Dickens, *The Pickwick Papers*, ed. James Kinsley (Oxford: Oxford University Press, 2008), 379; Owen Dudley Edwards, *Burke and Hare*, 3rd ed. (Edinburgh: Birlinn, Ltd., 2014), 290.

[121] To Wills, 31 August 1861, *Letters*, vol. 9, 451.

[122] Ruth Richardson, *Dickens and the Workhouse. Oliver Twist and the London Poor* (Oxford: Oxford University Press, 2012), 195.

[123] Madeline House and Graham Storey, Preface to *Letters*, vol. 1, x.

to be put next to Burke, in the Chamber of Horrors.'[124] Dickens's imitation book cover pushes discussions of the sublime and beautiful into the domain of the ridiculous. With the determined yet clever anti-intellectual stance he occasionally adhered to, Dickens mocks both the philosopher and the murderer by changing a minor detail in his 'imitation book-backs'. Other examples of his counterfeit titles, 'Kant's Ancient Humbugs', 'Drowsy's Recollections of Nothing', 'Heavisides Conversations with Nobody' or 'King Henry the Eight's Evidences of Christianity', mock philosophical discourse too.

Another use of the sublime appears in a letter to Forster:

> Mont Blanc, and the Valley of Chamounix, and the Mer de Glace, and all the wonders of that most wonderful place, are above and beyond one's wildest expectations. I cannot imagine anything in nature more stupendous or sublime. If I were to write about it now, I should quite rave – such prodigious impressions are rampant within me ...[125]

'Stupendous' and 'sublime' are the same words Dickens used to describe Glencoe five years earlier and when, in 1844, he travelled through Switzerland for the first time, he did indeed compare the ascent of the Simplon to Glencoe when 'well-sprinkled with Snow'.[126] His qualification in the second-last sentence breaks off the narrative, and despite Dickens's claim that if he 'were to write about it now, I should quite rave', he does not and decides to fade the sentence out. 'Raving' does not seem to be what Dickens wants to do, or at least not at the present moment, despite, or perhaps precisely because of those 'prodigious impressions [...] rampant' within him. He changes the topic instead, and speaks of the unusual mode of travel during this journey: 'You may suppose that the mule-travelling is pretty primitive. Each person takes a carpet-bag strapped on the mule behind himself or herself: and that is all the baggage that can be carried.' From 'anything more' stupendous or sublime, Dickens's mind turns to images of the 'pretty primitive', of detail, conciseness and scarcity. In *Little Dorrit*, he employs the same technique, describing 'little moving figures of men and mules, reduced to miniatures by the immensity around, [who] went with a clear tinkling of bells and a pleasant harmony of tongues'.[127]

[124] To Macready, 24 October 1846, *Letters*, vol. 4, 646.
[125] To Forster, 2 August 1846, *Letters*, vol. 4, 594.
[126] To Catherine Dickens, 23 November 1844, *Letters*, vol. 4, 228.
[127] Dickens, *Little Dorrit*, 439.

94 *Dickens and Switzerland*

In the letter about the Gotthard from 1845, Dickens relates his impressions from the safety of his carriage, or rather, from the inn he stays at later. The journey to the top itself is not perilous: the road is unremarkable but for its position 'between two massive snow walls'. Dickens has time to observe:

> The pass itself, the mere pass over the top, is not so fine, I think, as the Simplon; and there is no plain upon the summit, for the moment it is reached the descent begins. So that the loneliness and wildness of the Simplon are not equalled *there*'.[128]

And yet, he calls 'the whole descent [...] the highest sublimation of all you can imagine in the way of Swiss scenery' and considers 'the coming down from the Great St. Gothard with a carriage and four horses and only one postilion, as the most dangerous thing that a carriage and horses can do'.[129] Dickens's hyperbolic use of the term 'sublimation' is noteworthy: it is the only moment in which the sublime appears in this form in Dickens's letters. It is an odd choice, as 'sublime' itself can be prefixed with an article and thus become a noun. In contrast to 'the sublime', representing a state, according to 'sublimation' invokes an active process, action or transformation, and thus takes into account the progress of 'the whole descent'. 'Sublimation' is also a rare word in Dickens's fiction and only appears once, in *Dombey and Son*:

> Thereupon the Captain put his iron hook between his teeth, as if it were a hand; and with an air of wisdom and profundity that was the very concentration and sublimation of all philosophical reflection and grave inquiry, applied himself to the consideration of the subject in its various branches.[130]

Cuttle's 'concentration and sublimation of all philosophical reflection and grave inquiry' is reminiscent not only of the title Burke gave his study but also of its subject. All elements are there – the philosophy, the enquiry and even the sublime. Yet the Captain's philosophising is flawed, as is his 'nail biting': his hand is in fact a hook, and his reflection does not enable him to solve the problem, only bringing him to think of his friend Bunsby, who 'would deliver such an opinion on this subject, or any other that could be named, as

---

[128] To Forster, 15 June 1845, *Letters*, vol. 4, 320. Emphasis in original.
[129] Ibid., 321.
[130] Dickens, *Dombey and Son*, 213.

would give Parliament six and beat 'em'.[131] In 'Dickens and the Force of Writing', John Bowen discusses Dickens's ambiguous approach to philosophy, concluding that his 'fiction often sees philosophical inquiry as absurd and po-faced' and that this

> seems to occur in Dickens's work whenever it starts to think about the gaps between language and silence, sense and nonsense, the articulate and the inarticulable, commonly when people are stumped by the incomprehensibility of the world and the choices it presents.[132]

Incidentally, this is not too far from the sublime, a fact which Bowen notes as well: 'There is a way in which Dickens's work is sublime, in the sense that it is hard to comprehend it without a feeling of being overwhelmed.'[133] He points out:

> It is more usual of course to think of Dickens's writing as humorous rather than sublime, but it may be that the two – humour and sublimity – are not as different as we think. [...] It can be terrifying not to understand or be able to express something; it can also be ludicrously funny. [...] [Dickens's work] constantly reaches for sublime effects – seeking to raise our minds to the high and the noble, the awesome and the immense – and is equally able to invert the tide of emotional investment toward the low, the humorous and comic.[134]

This is particularly true for Dickens's way of narrating Switzerland. In *Pictures from Italy*, the language Dickens chooses to describe the same ascent is even closer to Burke's expectation of the sublime. Vocabulary invoking the terrible and threatening potential violence abounds:

> By degrees, the roar of water grew louder; [...] Then, even this was lost, in the thick darkness of a cavern in the rock, through which the way was pierced; the terrible cataract thundering and roaring close below it, and its foam and spray hanging, in a mist, about the entrance. Emerging from this cave, and coming again into the moonlight, and across a dizzy bridge, it crept and twisted upward, through the Gorge of Gondo, savage and grand beyond description, with smooth-fronted precipices, rising up on either hand, and almost meeting overhead. Thus we went, climbing on our rugged way,

---

[131] Ibid.

[132] John Bowen, 'Dickens and the Force of Writing', in *Palgrave Advances in Charles Dickens Studies*, ed. John Bowen and Robert L. Patten (Basingstoke: Palgrave Macmillan, 2006), 259; 260.

[133] Ibid., 261.

[134] Ibid.

higher and higher all night, without a moment's weariness: lost in the contemplation of the black rocks, the tremendous heights and depths, the fields of smooth snow lying, in the clefts and hollows, and the fierce torrents thundering headlong down the deep abyss.[135]

There is certainly nothing comical about this, and the tone is that of awe, a key term to Burke. Later in the description of this journey, Dickens speaks of 'the brink of a steep precipice', 'everlasting glaciers', 'horrible ravines', 'vast desolation of ice and snow', 'monstrous granite rocks' through which he travels 'deafened by the torrent plunging madly down'.[136] Dickens's fascination is not only with the roughness of the landscape but also its contrast with what surrounds it as well: the 'savage and grand' Gorge of Gondo rises up with 'smooth-fronted precipices' and the snow fields of smoothness.

In 'Dickens's Sublime Artefact', Ronald R. Thomas claims that Dickens 'makes a further and [...] fundamental change in the conception of the sublime by relocating it in the contemplation of human production rather than in the contemplation of natural or divine realms'.[137] This is often true, but not always. Moreover, I would propose replacing human 'production' with 'performance', as it considers Dickens's frequent use of the word in a theatrical environment. More often than not the human performance of Dickens's 'sublime' is related to acting: 'Pray', writes Dickens to Miss Coutts, 'let me recommend the Dragon in the Easter Piece to your particular regards. I look upon him as the most comic animal of modern times. When he gets drunk at the Fountain, he is Sublime'.[138] Elsewhere he describes some 'sublime acting', celebrates 'the sublime Williams', tells of someone 'exhibiting a sublime caricature' and mentions the treatment of a document 'with the most sublime contempt'.[139]

In *David Copperfield*, Dickens refuses to apply the term to the protagonist's recovery in Switzerland. The moment of healing, in which Copperfield says that 'great Nature spoke to me', is one of 'serenity' rather than sublimity.[140] The sublime, Dickens makes quite clear, does not play a part in Copperfield's recovery:

---

[135] Dickens, *Pictures from Italy*, 98.

[136] Ibid., 99.

[137] Ronald R. Thomas, 'Dickens's Sublime Artefact', *Browning Institute Studies* 14, The Victorian Threshold (1986): 74.

[138] To Miss Coutts, 24 April 1843, *Letters*, vol. 4, 475.

[139] To Forster, 20 November 1862, *Letters*, vol. 10, 163; to Macready, 24 July 1853, *Letters*, vol. 7, 119; to Forster, 15 March 1842, *Letters*, vol. 3, 134; to Forster, 11 October 1846, *Letters*, vol. 4, 633.

[140] Dickens, *David Copperfield*, 698.

> If those awful solitudes had spoken to my heart, I did not know it. I had found sublimity and wonder in the dread heights and precipices, in the roaring torrents, and the wastes of ice and snow; but as yet, they had taught me nothing else.[141]

Whereas Copperfield does not know whether 'those awful solitudes had spoken' to his heart, he is positive that the 'sublimity and wonder' he found had taught him 'nothing else'. Copperfield is unable to establish a connection with those 'awful solitudes', the 'dread heights and precipices', 'the roaring torrents, and the wastes of ice and snow', perhaps because they reflect the surface of his uneven yet static mind too closely. Indeed, with their own roughness and rigidity they are unable to present to Copperfield another form of existence. In contrast, the valley, with its 'softening influence awakened by its peace' in which Copperfield descends, and the village within it, offer a solution towards a state of being in balance with terror and beauty.

When he is imprisoned at the Marshalsea, *Little Dorrit*'s Arthur Clennam has a similar experience to that of Copperfield:

> Changeless and barren, looking ignorantly at all the seasons with its fixed, pinched face of poverty and care, the prison had not a touch of any of these beauties on it. Blossom what would, its bricks and bars bore uniformly the same dead crop. Yet Clennam, listening to the voice as it read to him, heard in it all that great Nature was doing, heard in it all the soothing songs she sings to man. At no Mother's knee but hers had he ever dwelt in his youth on hopeful promises, on playful fancies, on the harvests of tenderness and humility that lie hidden in the early-fostered seeds of the imagination; on the oaks of retreat from blighting winds, that have the germs of their strong roots in nursery acorns. But, in the tones of the voice that read to him, there were memories of an old feeling of such things, and echoes of every merciful and loving whisper that had ever stolen to him in his life.[142]

It is Amy Dorrit who is reading to Clennam here. The voices in *David Copperfield* are indistinct, probably those of shepherds, and 'great Nature' does indeed speak to him. Clennam only hears it in Amy's voice and yet the acts through which 'great Nature' approaches Man are the same: an oral performance. Both Clennam and Copperfield find in their future wives the love of their long-lost mothers.

[141] Ibid., 697.
[142] Dickens, *Little Dorrit*, 790.

98   *Dickens and Switzerland*

The passage in *David Copperfield* has been linked to Wordsworth's *Prelude*, yet among the academic community there does not seem a consensus as to how much of Wordsworth's work Dickens really read and the degree of appreciation in which he held the poet. Forster claims that

> Dickens had little love for Wordsworth, but he was himself an example of the truth the great poet never tired of enforcing, that Nature has subtle helps for all who are admitted to become free of her wonders and mysteries.[143]

The relevant entry in the *Oxford Reader's Companion to Dickens* is surprisingly short, noting that they only met once, in 1839, that the only poem 'we can be certain that Dickens actually admired' is 'We are Seven', that the two authors shared a fascination for childhood and innocence and that 'it could be argued that Dickens's novels represent an urbanisation of the Wordsworthian pastoral ideal'.[144] In 'Dickens's Reading', Philip Collins quotes the painter David Wilkie, who, on occasion of a dinner in 1839, remembered Dickens 'expressing "a very great admiration" for Wordsworth's genius', and considers the article in *Household Narrative* on 'The Prelude', which said that 'The portions of it which will probably strike most readers, and will certainly be read with peculiar interest just now are those descriptive of his residence at Cambridge, and its unfortunate effect upon him'.[145] Incidentally, the descriptions of Wordsworth's residence at Cambridge are in Book 5, called 'Cambridge and the Alps', which also describes the poet's subsequent journey to Switzerland.

In an article from 1998, Leon Litvak has shown that Dickens bought the 'Prelude' very shortly after it was published, in August 1850, 'at a time when he was working on the closing monthly numbers of *David Copperfield*'.[146] Litvak continues:

> While the poem cannot be seen to have guided the overall conception of *David Copperfield*, it is interesting to speculate on how Dickens's reading of Wordsworth at this time might have affected those portions of the novel following on the death of Dora (written by Dickens in August 1850). In chapter 58 (which opened the final double number in November 1850) David goes to the Alps, and engages in

---

[143] Forster, *Life of Dickens*, 447.
[144] Adam Roberts in Schlicke, *Oxford Reader's Companion to Dickens*, 604.
[145] Philip Collins, 'Dickens's Reading', *Dickensian* 60, no. 344 (1964): 139.
[146] Leon Litvak, 'What Books Did Dickens Buy and Read? Evidence from the Book Accounts with his Publishers', *Dickensian* 94, no. 445 (1998): 94.

a retrospective – but assertive – self-examination and spiritual awakening, which recalls for several critics the pattern adopted in 'The Prelude'.[147]

Among other critics, John Lucas, also quoted in Litvak, has pointed out some of the remarkable echoes of the 'Prelude' which seem to resonate in *Copperfield* and which, not only to him, 'seemed very strong'.[148]

There was, however, another moment in which Dickens was reminded of Switzerland while he was busy writing the final two numbers of *Copperfield*. Catherine Dickens had just given birth to Dora and was not with the rest of the family at Broadstairs. It was in this moment that Dickens wrote the letter to his wife, telling her that he could not sleep, 'walked about the house 'till 5' and 'was just as I was that night in Geneva'.[149] It may be mere coincidence, but while Dickens finds himself 'in that tremendous paroxysm of Copperfield – having my most powerful effect in all the Story, on the Anvil', he asks his friend Daniel Maclise, a painter, whether he 'would care to see what I am going to see at Highgate tomorrow, an asylum of Idiots'.[150] Only two weeks later, and still 'fort occupé, en ecrivant [*sic*] le dernier livraison de Copperfield', he wrote a letter of introduction to W. F. de Cerjat, still living in Lausanne, and to Dickens 'an inseparable part of dear old Switzerland to me' for the Reverend Chauncey Hare Townshend, 'who does not like to be near to you, and strange to you, after that'.[151] Suddenly, the voices of Charles Dickens and that of his alter ego David Copperfield blend in the letter, and exclaim: 'I wish I were at Rosemont, to come down the Hill with [Townshend], and ring your bell with my own hand!' In the next sentence he tells his friend of his intention to visit: 'Watson and I have threatened, twice, to make a descent on Lausanne. I really begin to think we shall do it, please God, next year. We have been dreadfully in earnest.'[152] Despite Dickens's assurance that both had been 'dreadfully in earnest', the trip would only take place in 1853 – without Watson, however, who had died the year before.

---

[147] Ibid.

[148] Ibid.

[149] To Catherine Dickens, 3 September 1850, *Letters*, vol. 6, 161.

[150] To W. H. Wills, 17 September 1850, *Letters*, vol. 6, 171; to Daniel Maclise, 19 September 1850, *Letters*, vol. 6, 173.

[151] To Count Alfred D'Orsay, 1 October 1850, *Letters*, vol. 6, 184.

[152] To W. F. de Cerjat, 1 October 1850, *Letters*, vol. 6, 183.

Contrasts, or Dickens, Switzerland and the Grotesque

As an 'essentially mixed or hybrid form', the grotesque is interested in heterogeneous shapes such as 'human forms, animal forms, the natural, the supernatural, the comic, the monstrous and misshapen' which it combines in 'unstable, conflicting, paradoxical relationships'.[153] A major influence for Dickens's understanding of the grotesque was – once more – the theatre: 'Everywhere what was praised in early nineteenth-century pantomime was the mixed art – comic, serious, playful, monstrous – of the grotesque.'[154] It shaped his way of seeing and describing the world as well as the style in which he would reproduce it. The grotesque is an essentially visual form, corresponding to Dickens's own style, which has often been described as cinematic.[155] Another aspect of the grotesque in Dickens is the significance he gives 'to human physiognomy as an index of character' and the 'overlap between Dickensian themes and the subjects of visual satire'.[156]

Many of Dickens's Swiss landscapes are grotesque:

> The bases of the mountains forming the gorge in which the little village lay, were richly green; and high above this gentler vegetation, grew forests of dark fir, cleaving the wintry snow-drift, wedge-like, and stemming the avalanche. Above these, were range upon range of craggy steeps, grey rock, bright ice, and smooth verdure-specks of pasture, all gradually blending with the crowning snow. Dotted here and there on the mountain's-side, each tiny dot a home, were lonely wooden cottages, so dwarfed by the towering heights that they appeared too small for toys. So did even the clustered village in the valley, with its wooden bridge across the stream, where the stream tumbled over broken rocks, and roared away among the trees.[157]

The large, 'cleaving' and 'stemming', is the active, wild, terrible, unpredictable part, which – at least for now – is protecting the 'tiny', 'dwarfed', passive, feminine, domestic village, which features wooden cottages 'too small for toys'. Describing his crossing of the Gotthard

---

[153] Michael Hollington, *Dickens and the Grotesque* (London: Croom Helm, 1984), 1.
[154] Ibid., 9.
[155] On Dickens and film, see Sergei Eisenstein, 'Dickens, Griffith, and the Film To-Day', in *Film Form*, ed. and trans. Jay Leyda (Orlando, FL: Harcourt, 1977), 195–255; Grahame Smith, *Dickens and the Dream of Cinema* (Manchester: Manchester University Press, 2003).
[156] Hollington, *Dickens and the Grotesque*, 13; 14.
[157] Dickens, *David Copperfield*, 697.

pass to Forster in 1845, Dickens employed the same vocabulary to characterise the Swiss towns and villages that he would use when describing women – or comestible goods.[158] He found the towns 'most charming: most fascinating: most delicious'.[159] The gigantic and the minuscule are united in a single, hermaphrodite landscape. The inherent tension which this description creates comes from the threat of violence posed by the wild gigantic which may give up its protective function any time and destroy the miniaturised domestic.

Dickens discovered many moments of extraordinary greatness and smallness in Switzerland: he describes 'the little baby-houses of inns' to Forster, there is a 'little toy church with a copper-coloured steeple' in the *Holly-Tree Inn*'s 'The Guest', and in *Little Dorrit*, the travellers' journey to the top of the St Bernard appears as if they were 'ascending the broken staircase of a gigantic ruin'.[160] In another letter, Dickens mentions the 'gigantic effort' it would be to transport a library over the Simplon and in yet another, he describes his observations of an 'immense Frenchman' and a 'very little Englishman' under the balcony of his hotel in Geneva. In the course of the narrative, the two characters turn into the 'Giant' and the 'Dwarf'.[161] The 'statue of St Peter in the street at Fribourg grasps the largest key that was ever beheld' while the Swiss cottages are 'glazed with small round panes of glass like crown-pieces'.[162] In 'Travelling Abroad', the boats with their sails on the lake seem 'like enormous magnifications of this goose-quill pen that is now in my hand'.[163] Dickens was fascinated with physical force and performance, but also attracted by seemingly opposite principles. John Carey remarks of Dickens's decision to ascend Vesuvius, ignore the warnings, climb right to the top and look down into the crater, that

> [the] anecdote is typical of Dickens. Typical of his disregard for other people – his 'hard and aggressive' nature, 'impetuous' and 'overbearing', in Forster's words; typical of his enormous and unquenchable desire for activity, for something which would use up his dynamic

---

[158] This rather derogatory commentary is not the only instance in Dickens's work in which female characters are objectified.

[159] To Catherine Dickens, 23 November 1844, *Letters*, vol. 4, 228; to Forster, 15 June 1845, *Letters*, vol. 4, 321.

[160] To Forster, 15 June 1845, *Letters*, vol. 4, 321; Dickens et al., *The Holly-Tree Inn*, 'The Guest', *Household Words*, Christmas number, 25 December 1855, 578; Dickens, *Little Dorrit*, 420.

[161] To Forster, ?October–November 1846, *Letters*, vol. 4, 652; to Thomas Beard, 21 October 1846, *Letters*, vol. 4, 640.

[162] Dickens, *Pictures from Italy*, 100.

[163] Dickens, 'Travelling Abroad', 95.

102   *Dickens and Switzerland*

energies; and typical of his fascination with fire as a beautiful and terrible destroyer, a visible expression of pure violence.[164]

This is one side of Dickens, certainly. But another, equally strong one is his sympathy for the helpless, vulnerable and tiny, the 'marvellously domestic, home-loving shape' of Dickens's nature, as Forster calls it.[165] In the description of this landscape, Dickens unites two potentially conflicting sides of his own personality. No wonder then that in this environment his fictional alter ego, David Copperfield, manages to reconcile the past and the present, Dora and Agnes, physical attraction and spiritual love.

The conglomeration of opposing principles belongs to the aesthetic form of the grotesque, which Dickens often feels attracted to. As mentioned in the Introduction, he describes the Inn at Fribourg as having 'a German bedstead in it, about the size and shape of a baby's linen-basket' and contrasts this smallness in the next sentence with a hyperbole: 'Butter is so cheap hereabouts, that they bring you a great mass, like the squab of a sofa, for tea.'[166] Dickens delights in the contrast between excess and restraint, and the threat of an organised but unstable system to collapse and fall apart.

In his references to Switzerland, Dickens is rarely able to avoid the grotesque. *Pictures from Italy* feature a precursor to the description of the cottages in *David Copperfield*: 'I will not recall', he says, '(though I am sorely tempted) how the Swiss villages, clustered at the feet of Giant mountains, looked like playthings, or how confusedly the houses were heaped and piled together.'[167] Once more we find a gargantuan force threatening, aestheticising and towering over an anarchically assembled entity of smallness resembling 'playthings'. These houses belong to the same domain as some of Dickens's female characters who occupy the ambiguous space between 'child' and 'woman'. The cottages ooze an irresistible mixture of mature order, domesticity and harmony, but at the same time retain a childlike quality of purity and innocence. They are as yet uncorrupted but live in the constant danger of being destroyed. Dickens's fascination with the corruption of innocence obviously does not stop at young women.

Note the capital in 'Giant mountains', as if the mountains were characters themselves. The narrative also drifts towards biblical

---

[164] Carey, *The Violent Effigy*, 12.
[165] Forster, *Life of Dickens*, 922.
[166] To Catherine Dickens, 23 November 1844, *Letters*, vol. 4, 229.
[167] Dickens, *Pictures from Italy*, 99.

legend and fairy tale in *Little Dorrit*, suggesting at least two under-lying stories of Arks, Giants and castles. Caves and cellars act as 'whispers of the perils of the place', 'never-resting wreaths and mazes of mist' which wander about, 'hunted by a moaning wind'.[168] This landscape is personalised, inhabited, a part of the parallel exist-ence of fairy tales and ghosts neither the travellers nor the narrator seem to have full access to. Dickens presents us with broken narra-tives, embodied in the illusion of the 'broken staircase of a gigantic ruin' – perhaps Babel, which is invoked earlier, but perhaps simply the remains of another, now inaccessible myth. The travellers see the 'Blackened skeleton arms of wood by the way', which point 'upward to the convent as if the ghosts of former travellers overwhelmed by the snow haunted the scene of their distress'.[169] These moments are also narrative possibilities, as if he wanted to test his subject in dif-ferent genres. The broken narratives are all linked to the space they inhabit and foreshadow the chance meeting of the characters on top of the mountain, whose separate stories will henceforth be linked through the encounter at this junction.

Unclear distinctions between animate and inanimate nature are a widespread phenomenon in Dickens's writing. A frequently used simile appears in *Martin Chuzzlewit*, where the 'slighter branches cracked and rattled as they moved, in skeleton dances' to the 'moaning music' of an autumnal wind, and is also repeated elsewhere in Dickens's descriptions of Alpine travel. Later in *Little Dorrit*, Blandois's sinister look haunts Amy on the way to Martigny, and even 'when the convent was gone and some light morning clouds veiled the pass below it, the ghastly skeleton arms by the wayside seemed to be all pointing up at him'.[170] In 'Shy Neighbourhoods', the narrator catches himself 'looking about for wooden arms to point the right track up the mountain', and in 'Lying Awake', he remembers 'the same black wooden arms pointing the way' up to the pass.[171] In 'A Message from the Sea', 'the bleached and barren skeletons of a forest of pines varied the desolate monotony'.[172]

The episode in *Little Dorrit* on the St Bernard is one of the most prominent examples of Dickens's writing on Switzerland. It stands at the beginning of a new chapter in a new, second book, and Dickens makes sure we understand it as such: the characters remain unnamed

---

[168] Dickens, *Little Dorrit*, 420.
[169] Ibid., 421.
[170] Ibid., 443.
[171] Dickens, 'Shy Neighbourhoods', 118; 'Lying Awake', 91.
[172] Dickens, 'The Club-Night', 599.

until the very end of this first chapter, as if they were unfamiliar, and as if the temporal and geographical gap which occurs between the books had made them as foreign to us as the country they are travelling in. On the St Bernard, the Dorrits's fortunes reach a literal and metaphorical peak, but only seemingly so, as the view is clouded from the start and, at least for a while, their luck will only go downhill from there. As Edwin Eigner observes in his *Dickens Pantomime*, it is in the third quarter of the novel – the beginning of the second book – that 'the family degenerates in Italy as redemptive power seems to drain out of Amy, and at home Mr. Merdle's complaint becomes the condition of England'.[173]

Even the new beginning is only one in part – we soon understand that we are already familiar with these unnamed characters ascending the mountain. And surely, there has been a chapter called 'Fellow Travellers' before? The narrative is taking a break, quite literally. The Dorrits's trip to the St Bernard is a circular one, going nowhere. Even though the mountain is a pass to Italy, the family start and end their mountain excursion in Switzerland. The journey is also a passage through various forms of boundaries, such as that between the living and the dead: figuratively, with the 'Blackened skeleton arms of wood' pointing 'upward to the convent, as if the ghosts of former travellers overwhelmed by the snow, haunted the scene of their distress' and literally, with the morgue full of 'dead travellers found upon the mountain'.[174]

The second book opens with a vintage scene. It is a piece of writing Dickens would rework and adapt in *The Tale of Two Cities* three years later, extending it both in length and symbolism.[175] In *Little Dorrit*, the passage forms the opening to the reader's first encounter with Switzerland:

> In the autumn of the year, Darkness and Night were creeping up to the highest ridges of the Alps.
> It was vintage time in the valleys on the Swiss side of the Pass of the Great Saint Bernard and along the banks of the Lake of Geneva.

---

[173] Edwin Eigner, *Dickens Pantomime*, 31.
[174] Dickens, *Little Dorrit*, 420; 421.
[175] Charles Dickens, *A Tale of Two Cities* (Oxford: Oxford University Press, 2008), 32. This powerful scene also inspired Dickens's admirer Leo Tolstoy to write a similar passage in his *Cossaks*. In contrast to Dickens's condensed scene, Tolstoy's is much longer and the tone is quite different. Leo Tolstoy, 'Cossacks', in *Tales of Army Life*, trans. Louise and Aylmer Maude (London: Oxford University Press, 1932), 409; for a short introduction, see Galina Alekseeva, 'Dickens in Leo Tolstoy's Universe', in Hollington, *The Reception of Charles Dickens in Europe*, vol. 1, 91.

The air was charged with the scent of gathered grapes. Baskets, troughs, and tubs of grapes, stood in the dim village doorways, stopped the steep and narrow village streets, and had been carrying all day along the roads and lanes. Grapes, spilt and crushed under foot, lay about everywhere. The child carried in a sling by the laden peasant-woman toiling home, was quieted with picked-up grapes; the idiot sunning his big goitre under the eaves of the wooden chalet by the way to the waterfall, sat munching grapes; the breath of the cows and goats was redolent of leaves and stalks of grapes; the company in every little cabaret were eating, drinking, talking grapes.[176]

In *Dickens and the Grotesque*, Michael Hollington observes that Dickens 'exemplifies the 'vulgar' side of Italy' in *Little Dorrit*, 'representing social and political realities that the classical tourist ignores', an issue he describes as Dickens's 'new picturesque'.[177] In his writing about Switzerland, the matter is more complex. Whereas Dickens occasionally finds inspiration in the aestheticism of the 'new picturesque', he is also not afraid to revert to the traditional picturesque in order to create effect. In the quotation from *Little Dorrit* above we find both: the two opening sentences with their wide, panoramic perspective are part of the traditional picturesque tableau. Nonetheless, the capitalised initial letters in 'Darkness' and 'Night' suggest personification, and the fact that they are 'creeping up' further encourages the image of two animate forces. On first glance, the scene may look picturesque, bordering on the sublime perhaps, but on second, there is a grotesque, uncanny, threatening element to it.

The vintage scene is both romantic and grotesque because it focuses on the visual and the 'aesthetics of ugliness', as Michael Hollington has argued.[178] Hollington discusses Dickens in terms of the German Romantic grotesque and defines this kind of aesthetics as 'how beauty could be constructed, paradoxically, from the most intractable materials, including, most importantly, the unpleasant but fantastic realities of a new urban and incipiently industrial society'.[179] Certainly, society here is neither 'urban' nor 'incipiently industrial', but rustic and rural. It is a world unfamiliar to the urban eye, which therefore may find it easy to discover a grotesque aesthetic in the chaos of vintage time. Note, however, how the scene takes place in 'the dim village doorways', the 'steep and narrow

---

[176] Dickens, *Little Dorrit*, 419.
[177] Hollington, *Dickens and the Grotesque*, 146.
[178] Ibid., 18.
[179] Ibid.

106 *Dickens and Switzerland*

village streets', the 'roads and lanes': this is not London or Paris, of course, but the largest conglomeration of people in the area surrounding the St Bernard.[180]

Following the grapes' trace allows Dickens to penetrate every corner of the village society he describes. As it did in Italy, the narrator's glance also deviates from the beaten track in Switzerland, and discovers vulgarity and distortion beyond the picturesque backdrop of the 'Mountain-peaks of great celebrity'.[181] The same is true when the narrator redirects his focus on top of the St Bernard from the main characters and studies the frozen bodies in the morgue. His attention wanders away from the main plot to offer a broader perspective, but also to create an atmosphere, an expectation and a break, and not least, a moment of strong emotion.

The fact that both travel and the grotesque can function as catalysts for reversing the established order and challenging authority are clearly visible here, and must have been immensely attractive to Dickens. Judith Adler notes: 'Insofar as travel can anchor visions of reality in particularly vivid or pleasurable personal experience, pursued in seeming freedom from the coercion of authority, its powers of ideological transformation and confirmation may be unusually potent.'[182] In the vintage scene, sequences become illogical and orders distorted: the grapes, causing the overflow, only become the grammatical subject matter of the fourth sentence of this paragraph. Before this, the emphasis is on the scent-charged air, the baskets, troughs and tubs. There is little evidence of a functional social hierarchy – something Dickens usually praises about Switzerland – in this list. The sequence – child, peasant-woman, 'idiot' –is, if anything, a sequence from bottom to top, and assymetrical. After all, the woman carrying the child is not their 'mother', but a 'peasant-woman toiling home'. The narrator's focal point is irregular too, with an omniscient perspective penetrating every possible corner of the 'valleys' and 'along the banks of the Lake of Geneva', but also offering a close-up of 'the child', the 'peasant-woman', the 'idiot' and the interiors of 'every little cabaret'.[183] At the same time, it is a sequence starting with the most unspoiled element in the chain, the child and his mother, and ending with grotesque deformation in the human body. Read as the alarming beginning of a process of

[180] Martigny had about 2,500 permanent residents in 1850. *Historisches Lexikon der Schweiz*, s.v. 'Martigny'.
[181] Dickens, *Little Dorrit*, 419.
[182] Adler, 'Travel as Performed Art', 1383.
[183] Dickens, *Little Dorrit*, 419.

degeneration, the sequence ends with a hint at the animalistic and beastly in the shape of cows and goats. The sequence, however, ends only with the 'breath of cows and goats', rather than the physical appearance of the animals themselves, as if this development was not quite sure which physical form it will eventually take.

The vintage scene is also another one of the moments in which Dickens puts great emphasis on the oral. John Carey notes that 'Food consumption, for instance, is an indispensable accompaniment of Dickensian bliss'.[184] Once more, as Ian Watt puts it, the 'sucking, eating, and speaking', which 'employ the same organs and reflexes – the lips, the tongue, the jaws, the throat, the breathing apparatus' are not only present, but the focus.[185] The child, 'quieted with picked-up grapes', young enough still to be 'carried in a sling' is sucking, the 'idiot' is 'munching' and the animals' breath is 'redolent of leaves and stalks of grapes'. The difference between Watt's list and the one Dickens presents here is that the first traces a progression from bottom (sucking when a child) to top (controlled breathing during speech), whereas the second is that of a carnivalesque regression from top to bottom in which the order of activity – sucking, eating, breathing – remains the same, but the performers decline from human into beast.

A transformation of the grapes into wine remains almost fruitless. Despite the presence of a 'generous abundance' both in raw material and workforce, the scene is everything but productive. Disorder and chaos reign instead. Rather than being contained in vats, the grapes are 'spilt and crushed under foot, lay about everywhere' and the people are not hard at work, but 'toiling home', 'sunning' their goitre and sitting in cabarets 'eating, drinking, talking grapes' rather than processing them. No wonder that 'no ripe touch of this generous abundance could be given to the thin, hard, stoney wine, which after all was made from the grapes!'

There seems to exist an odd connection between wine and Switzerland in some of Dickens's writing: in *No Thoroughfare*, the first Walter Wilding owns a wine business in London, the stock of which appears to be at least partly bought in Switzerland. This triggers Vendale and Obenreizer's journey to Neuchâtel, where the legitimate right to the wine business becomes a question of identity, that is the right kind of blood. Yet at least some of the grapes grown in Switzerland seem to be strangely fruitless: the notary Maître

---

[184] Carey, *The Violent Effigy*, 25.
[185] Watt, 'Oral Dickens', 174.

108 *Dickens and Switzerland*

Voigt once dealt with a legal case over 'half an acre of vineyard that seldom bore any grapes'.[186] However, unless Dickens is being ironic here, not all Swiss wine growers are equally unsuccessful: the supper which the Dorrits, the Gowans and the rest of the company enjoy on top of the St Bernard 'was like the supper of an ordinary Swiss hotel, and good red wine grown by the convent in more genial air was not wanting'.[187] Given Dickens's usual dislike of anything Catholic, this assessment is almost complimentary. Wine also plays an important role in Scott's *Anne of Geierstein*, a likely source for *No Thoroughfare*.[188] Additionally, in Scott's novel, the English protagonist and his father disguise themselves as merchants when they travel through Switzerland, in order to hide their true identity. It would be an astonishing coincidence if they had not figured as a template for Vendale, the wine merchant.

In 'To Be Read At Dusk', wine undergoes a similar metamorphosis to that of *Little Dorrit* and *A Tale of Two Cities*, only that it turns into dusk rather than blood:

> Five couriers, sitting on a bench outside the convent on the summit of the Great St Bernard in Switzerland, looking at the remote heights, stained by the setting sun as if a mighty quantity of red wine had been broached upon the mountain top, and had not yet had time to sink into the snow.

A little later, the 'wine upon the mountain top soaked in as we looked'.[189] Alpine landscape at dusk is one of the recurring patterns in Dickens's Switzerland. Copperfield too, 'came, one evening before sunset, down into a valley, where I was to rest'.[190] The first sentence of the following paragraph puts another emphasis on this: 'I came into the valley, as the evening sun was shining on the remote heights of snow, that closed it in, like eternal clouds.'[191]

Whereas Dickens explored the atmosphere of vintage in *Little Dorrit*, he extended and reimagined the scene in the moment the wine has spilled in *A Tale of Two Cities*. Both scenes, I would like to suggest, function as allegories and also form a sequence. Their common source is Hans Holbein and his illustrations of the *Dance of Death*. Holbein's *Dance* was one of Dickens's favourite books

---

[186] Collins and Dickens, *No Thoroughfare*, 214.
[187] Dickens, *Little Dorrit*, 427.
[188] See Chapter 1, 25.
[189] Dickens, 'To Be Read at Dusk', 66.
[190] Dickens, *David Copperfield*, 697.
[191] Ibid.

and he acquired a copy in 1833.[192] It was, according to Michael Hollington, 'a continual reference point' in Dickens's writing.[193] The edition Dickens read, edited by Francis Douce, mentions a dance of peasants attributed to Holbein, but probably not by him.[194] The carnivalesque release and all-encompassing exuberance in both scenes is reminiscent of Holbein's template. In contrast to *Little Dorrit*, the link between wine and blood is made explicit in the passage from *A Tale of Two Cities*:

> The wine was red wine, and had stained the ground of the narrow street in the suburb of Saint Antoine, in Paris, where it was spilled. It had stained many hands, too, and many faces, and many naked feet, and many wooden shoes. The hands of the man who sawed the wood, left red marks on the billets; and the forehead of the woman who nursed her baby, was stained with the stain of the old rag she wound about her head again. Those who had been greedy with the staves of the cask, had acquired a tigerish smear about the mouth; and one tall joker so besmirched, his head more out of a long squalid bag of a nightcap than in it, scrawled upon a wall with his finger dipped in muddy wine-lees—BLOOD.[195]

Among a greater anonymous mass, described in a wonderful *pars pro toto* of loose body parts as 'many hands', 'many faces' and 'many naked feet', we find a similar array of characters as on the foot of the St Bernard. The cast seems more diverse in Paris, however. New to the company is the 'man who sawed the wood', but we have met the 'woman who nursed her baby' and the 'tall joker' before in Switzerland. The tall joker may not appear as double of the Swiss 'idiot' at first glance, but he too is defined by a grotesque distortion with his 'head more out of a long squalid bag of a nightcap than in it'. The nightcap becomes as much part of the 'joker's' body as the 'idiot's' goitre, but his bodily extension has moved from the lower part of the face to the top of it. If we read figures through the lens of the pantomimic character of the clown, the descriptions of the 'idiot' and the 'joker' both make sense. There are notions of the beastly, in the 'tigerish smear about the mouth' on those who were too greedy.

The symbolism of wine turned to blood is also an echo of the Catholic belief of transubstantiation, that is, that the wine and bread served during mass transform into the blood and body of Christ.

---

[192] Michael Hollington, 'Dickens and the Dance of Death', *Dickensian* 76 (1980): 67.
[193] Hollington in Schlicke, *Oxford Reader's Companion to Dickens*, 255.
[194] Holbein, *The Dance of Death*, 80.
[195] Dickens, *A Tale of Two Cities*, 32.

110 *Dickens and Switzerland*

Dickens, who was 'perfectly convinced that Roman Catholicism embodied the worst evils of the past, that it was the epitome of ignorance and superstition, slavish obedience to priestly authority, and unwholesome asceticism', saw the same flaws in Switzerland's Catholic cantons as he had observed in his *Pictures from Italy*.[196] There, his 'taste for the macabre is well satisfied by multitudes of relics and skeletons of saints dressed up in rich vestments and jewels'.[197]

In Switzerland, the matter was much more complex in that the country was, and is, split between Catholic and Protestant cantons. During the very same years of Dickens's first three visits, there was a build-up to the final war on Swiss soil to date: a civil war, the 'Sonderbund', or War of the Separate League. The skirmishes in Geneva which Dickens reports in his letters all belong to this conflict. Very broadly speaking, they emerged between Catholic and the Protestant cantons and culminated in the 'Year of Revolutions' in 1848. In *A Very Civil War*, Joachim Remak points out that unlike the other revolutions taking place in the same year, in Switzerland 'it was the reformers who won, and they made their victory incontrovertible, creating democratic institutions that would long outlast them'.[198] Needless to say that even though Dickens felt that it was 'a horribly ungentlemanly thing to say', his sympathy was 'all with the radicals'.[199] 'I don't know any subject', he explained, 'on which this indomitable people have so good a right to a strong feeling as Catholicity – if not as a religion, clearly as a means of social degradation'.[200] Earlier, he had written:

> I don't know whether I have mentioned before, that in the valley of the Simplon hard by here, where [...] this Protestant canton ends and a Catholic canton begins, you might separate two perfectly distinct and different conditions of humanity by drawing a line with your stick in the dust on the ground. On the Protestant side, neatness; cheerfulness; industry; education; continual aspiration, at least after better things. On the Catholic side, dirt, disease, ignorance, squalor and misery.[201]

---

[196] Robert Newsom in Schlicke, *Oxford Reader's Companion to Dickens*, 510.
[197] Ibid.
[198] Joachim Remak, *A Very Civil War. The Swiss Sonderbund War of 1847* (Boulder, CO: Westview Press, 1993), xiii.
[199] To Forster, 11 October 1846, *Letters*, vol. 4, 632.
[200] Ibid.
[201] To Forster, 24 and 25 August 1846, *Letters*, vol. 4, 611.

The 'dirt, disease, ignorance, squalor and misery' is clearly visible in Dickens's description of vintage time in the – Catholic – 'valleys on the Swiss side of the Pass of the Great Saint Bernard'.[202] The symbolism of the blood-wine in this scene not only represents Dickens's uneasiness about Catholicism, but also introduces a cannibalistic dimension.

What the Waves Were Always Saying, or Water and the Oral

Dickens's affinity for the oral has already emerged in Chapter 1.[203] Orality in all its aspects is a key ingredient to Dickens's texts about Switzerland. References to food and drink – grotesque, odd and comic – are the most straightforward ones and I have already mentioned the uncommercial traveller's arrival into the 'land of wooden houses, innocent cakes, thin butter soup, and spotless little inn bedrooms with a family likeness to Dairies' in the last chapter.[204] Food, drink and death are often curiously linked in Dickens, and Obenreizer's drugging of Vendale's brandy in *No Thoroughfare* is no exception. The narrator of 'Shy Neighbourhoods' in *The Uncommercial Traveller* is out on a walk in England 'to breakfast', but cannot 'disembarrass myself of the idea that I had to climb those heights and banks of cloud, and that there was an Alpine Convent somewhere behind the sun, where I was going to breakfast'.[205] That 'Alpine Convent' not only welcomes travellers and provides for them but, as we have already seen in *Little Dorrit*, also stores the dead bodies of those in a frozen morgue who did not make it to breakfast in time.

The very first sentence of *Dombey* compares little Paul's constitution to food: the child is 'carefully disposed on a low settee immediately in front of the fire and close to it as if it were analogous to that of a muffin, and it was essential to toast him brown while he was still new'.[206] This is one of the several instances which confirms John Carey's observation that a 'form of violence more exotic and, to Dickens' way of thinking, more amusing than capital punishment

---

[202] Dickens, *Little Dorrit*, 419.
[203] See Chapter 1, 31.
[204] Dickens, 'Travelling Abroad', 94; see also Chapter 1, 78.
[205] Dickens, 'Shy Neighbourhoods', 118.
[206] Dickens, *Dombey and Son*, 1.

112   *Dickens and Switzerland*

was cannibalism'.[207] Harry Stone has pointed out that Dickens's 'fascination with cannibalism and his profound anxieties concerning it were rooted, as he himself proclaimed, in his earliest days'.[208] Michael Hollington has pointed out that

> The very frequent association of human flesh with food may originate in a childhood memory. An interesting autobiographical sketch in *The Uncommercial Traveller* recalls a childhood visit to some dead infants which had the effect of 'reminding me by a homely association, which I suspect their complexion to have assisted, of pigs' feet as they are usually displayed at a neat tripe-shop.'[209]

It is unsurprising then, that it would resurface when Dickens was thinking about childhood in *Dombey*.

An interesting variation of cannibalism can also be found in *The Battle of Life*, where the moon looks upon the fallen knights who are lying 'with upturned faces that had once at mother's breasts sought mother's eyes, or slumbered happily'.[210] The once blood-soaked 'guilty battle-ground' is farmed and yields crops, which feed new generations:

> Crops were sown, and grew up, and were gathered in; the stream that had been crimsoned, turned a water-mill; men whistled at the plough; gleaners and haymakers were seen in quiet groups at work; sheep and oxen pastured; boys whooped and called, in fields, to scare away the birds; smoke rose from cottage chimneys; Sabbath bells rang peacefully; old people lived and died; the timid creatures of the field, and simple flowers of the bush and garden, grew and withered in their destined terms: and all upon the fierce and bloody battle-ground, where thousands upon thousands had been killed in the great fight.[211]

The fertilised soil, however, is tainted, as 'deep green patches' appeared in the corn 'at first, that people looked at awfully' and the berries growing there are 'believed to leave too deep a stain upon the hand that plucked them'.[212] The connection between the bloodshed and the field is eventually almost forgotten, and the 'deep

[207] Carey, *The Violent Effigy*, 22.
[208] Stone, *Night Side of Dickens*, 15.
[209] Hollington, *Dickens and the Grotesque*, 53n28.
[210] Dickens, *Battle of Life*, in *The Christmas Books, Vol. 2: The Cricket on the Hearth, The Battle of Life, The Haunted Man*, ed. Michael Slater (London: Penguin, 1971), 136.
[211] Ibid., 137.
[212] Ibid., 138.

green patches were no greener now than the memory of those who lay in dust below'.[213] The overt emphasis on death and consumption throughout the opening of the story is continued in the apple pickers who watch Marion and Grace dance. There is the same uneasiness about food and drink production, gathering and consumption as in *Little Dorrit*'s vintage scene above.

Equally fascinating to Dickens are breastfed babies. Eating directly from their mother's body, Dickens seems to at least scent a hint of cannibalism there as well. Their bodies are seldom distinct and can hardly be told apart. In *The Uncommercial Traveller*'s 'Travelling Abroad', the narrator meets 'a hundred women in bodices', who 'sold eggs and honey, butter and fruit'. This is nothing out of the ordinary, had Dickens not continued: 'and suckled their children as they sat by their clean baskets, and had such enormous goitres (or glandular swellings in the throat) that it became a science to know where the nurse ended and the child began'.[214] The mothers' 'glandular swellings in the throat' somehow blur the boundaries between their own bodies and that of their child. Dickens is not pointing out a singular occurrence here, but in a hyperbolical fashion typical of him, he turns it into a mass phenomenon. Every single one of the 'hundred women in bodices' seems to suffer from the same condition. Nourishment and disease seem to go hand in hand in this passage and link it to its predecessor in *Little Dorrit*. The abundance of food available contrasts with the mothers' 'glandular swellings in the throat'.

Dickens was riveted by goitres. They appear in many of his Swiss texts, but always remain a marginalised comment with a comic and grotesque effect. During Dickens's lifetime, goitres were thought to originate from static air or 'unhealthy waters'. An article written by Eliza Lynn Linton which appeared in *Household Words* in 1858 supports this idea and links melted snow and seawater to 'cretinism' and goitres:

> Some chemists say, that it is the confined waters of Switzerland, and their mixture with melted snow-water, which is almost absolutely destitute of iodine, that helps to make so many cretins. Of course they do not assert that the water is the sole cause. The want of a free circulation of air in the deep valleys, and the want of a free and generous diet, together with the close intermarriages common even in Roman Catholic mountainous districts – all these causes count

[213] Ibid.
[214] Dickens, 'Travelling Abroad', 94.

114 *Dickens and Switzerland*

for much in this malady; [...] But, at all events, it requires very little chemical courage to say that melted snow-water is bad, owing to its absence of iodine; iodine being, the grand specific against scrofula, glandular swelling, and the like. [...] The melted ice of sea-water has no saltness, and is sweet and pleasant; but unwholesome, causing glandular swellings in the throat, arriving in fact to the condition of snow-water which has been congealed and locked up without atmospheric air.[215]

Murray's Handbook for Travellers in Switzerland dedicates an entire section to 'Goitre and Cretinism' in its 'Introductory Information' and opens with a noteworthy antagonism:

> It is a remarkable fact that, amidst some of the most magnificent scenery of the globe, where nature seems to have put forth all her powers in exciting emotions of wonder and elevation in the mind, man appears, from a mysterious visitation of disease, in his most degraded and pitiable condition. Such, however, is the fact. It is in the grandest and most beautiful valleys of the Alps that the maladies of *goitre* and *cretinism* prevail.[216]

The *Murray* may also explain why 'cretinism' and goitre frequently appear together in Dickens's narratives of Switzerland, as it was believed that the two arise 'from the same cause, whatever it may be'. The 'crétin', we learn, 'is an idiot – a melancholy spectacle – a creature who may almost be said to rank a step below a human being'.[217] Rather unsurprising, then, that Dickens's interest was aroused. Despite his frequent references to goitres and 'idiots' in his fiction, there is no evidence in his surviving letters that Dickens ever met people suffering with these afflictions outside Haldimand's asylum during his stay in Switzerland. In fact, the word 'goitre' appears only once in the whole of his surviving collection of letters, which suggests that their frequent appearance in his fiction is as much the result of grotesque effect rather than a realistic representation of what he saw.[218]

In an article with the unflattering title 'Idiots', Dickens and William Henry Wills explore popular notions of 'idiots' and observe:

> In association with Switzerland, it suggests a horrible being, seated at a chalet door (perhaps possessing sense enough to lead the way

---

[215] Eliza Lynn Linton, 'Water', *Household Words*, 23 October 1858, 365.
[216] Murray, *Handbook for Travellers in Switzerland 1838*, lviii.
[217] Ibid.
[218] To Forster, 13 November 1846, *Letters*, vol. 4, 656.

to a neighbouring waterfall), of stunted and misshapen form, with a pendulous excrescence dangling from his throat, like a great skin bag with a weight in it.[219]

They mention Dr Guggenbühl, the 'devoted and distinguished founder of the asylum on the Abendberg, in Switzerland' and provide several examples of the institution's inmates. In this article, however, there is no indication that water might be causing the condition. They write:

> The causes of idiocy are as yet imperfectly understood. Little is known of the origin of the disorder, beyond the facts that idiocy is sometimes developed during the progress of dentition, and that it would seem to be generally associated with mental suffering, fright, or anxiety, or with a latent want of power, in the mother.[220]

With the 'progress of dentition' we discover yet another oral phenomenon.

In 'Travelling Abroad', many of the elements Dickens employs to create grotesque effect come together when the narrator reaches Switzerland. The passage is typical of many of Dickens's fictional representations of Switzerland as it begins on a picturesque note – 'the cluster of chalets where I had to turn out of the track to see the waterfall' – which suddenly turns into a scene of the grotesque. It is certainly noteworthy that the grotesque only manifests itself once the narrator 'had to turn out of the track' and leave the beaten path, as it were:

> By such ways and means, I would come to the cluster of chalets where I had to turn out of the track to see the waterfall; and then, uttering a howl like a young giant, on espying a traveller – in other words, something to eat – coming up the steep, the idiot lying on the wood-pile who sunned himself and nursed his goitre, would rouse the woman-guide within the hut, who would stream out hastily, throwing her child over one of her shoulders and her goitre over the other, as she came along.[221]

The several attempts of seeing and eating – that of the tourist who wants to 'see the waterfall', the 'idiot' who was 'sunning himself' and 'nursing his goitre' and turns into a 'young giant' discovering 'something to eat' – are interrupted or distorted. The 'idiot' howls to

---

[219] Dickens and William Henry Wills, 'Idiots', *Household Words*, 4 June 1853, 313.
[220] Ibid., 317.
[221] Dickens, 'Travelling Abroad', 95.

116   *Dickens and Switzerland*

alert his mother for 'something to eat', thereby making a direct link between the traveller and the subsequent promise of food. The water this family is living off both literally, by drinking it, and figuratively, by showing it to travellers for money, carries a disease.

A little earlier in 'Travelling Abroad', when the narrator is still imagining himself in Paris, he is 'dragged by invisible force into the Morgue. I never want to go there, but am always pulled there'.[222] There, he sees

> a large dark man whose disfigurement by water was in a frightful manner, comic, and whose expression was that of a prize-fighter who had closed his eyelids under a heavy blow, but was going immediately to open them, shake his head, and 'come up smiling'. O what this large dark man cost me in that bright city![223]

The Swiss scene is an awkward, twisted double of the experience in the Paris morgue. As with the goitre-ridden mother later in Switzerland, the dead man suffers from 'disfigurement by water'. Just as the 'idiot', who is 'lying on a wood-pile', suns himself and nurses his goitre, so the bodies in the morgue are all laid out, like the 'old grey man lying all alone on his cold bed, with a tap of water turned on over his grey hair'.[224] The large dark man is both 'frightful' and 'comic', just as the 'idiot' when he utters 'a howl like a young giant, on espying a traveller – in other words, something to eat'. The woman-guide does not run or fly out of the chalet, but will 'stream out hastily', at the prospect of earning some money, strengthening the connection between herself and the waterfall. She has already adopted one of the qualities of the water on which she depends.

We never learn the Swiss woman's attitude towards the waterfall, but the same set of objects – the chalet, the waterfall, the 'idiot' and goitres – reappear in a variety of combinations in Dickens's fiction. The goitre-bearer is not always identical with the 'idiot', but if one is present, the other is not far off. Obenreizer's recollection of his childhood in *No Thoroughfare* follows the same pattern:

> I drew a word-picture of my sordid childhood. Of our poor hut, by the waterfall which my mother showed to travellers; of the cow-shed where I slept with the cow; of my idiot half-brother always sitting at the door, or limping down the Pass to beg, of my half-sister always spinning, and resting her enormous goitre on a great stone; of my

---

[222] Ibid., 88.
[223] Ibid.
[224] Dickens, 'Travelling Abroad', 88.

being a famished naked little wretch of two or three years when they were men and women with hard hands to beat me, I, the only child of my father's second marriage – if it even was a marriage.

Cut out here, of course, is the emphasis on food and eating. In this grotesque image, contrary to appearances and similar to the disappointingly 'stoney wine' produced from the rich abundance of grapes in *Little Dorrit*, the landscape of Obenreizer's childhood, picturesque enough to attract a certain amount of tourists, does not yield a satisfactory amount of output to maintain the family. The abundance of food has been replaced with total dependence on money from tourists and the comedy is gone. The 'Mimic water [...] dropping off a mill-wheel under the clock' which Vendale observes in Obenreizer's apartment functions both as a domestic trinket and also a constant reminder of its owner's 'sordid childhood' – as if Obenreizer was as obsessed with his past as his creator.[225]

Secret Intelligence, or Dickens on Switzerland

This chapter has discussed Switzerland in its most well-known and prominent form in Dickens's writing. It is visible, sometimes even ostentatious, because of the various lenses, some of which are typical of a narrative of the country, through which Dickens narrates it: he mocks the sublime, focuses on grotesque transformations and highlights uncanny relationships between death and food, for example. Through the plays he had seen and the travel books he had read, Dickens was familiar with the popular ways of writing about Switzerland. His texts often acknowledge these narratives and take inspiration from them, but Dickens plays with and transforms them to develop his own style. Dickens's representation of Switzerland is distinctive because even though he is interested in descriptions of its landscape and the sensation of the sublime, he is more often drawn to topics which we recognise as typically 'Dickensian': the oral, the comic and the grotesque. The connections established in this chapter are perspectival and frequently only semi-voiced in Dickens's texts due to the strong associative nature of his writing in general, and on Switzerland in particular.

Switzerland in Dickens is a place of invention and reinvention, of discovery and self-discovery. Despite his suffering and the alleged

---

[225] Collins and Dickens, *No Thoroughfare*, 137.

'need for streets', he conceived an astonishing amount of material during his 1846 stay in Lausanne, which he put to great effect in his later fiction. Switzerland was also a place in which Dickens was greatly concerned with fictional and factual 'life' writings. During his stay in Switzerland, he was so busy with reflections on the past, memory, childhood and death that the country eventually became a trigger itself for this kind of occupation. His approach to writing on Switzerland seems intuitive and often seemingly semi-conscious, hence the many short and experimental but often rather revealing autobiographical pieces in which the country appears. In many ways and just like the Blacking Warehouse, Switzerland seems to have resisted fictionalisation, most likely because of Dickens's deep personal investment in the memory of it. An exception to this is perhaps the grotesque, the one lens he most systematically employs to narrate Switzerland.

Many of the Swiss references in Dickens's writing remain marginal or invisible without a look into the paratext and the context of his fiction. Even though the number of direct references to Switzerland is comparatively modest in Dickens's fiction overall, it is nonetheless a regular appearance which resurfaces and occasionally intrudes in the most unexpected of moments of writing. One of the reasons for this is clearly the distressing, unexplained and perhaps inexplicable but undoubtedly seminal experience he had during his stay in 1846. The event not only provided creative material for the fiction he was writing at the time but also had an influence on his texts for many years to come. It triggered a painful and intense personal introspection which manifested itself in the form of an almost obsessive reassessment of his own childhood, a fascination with death and the inspiration to write his autobiography. If we have focused on the most visible representations of Switzerland in this chapter, the next will discuss the most invisible and hidden side of Dickens's attitude towards and writing on Switzerland.

Chapter 3

Uncovering Switzerland

I have now recalled all that I think it needful to recall here, of this term of absence – with one reservation. I have made it, thus far, with no purpose of suppressing any of my thoughts; for, as I have elsewhere said, this narrative is my written memory. I have desired to keep the most secret current of my mind apart, and to the last. I enter on it now.

David Copperfield, Chapter 58

Some Old Scenes and Some New People, or Switzerland in Later Dickens

Dickens, it is well known, visited Switzerland four times: in 1844, 1845 and 1846, and a last time in 1853, when he travelled the country with his friends, the writer Wilkie Collins and the painter Augustus Egg. There is, however, a surprising reverberation of Switzerland in Dickens's later life and writing. From the 1850s onwards, Switzerland becomes an enigmatic presence both in his letters and his fiction. This unexpected and often problematic presence of Switzerland in Dickens's later work confirms Forster's statement that his visits had a long-lasting influence and that – as we began to outline in Chapter 1 – we need to widen our focus beyond the years of Dickens's known journeys to the country in order to get a fuller picture of its influence upon his works.[1]

During the late 1850s and early 1860s, Switzerland was still on Dickens's mind. It manifests itself as a memory, 'ever fresh', as a

[1] Forster, *Life of Dickens*, 446.

120 *Dickens and Switzerland*

good setting for some of his works, but also as 'a most horribly lying pretext', when he does not want to meet someone.[2] In the *Oxford Reader's Companion to Dickens*, Michael Hollington concludes that 'Switzerland [...] figures quite frequently in Dickens's imaginative work', and virtually every novel since *Dombey*, which he began in Switzerland, features at least one Swiss reference. They are minor, of course, and occasionally implicit, but they are there. The novel which followed *Dombey* was *David Copperfield*, where the protagonist travels to Switzerland where he is healed from his sorrow and discovers his love for Agnes. *Bleak House* seems to stand out here, and yet it has a very odd connection, as we will see below, and *Hard Times*, the novel which followed *Bleak House*, has a popular culture reference to the country through Sleary's circus programme, as outlined in Chapter 1. *Little Dorrit*, of course, features the largest description of Switzerland in any of Dickens's major texts. The Swiss connections of *A Tale of Two Cities* have been discussed in the last chapter and *Our Mutual Friend* as well as *The Mystery of Edwin Drood* will be considered below.

A surprising number of allusions occur in the 1850s and the early 1860s: there are several more or less indirect connections in *Our Mutual Friend*.[3] About a third of *No Thoroughfare* is set in Switzerland. At least two of *The Uncommercial Traveller*'s chapters from 1860, 'Travelling Abroad' and 'Shy Neighbourhoods', carry references to the country. A ghost story takes place at an inn in Switzerland in 'A Message from the Sea', and there are several as yet unattributed articles on or set in Switzerland in *All the Year Round*.[4] Most unexpected, perhaps, is Dickens's reference to the canton of Vaud in *A Child's History of England*, which appeared in three 'volumes' in *Household Words* between 1851 and 1853.[5]

Even his relationship with Ellen Ternan bears a literary connection with Switzerland. Dickens met Ternan in 1857, and began a relationship with her which, as far as we are aware, lasted until his death in 1870. Ternan translated a book about Zermatt, a town in the Swiss canton of Valais, from French into English in 1894.[6] It is not

---

[2] To Cerjat, 25 October 1864, *Letters*, vol. 10, 445; to Sir Joseph Oliffee, 18 January 1863, *Letters*, vol. 10, 196.

[3] Hollington in Schlicke, *Oxford Reader's Companion to Dickens*, 558.

[4] For example: Fyfe, 'Grandfather Blacktooth', 111; E. S. Dixon, 'A Dangerous Hand', *All the Year Round*, 17 November 1866, 456; Mrs Carvick, 'The Unlucky Captain', *All the Year Round*, 5 October 1867, 346; 'The Prisoner of Chillon', *All the Year Round*, 16 July 1870, 150.

[5] Dickens, *A Child's History of England*, 490.

[6] Emile Yung, *Zermatt and the Valley of the Viège*, trans. Wharton Robinson (London: J. R. Gotz, 1894).

known how or even whether Ternan became acquainted with Emile Yung, the author of this book. A possible connection might have been animal magnetism, as Yung, doctor of sciences and associate professor at the University of Geneva, had published another book earlier on 'normal' and 'pathological' sleep, in which he discusses the subject.[7] Dickens too was interested in mesmerism and was friends with John Elliotson, a well-known mesmerist. After Dickens's death, Ternan married clergyman George Wharton Robinson in 1876, and reduced her age by a full fourteen years on the 1881 census.[8] By 1894, the Wharton Robinsons had two boys and were living in London. Whether it was indeed financial worry which induced Ellen to translate the book must remain a mystery, like much else in the Dickens/Ternan relationship.[9] As far as we know Dickens never visited Zermatt, and there are no indications of it in his letters and his other writing. The place is never mentioned in *Household Words* and only appears on a single occasion in an article by Albert Smith in *All the Year Round*.[10] Ellen Ternan visited Switzerland at least once with her husband in the 1880s, where they joined her sister Fanny and her husband Thomas Adolphus Trollope, Anthony's brother.[11]

The common denominator between Dickens's 'Swiss' texts and Ellen Ternan's translation of a book about Zermatt is their unexpected and unexplained references to Switzerland. In most cases, Dickens's references to Switzerland in his fiction are subtle and appear as spontaneously as in his later letters. The act of disguising Switzerland, of saying and not saying, goes back to one of the earliest mentions of the country in Dickens's writing. In *Pictures from Italy*, Switzerland ought to vanish and disappear behind the grander narrative of the journey to and through Italy. It is 'not there' in a double sense: it neither figures in the title nor does the author seem to want to recall it. Switzerland becomes an – unsuccessful – act of mental suppression.[12] Nathalie Vanfasse has remarked on Switzerland's paraliptic quality in the *Pictures* as well, pointing out how the sights are listed in a brief and orderly manner, and how Dickens, in contrast to accounts of other countries, refuses to give a more detailed description.[13]

---

[7] Emile Yung, *Le Sommeil Normal et le Sommeil Pathologique. Magnétisme Animal, Hypnotisme, Névrose Hysterique* (Paris: Octave Doin, 1883).

[8] Claire Tomalin, *The Invisible Woman* (London: Penguin, 1991), 220.

[9] John Bowen, 'Acts of Translation', *Times Literary Supplement*, 2 November 2007.

[10] Albert Smith, 'A Piece of China (i)', *All the Year Round*, 30 April 1859, 17.

[11] Tomalin, *Invisible Woman*, 221.

[12] See Chapter 2, 71.

[13] Vanfasse, *La Plume et la route*, 42.

122   *Dickens and Switzerland*

Yet Switzerland stubbornly resists erasure and keeps popping into the narrative, in the same way and equally 'for no reason on earth that I can find out', as it will four years later in 'Lying Awake'.[14]

It is often a game of telling and not telling when Dickens set his plot in Switzerland: in *David Copperfield*, the valley in which he finds 'some long-unwonted sense of beauty and tranquillity, some softening influence awakened by its peace' is never named and impossible to identify due to the lack of detail and its generic nature.[15] In *Little Dorrit*, Dickens introduced a new twist: whereas the location of the opening of the second book is revealed within the first two sentences, the identity of the travellers is only disclosed at the very end of the first chapter. In the form of a guestbook entry, and in a later chapter in Martigny, we meet the 'new' Dorrits symbolically as well as literally on the highest top, as if their wealth had set them apart from the 'old' Dorrits in the first book.

I Enlarge My Circle of Acquaintance, or Swiss Murderers

Dickens's points of contact with Switzerland were not only the performances on stage and his own travels. Dickens also met – if only indirectly – Swiss subjects in England. In an ironic reversal of the melodramatic theatricals Dickens saw when he was younger, the most prominent Swiss he encountered in London were no innocent maids or poor peasants oppressed by foreign villains, but genuine criminals. As early as 1912, a disappointed Gustav Schirmer noted that 'it is truly not nice of Dickens' to make the greatest villains Swiss both in *Little Dorrit* and in *No Thoroughfare*.[16] Yet the various allusions to murder and violence in relation to Switzerland in Dickens's fiction are no coincidence. 'Dickens', Jan-Melissa Schramm points out, 'attended a number of public executions in the course of his career – most notably those of Courvoisier in 1840 and Frederick and Maria Manning in 1849'.[17] What she fails to point out is that both Courvoisier and Maria Manning were Swiss.[18]

---

[14] Dickens, 'Lying Awake', 91.

[15] Dickens, *David Copperfield*, 697.

[16] Schirmer, 'Charles Dickens und die Schweiz', 11. The author's translation.

[17] Jan-Melissa Schramm, 'Dickens and the Law', in *A Companion to Charles Dickens*, ed. David Paroissien (Oxford: Blackwell, 2008), 288.

[18] The *Pilgrim* editors give the name as 'Maria' throughout, but the *Oxford Dictionary of National Biography* calls her 'Marie'. The *Times* refer to her as 'Maria' and she

Mischief, or Courvoisier

Born 'of decent parents in Switzerland' and after having received a 'moderately good education', François Benjamin Courvoisier was 'reported to have come to England to his uncle, [...] through whose instrumentality he obtained several most respectable situations'.[19] The last of these employments was in Lord John Russell's uncle's household, Russell being a friend of Dickens. Courvoisier was twenty-three years old and had only been employed as a valet for five weeks, when one morning his master, Lord William Russell, was found in his bed with his throat cut. Soon, Courvoisier was identified as the murderer. The motive for the deed was identified as 'that of avarice', though in one of the several confessions Courvoisier made in prison, he also speaks of a dislike of his master.[20] As 'an alien', he 'elected to be tried by a jury of Englishmen' and was sentenced to death after a trial which took three days and had caused immense public interest.[21] The 1841 *Newgate Calendar*'s introductory sentence to Courvoisier's case thus runs: 'For a considerable number of years, scarcely any circumstance occurred in the metropolis which created a greater degree of consternation and interest than the tragical event which it now becomes our duty to record.'[22]

While having dinner with friends the evening before Courvoisier's execution, Dickens decided, apparently on a whim, to 'see what was being done by way of preparation'.[23] At 'about one o'clock in the morning' he reported from what was probably the first execution he witnessed: 'I should like to watch a scene like this, and see the end of the Drama.'[24] This is an interesting sentence, because what Dickens enjoyed doing himself he would later criticise in other spectators: watching the spectacle of death. Fred Kaplan notes the theatrical vocabulary Dickens uses: from the room Dickens and his friends rented to oversee the spectacle, he must have 'felt that he was both

---

is 'Maria' in the title of Robert Huish's *The Progress of Crime, or The Authentic Memoirs of Maria Manning* (London: M'Gowan & Co., 1849), but 'Marie' in the narrative. There seems to be no consensus, so I will be using the seemingly more frequent 'Maria'.

[19] Camden Pelham, *The Chronicles of Crime; or, The New Newgate Calendar* (London: Bradbury and Evans, 1841), vol. 2, 582.

[20] Ibid.

[21] Ibid., 569.

[22] Ibid., 563.

[23] Philip Collins, *Dickens and Crime* (London: Macmillan, 1964), 225.

[24] Ackroyd, *Dickens*, 313.

124   *Dickens and Switzerland*

part of the crowd and an objective observer of that live performance no other theatre could provide'.[25] Just as Courvoisier's murder 'seems to have been rather the result of a sudden impulse than of predetermined malice', Dickens's own decision to watch the hanging was an abrupt resolve.[26]

His immediate reaction to the execution was to write two letters to the *Morning Chronicle*, which he wrote under the pseudonym 'Manlius'.[27] In terms of the event itself, Philip Collins argues that 'Memories of it affect *Barnaby Rudge*, [...] but it was not until 1846 that he wrote explicitly about the Courvoisier hanging in a letter to the *Daily News*'.[28] There is no indication in any of Dickens's writings that he thought Courvoisier's foreign origin important. Nor does the *Newgate Calendar* cite the murderer's 'alien' status as a reason for his deed. In fact, from a contemporary perspective, it is surprising how little attention was paid to his foreign origins. In this respect, Courvoisier certainly does not seem to have been a model for *Little Dorrit*'s Rigaud, whose patched-up Swiss-French-English nationalities precisely seems to allow him to adopt different identities.

Louis, the Swiss murderer from the *Holly-Tree Inn* remains generic, as no detailed description is given of him. More attention is paid to the discovery of the murder through the 'terrible Bantam crowing on the wood-stack' who causes the discovery of the crime and Louis's subsequent execution.[29] Henri's murder is once more not part of the main plot, but surfaces in one of the stories told within the story. The description of this Swiss execution is so accurate that it leads John Carey to assume that the event was a real one and that 'In Switzerland [Dickens] went to see a man beheaded'.[30] Philip Collins, too, asserts that 'this episode has the ring of truth in it, and there are several possible occasions when Dickens was in Switzerland during the winter months and could thus have "come upon this murderer sitting ... on a scaffold".'[31] Collins claims that the supposedly last of Dickens's sojourns in Switzerland, in 1853, 'seems the most likely date for this episode', but does not provide any further support for this.[32] It seems very unlikely to me that Dickens saw a

---

[25] Fred Kaplan, *Dickens. A Biography* (New York: William Morrow & Co., 1988), 199.
[26] Pelham, *Chronicles of Crime*, 582.
[27] To the Editor of the *Morning Chronicle*, ?21 June 1840, *Letters*, vol. 2, 86ff; to the Editor of the *Morning Chronicle*, 26 June 1840, *Letters*, vol. 2, 90ff.
[28] Collins, *Dickens and Crime*, 225.
[29] Dickens et al., *The Holly-Tree Inn*, 578.
[30] Carey, *The Violent Effigy*, 21.
[31] Collins, *Dickens and Crime*, 235.
[32] Ibid., 253n35; 344.

Uncovering Switzerland   **125**

man beheaded in Switzerland either in 1846 or 1853. Throughout the 1840s, his letters and accounts to Forster seem fairly comprehensive, and at this point their friendship was still very close. There is no reason why Dickens would not have told Forster of an execution in 1846. Even though the 1850s marked a slow but steady change in their friendship, he still wrote to Forster from Switzerland.[33] In none of the many letters Dickens sent to friends and family at the time – or indeed at any time later – is there evidence that he saw a beheading there. Had he seen an execution in Switzerland, it would have been odd and very much out of character if Dickens had not mentioned it.

It is possible, however, that Dickens was retelling an experience he had had ten years earlier and which he already described in *Pictures*. During his stay in Rome, he went to see a man beheaded. In contrast to Courvoisier's hanging, there were 'not many people lingering about' in Rome.[34] Both in *Pictures* and the *Holly-Tree Inn*, Dickens pays particular attention to the killing instrument. In *Pictures*, the sword is 'charged with a ponderous mass of iron, all ready to descend, and glittering brightly in the morning sun, whenever it looked out, now and then, from behind a cloud'.[35] It is an odd sentence as the focus shifts from the weapon to the sun, as if neither could be looked at for too long and they resisted closer examination. In the *Holly-Tree Inn*, the 'great sword (loaded with quicksilver in the thick part of the blade), swept round him like a gust of wind, or fire, and there was no such creature in the world'.[36] Before the reader is aware of it, the deed is done and the act of killing is over. In the *Holly-Tree Inn*, Dickens adds a biting humorous remark: 'My wonder was, not that he was so suddenly dispatched, but that any head was left unreaped, within a radius of fifty yards of that tremendous sickle.'[37] As if the action were impossible to describe and vanished behind its setting, the text is almost exclusively descriptive. The total absence of an executioner at the crucial moment in both accounts makes the scenes even more immediate and unsettling. In the *Pictures*, neither he nor the instrument of killing seem to have anything to do with the victim's death. The link is entirely implicit:

> He kneeled down, below the knife. His neck fitting into a hole, made
> for the purpose, in a cross plank, was shut down, by another plank

---

[33] To Forster, 20 October 1853, *Letters*, vol. 7, 167ff.
[34] Dickens, *Pictures from Italy*, 141.
[35] Ibid.
[36] Dickens et al., *The Holly-Tree Inn*, 578.
[37] Ibid.

126 *Dickens and Switzerland*

above; exactly like the pillory. Immediately below him was a leathern bag. And into it his head rolled instantly.[38]

On the occasion of Courvoisier's execution, Dickens said: 'I should have deemed it impossible that I could have ever felt any large assemblage of my fellow-creatures to be so odious.'[39] If, at Courvoisier's hanging, Dickens was disgusted by the mass of people and the 'ribaldry, debauchery, levity, drunkenness, and flaunting vice in fifty other shapes', the absence of a rowdy crowd in Rome did not improve the situation either: 'Nobody cared, or was at all affected. There was no manifestation of disgust, or pity, or indignation, or sorrow.'[40] Parallels to theatre pervade both texts and are an expression of disgust when relating to the audience. From London, Dickens reported:

> I hoped, for an instant, that there was some sense of Death and Eternity in the cry of 'Hats off!' when the miserable wretch appeared; but I found, next moment, that they only raised it as they would at a Play – to see the Stage the better, in the final scene.[41]

As there was no large audience in Rome, Dickens had to redirect his focus. Rather than the spectators, he attacks the purpose of the event and draws his comparison to a stage performance there: 'It was an ugly, filthy, careless, sickening spectacle; meaning nothing but butchery beyond the momentary interest, to the one wretched actor.'[42] In an awkward reversal, the prisoner, who is the only subject forced into passivity in the present group of people, becomes the agent and actor in the most literal sense of meaning.

I Am Shown Two Interesting Penitents, or The Mannings

If Courvoisier's direct presence is difficult to trace in Dickens's fiction, that of the Mannings is even more so. Dickens briefly mentioned George Manning in 'Pet Prisoners' and 'The Demeanour of Murderers', two leading articles he had written for *Household*

---

[38] Dickens, *Pictures from Italy*, 143.
[39] Collins, *Dickens and Crime*, 226.
[40] Dickens, *Pictures from Italy*, 144.
[41] Collins, *Dickens and Crime*, 226.
[42] Dickens, *Pictures from Italy*, 144.

Words in 1850 and 1856.[43] Maria Manning features in Dickens's 'A Detective Police Party', and, together with her husband, in articles by other authors, including 'Rogue's Walk' by Albert Smith. 'Foolish Fashion' as well as 'Calamity-Mongering' appeared in *All the Year Round* and confirmed Smith's statement that black satin went out of fashion after 'the precious murderess, Mrs. Manning' had chosen it as the garment 'in which it would be most becoming for her to present herself "on the drop".'[44] 'Railway Thoughts' from 1868 claimed that 'there is nothing which interests mankind so deeply as murder' and the only murder mentioned is that 'of Mr. O'Connor by Mrs. Manning'.[45] She has a cameo appearance under her own name in Wilkie Collins's *Woman in White* when the incomparable Marian Halcombe expresses her dislike of 'corpulent humanity' and stresses that 'Mr. Murderer and Mrs. Murderess Manning were […] both unusually stout people'.[46]

But Dickens himself also had some literary plans of his own for Maria Manning: it is the general consensus that she was the model for Hortense in *Bleak House*.[47] Yet, to some scholars, her origins seem to have caused confusion. A 1923 article in the *Dickensian* claimed she 'came from Sweden', another one from 1971 as well as Philip Collins in *Dickens and Crime* maintained that she was 'a Belgian'.[48] Neither of these claims is true. Maria Manning, née Roux, was born in 1821 in Switzerland. Despite this, she earned herself an entry in the *Oxford Dictionary of National Biography*, most likely because she was married to a British citizen when she committed the deed.[49]

In contrast to Courvoisier, she 'made a plea that as a foreigner she was not subject to the jurisdiction of an English court; this was dismissed because of her marriage to a British subject'.[50] She had come to England for domestic service – just as Courvoisier had done.

---

[43] Dickens, 'Pet Prisoners', *Household Words*, 27 April 1850, 100; Dickens, 'The Demeanour of Murderers', *Household Words*, 14 June 1856, 507.

[44] Dickens, 'A Detective Police Party', *Household Words*, 27 July 1850, 410; Albert Smith, 'Rogue's Walk', *Household Words*, 12 September 1857, 263; 'Calamity Mongering', *All the Year Round*, 3 March 1866, 187; 'Foolish Fashions', *All the Year Round*, 27 June 1868, 65.

[45] 'Railway Thoughts', *All the Year Round*, 4 January 1868, 83.

[46] Collins, *The Woman in White*, 218.

[47] Collins, *Dickens and Crime*, 235; Slater, *Charles Dickens*, 346; also to John Leech, 7 November 1849, *Letters*, vol. 5, 642.

[48] Philip Hale, 'Hortense and the Mannings', *Dickensian* 1, no. 19 (1923): 22; Collins, *Dickens and Crime*, 235; James Davies, 'John Forster at the Mannings' Execution', *Dickensian* 67, no. 363 (1971): 12.

[49] *Oxford Dictionary of National Biography*, s.v. 'Manning, Marie'.

[50] Ibid.

128   *Dickens and Switzerland*

With her husband, she murdered a wealthy friend – and probably her lover – and buried him in a pit of quicklime under their kitchen. The murder itself was spectacular, particularly because the couple had worked together, the victim was said to be her lover and their motive seems to have been sheer greed. Maria Manning's behaviour during and after the trial stirred even more interest, as did her general appearance and flashy dressing style. The *Times* described her as

> rather above the middle height, and her figure is stout, without being clumsy. It would, however, be a mistake to call her either handsome or beautiful. [...] Her features are neither regular nor feminine, yet the general expression of her face is rather pleasing than otherwise, and she has evidently been a comely woman. [...] She has dark hair and eyes, and by her cast of countenance would be set down as either a German or an English woman.[51]

This account confirms, on the one hand, how common such detailed physical and physiognomic descriptions were at the time and shows, on the other, how particular features were attributed to certain nationalities. Maria Manning does not seem to meet the expectations readers or at least the author of the article above would have of the appearance of a 'Swiss' woman. She resembles a 'German', or, what is perhaps more unsettling for the readership of the *Times*, an 'English' woman, as if even in her physical appearance she refused to give away what she really was, a foreigner, and a murderess.

The description of Hortense is similar, with some striking differences, however:

> My Lady's maid is a Frenchwoman of two and thirty, from somewhere in the southern country about Avignon and Marseilles, a large-eyed brown woman with black hair who would be handsome but for a certain feline mouth and general uncomfortable tightness of face, rendering the jaws too eager and the skull to prominent. There is something indefinably keen and wan about her anatomy and she has a watchful way of looking out of the corners of her eyes without turning her head which could be pleasantly dispensed with, especially when she is in an ill humour and near knives. Through all the good taste of her dress and little adornments, these objections so express themselves that she seems to go about like a very neat she-wolf imperfectly tamed. Besides being accomplished in all the knowledge appertaining to her post, she is almost an Englishwoman in her acquaintance with the language;[52]

[51] 'The Bermondsey Murder', *The Times*, 25 August 1849.
[52] Dickens, *Bleak House*, 187.

Like Rigaud, Hortense has connections to the south of France, though she does not commit her murder there. Hortense is likened to a threatening mixture between a cat and a she-wolf from the start. Just as Maria Manning, she blends in and is knowledgeable of her duty as a maid and the expectations of her environment, while her physical attractiveness is elusive and unclear. She 'would be handsome', were it not for certain defects, though it remains unclear whether it is at all in her power to amend these. Hortense, however, is not stout, but also has a 'certain grace and propriety'.[53] This changes when she is attacked and becomes upset: '"Upon my soul I wonder at you!" Mr. Bucket remonstrates. "I thought the French were a polite nation, I did, really. Yet to hear a female going on like that before Sir Leicester Dedlock, Baronet!"'[54] Esther describes Hortense's face as 'not an agreeable one, though it was handsome', somewhat qualifying the earlier description.[55] Yet, the *Times* also gave contradictory accounts of Maria Manning's physical appearance and stated that there 'has been a diabolical energy of character displayed by her throughout, which has attracted to her conduct a still larger share of public attention than to that of Manning. Her handsome figure, foreign origin, and various other considerations, contributed to this effect'.[56]

We do not know why Dickens decided to watch the execution of the Mannings. He had not wanted to go at first, but then changed his mind.[57] In a letter to his friend John Leech, who was going to watch the event with him, he adopted an informal, humorous tone. They decided to make quite a night of it and Dickens proposed to meet for supper the evening before.[58] After the execution had taken place, the merry tone had gone and – in hindsight – Dickens had now found himself a reason for attending. He wrote a letter to the *Times*, claiming that he had gone 'with the intention of observing the crowd gathered to behold it' and that he had 'excellent opportunities of doing so'.[59] His indignation at what he had seen was once more directed at the crowd. The most surprising and uncanny effect, however, was that at least to Dickens and Forster, Maria Manning seems to have appeared more appealing dead than alive. In a letter to Bulwer Lytton, Forster noted that she

[53] Ibid., 368.
[54] Ibid., 832.
[55] Ibid., 290.
[56] 'The Bermondsey Murder', *The Times*, 14 November 1849.
[57] Collins, *Dickens and Crime*, 236.
[58] To John Leech, 12 November 1849, *Letters*, vol. 5, 643.
[59] To the Editor of *The Times*, 13 November 1849, *Letters*, vol. 5, 645.

was *beautifully dressed*, every part of her noble figure finely and fully expressed by close fitting black satin, spotless white collar round her neck loose enough to allow the rope without its removal, and gloves on her manicured hands. [...] But there was nothing hideous in her as she swung to and fro afterwards. The wretch beside her was as a filthy shapeless scarecrow – she had lost nothing of her graceful aspect! This is heroine-worship, I think![60]

Forster seemed smitten with Manning's appearance which was caused not only by her 'noble' figure, but also the propriety of her clothing and overall style. For Forster she is graceful – sexy, perhaps, in modern terms – even in her death. That imagination is – at least in parts – taking over here, becomes obvious in the description of her 'gloves on her manicured hands'. Forster, just like Dickens, only ever saw the Mannings from the rooftop they hired for observing the execution. He was never close to her bare hands, as not only would she have been too far away for a detailed inspection but she was also wearing gloves. In a later letter, Forster claims that the doctor who examined the body after her death said that 'he had never seen so beautiful a figure, compared her feet to those of a marble statue'.[61] James Davies describes Forster's reaction to her appearances as containing 'undertones of suppressed sexuality' and explains them as the typical response 'of a thirty-seven-years-old bachelor in a society that imposed at least a surface respectability'.[62] Yet, I read no 'undertones of suppressed sexuality' but see this as a rather straight-forward account of a weirdly attractive corpse.

Dickens's own reaction is less clear, but there is a piece of writing in which he remembers the Mannings's execution. Interestingly, it also features a connection to Switzerland. It is an odd connection in an odd piece: 'Lying Awake' appeared in *Household Words* in 1852, and could be seen as a precursor to 'Travelling Abroad' in content and style. It has been described well as an 'insomniac reverie', in which Dickens 'mingles memories of his travels [...], with a vivid childhood reminiscence and with more recent news items'.[63] Just as in 'Travelling Abroad', the narrator finds himself in a state between waking and dreaming, only that in 'Lying Awake' the recollections are less chronological, more erratic, involuntary and upsetting, as they prevent the narrator from sleeping. As the narrator

---

[60] Davies, 'John Forster at the Mannings' Execution', 15. Emphasis in original.
[61] Ibid., 13.
[62] Ibid., 15.
[63] Dickens, 'Lying Awake', 88.

Uncovering Switzerland **131**

contemplates the similarities in every human experience of life, he concludes that

> It is probable that we have all [...] committed murders and hidden bodies. It is pretty certain that we have all desperately wanted to cry out, and have had no voice; that we have all gone to the play and not been able to get in; that we have all dreamed much more of our youth than of our later lives; that – I have lost it! The thread is broken.[64]

The thread, however, is not broken, but shifts from one association to the next, as random thoughts have a tendency to do. A paragraph, and Dickens is in Switzerland: 'up I go, for no reason on earth that I can find out, and drawn by no links that are visible to me, up the Great Saint Bernard!'[65] The reason for this jump may not be visible to the narrator – or even Dickens himself – but there is, of course at least the link of death. Metaphorical as they seem, the 'committed murders' and 'hidden bodies' become quite literal in Dickens's experiences of Switzerland. He had seen both Courvoisier and Maria Manning hanged – for murder – and it was on top of the St Bernard that he discovered the 'hidden bodies' of frozen travellers which he describes in *Little Dorrit* and elsewhere. Conspicuously, Dickens does not mention the bodies on top of the mountain in 'Lying Awake', but death is mentioned a suspicious number of times: he thinks of 'the same happy party' with which he ascended the pass and interjects 'ah! Two since dead, I grieve to think'.[66] He remembers 'the same track, with the same black wooden arms to point the way' and even though he does not liken them to 'skeleton' arms as he does in *Little Dorrit*, they seem to result from the same memory. He remembers 'the same breed of dogs fast dying out' and 'the same lone night in a cell' – after which, incidentally, he wrote to Forster that when he woke up he thought he had died.[67]

In the next paragraph he tells of a figure he 'once saw, just after dark, chalked upon a door in a little back lane near a country church – my first church'. The figure horrified him 'so intensely – and in connection with a churchyard [...] that it is still vaguely alarming to me to recall'.[68] The figure Dickens describes seems to be a grotesque. However, the fact that it scared him 'in connection with the graveyard' almost disappears behind Dickens's description of it, yet

---

[64] Davies, 'John Forster at the Mannings' Execution', 88.
[65] Dickens, 'Lying Awake', 91.
[66] Ibid., 91.
[67] To Forster, ?6 September 1846, *Letters*, vol. 4, 618.
[68] Dickens, 'Lying Awake', 91.

132   *Dickens and Switzerland*

this seems to be the crucial – and terrifying – connection. 'It lays', the narrator admits, 'a disagreeable train'. Consequently, he tries to think of something else, something 'on the voluntary principle' and comes to think of the 'balloon ascents of this last season'.[69] Yet, he is aware that he

> must hold them tight though, for I feel them sliding away, and in their stead are the Mannings, husband and wife, hanging on the top of Horsemonger Lane Jail. In connexion [*sic*] with which dismal spectacle, I recal [*sic*] this curious fantasy of the mind. That, having beheld that execution, and having left those two forms dangling on the top of the entrance gateway – the man's, a limp loose suit of clothes, as if the man had gone out of them; the woman's a fine shape, so elaborately corseted and artfully dressed, that it was quite unchanged in its trim appearance as it slowly swung from side to side.[70]

The narrator's resolution of keeping control of his thoughts is thwarted almost as soon as he utters them, as what follows immediately afterwards is the next association of the balloon with the Mannings. Dickens does not make explicit the cause of the association, but the woman's body and her artful dress may, in a metaphor, certainly come to resemble a balloon with its many ropes that equally swings 'from side to side' and, from a distance, appears as 'elaborately corseted and artfully dressed'. Just like the dead on top of the St Bernard and the chalk figure near a churchyard, the hanging of the Mannings, the narrator – or Dickens? – confesses, pursued him in his thoughts and he 'never could, by my utmost efforts, for some weeks, present the outside of that prison to myself (which the terrible impression I had received continually obliged me to do) without presenting it with the two figures still hanging in the morning air'.[71] Note how the Mannings now turn into 'figures' as well, just like the one he had seen near the church as a young boy.

Tempest, or Letters from the 1850s

Throughout the 1850s there are letters which suggest that Dickens was thinking about returning to Switzerland. On a handful of occasions in the 1860s he even indicated that he was planning to travel, but then evidently did not. One of the most moving letters which tell

[69] Ibid., 92.
[70] Ibid.
[71] Ibid.

of Dickens's intention to go back to Switzerland, dates from 1851. Forster reproduces it in his biography:

> I very nearly packed up a portmanteau and went away, the day before yesterday, into the mountains of Switzerland, alone! Still the victim of an intolerable restlessness, I shouldn't be at all surprised if I wrote to you on one of these mornings from under Mont Blanc. I sit down between whiles to think of a new story, and, as it begins to grow, such a torment of desire to be anywhere but where I am; and to be going I don't know where, I don't know why; takes hold of me, that it is like being *driven away*. If I had had a passport, I sincerely believe I should have gone to Switzerland the night before last. I should have remembered our engagement – say, at Paris, and have come back for it; but should probably have left by the next express train.[72]

Not only was Dickens longing to return to Switzerland, but he had very clear plans of executing his idea. He was aware of the time frame a journey to Switzerland required in 1851 and 'sincerely' believed that he should have gone – had he had the necessary documents. His 'desire to be anywhere but where I am' is strongly connected to the creative process of inventing the new story which would become *Bleak House*. The restlessness Dickens experienced in the mid-1850s seems to bear parallels with the one he experienced in Switzerland in 1846, yet he longed to go back. It is curious indeed that Dickens should have wished to return to the very place where he had felt 'sick, giddy, and capriciously despondent', had 'bad nights' and was 'full of disquietude and anxiety' when writing *The Battle of Life* and *Dombey*.[73] Yet, the letter also shows that in the long term, Dickens felt that despite his lament of the 'absence of streets', his stay in Switzerland had not been the cause of his crisis but part of its solution. Forster's commentary about the letter reveals an even closer connection between the genesis of a new book and Dickens's urge to return to Switzerland. Forster reminds us that Dickens's

> own restlessness with fancies for a new book had arisen beyond bounds, and for the time he was eager to open it in that prettiest quaintest bit of English landscape, Strood valley, which reminded him always of a Swiss scene.[74]

---

[72] To Forster ?late September 1851, *Letters*, vol. 11, 501.

[73] To Forster, 26 September 1846, *Letters*, vol. 4, 625.

[74] Forster, *The Life of Charles Dickens* (London: Chapman and Hall, 1873), vol. 2, 411. The remark in which this paragraph figures was removed in later editions. It also included a quote from one of the letters in which Dickens stated his longing to return to Switzerland.

134   *Dickens and Switzerland*

The *Pilgrim* editors note that on this instance, Forster was confusing Strood with Stroud in Gloucestershire, but this does not affect Dickens's association of the place with Switzerland, of course.[75]

His 1853 trip does not seem to have eased Dickens's urge to return to Switzerland whenever life became difficult. In autumn 1854, he told Forster:

> I have had dreadful thoughts of getting away somewhere altogether by myself. If I could have managed it, I think possibly I might have gone to the Pyreennees (you know what I mean that word for, so I won't re-write it) for six months! I have put the idea into the perspective of six months, but have not abandoned it. I have visions of living for half a year or so, in all sorts of inaccessible places, and opening a new book therein. A floating idea of going up above the snow-line in Switzerland, and living in some astonishing convent, hovers about me. If *Household Words* could be got into a good train, in short, I don't know in what strange place, or at what remote elevation above the level of the sea, I might fall to work next. Restlessness, you will say. Whatever it is, it is always driving me, and I cannot help it. I have rested nine or ten weeks, and sometimes feel as if it had been a year – though I had the strangest nervous miseries before I stopped. If I couldn't walk fast and far, I should just explode and perish.[76]

The key element in this passage is a desire for solitude. When Dickens visited the St Bernard in 1846, he was in the company of family and friends. Yet, in his mind, Dickens imagines himself in 'inaccessible places' and 'astonishing convents', possibly forgetting that both monasteries, that on the Simplon and the one on the St Bernard, were built along ancient pass routes and therefore 'accessible' in essence. Once more, the idea of an 'opening of a new book' is the driving force behind Dickens's longing for an absence. Given his strong anti-Catholic sentiment, Dickens's desire to spend time among the monks is surprising, even though he admitted to his wife in 1844 that if 'all Monks [*sic*] devoted themselves to [providing for travellers on top of the mountains], I should have little fault to find with them'.[77]

His *Memoranda* feature an entry which may be related to Dickens's own, unhappy situation in the 1850s. It reads:

> The man who is incapable of his own happiness. One who is always in pursuit of happiness. Result. Where is happiness to be found

[75] To Forster, 26 September 1846, *Letters*, vol. 4, 625n2.
[76] To Forster, ?29 September 1854, *Letters*, vol. 7, 428.
[77] To Catherine Dickens, 23 November 1844, *Letters*, vol. 4, 228.

Uncovering Switzerland   135

then. Surely not everywhere? Can that be so, after all? Is *this* my experience?[78]

Dickens had experimented with his own fictionalised biography in *David Copperfield*. There, the protagonist found, if not his happiness, at least comfort, hope and contentment in a Swiss valley. Fred Kaplan considers that

> Though this entry does not seem to relate to any character in his fiction, it does suggest Dickens' own frenetic 'pursuit of happiness' and his frequent restlessness, especially keen in the [*Little Dorrit*] period. [...] [The entry] may be basically autobiographical. If so, it is one of the rare instances in the notebook of Dickens' looking within himself rather than outward for character possibilities.[79]

To the Dorrit family, Switzerland no longer offers the same comfort as it did to Copperfield. Their travels seem restless, erratic and blurred throughout. Instead of finding peace and being able to cancel their own 'mistaken past', as Copperfield does, they seem to be haunted by prisons, no matter where they go. Even on top of the St Bernard, a reminder of their Marshalsea past is awaiting them.

Two years later, Dickens told Forster that he was still 'beset by my former notions of a book whereof the whole story shall be on the top of the Great St. Bernard. As I accept and reject ideas for *Little Dorrit*, it perpetually comes back to me'.[80] Yet, fiction suddenly turned to fact in Dickens's mind, as he continued:

> Two or three years hence, perhaps you'll find me living with the Monks and the Dogs a whole winter – among the blinding snows that fall about that monastery. I have a serious idea that I shall do it, if I live.[81]

The monks, whom he did still 'mourn to know as humbugs', the 'breed of dogs fast dying out' and the 'intensely cold convent with its menagerie smell' (which he described in 1852) had now become desirable company for the writing of a new book which only ever existed in Dickens's fancies.[82] Of course, *Little Dorrit*'s second book opens on the pass which Dickens mentions – but it is by no

[78] Dickens, *Charles Dickens' Book of Memoranda*, ed. Fred Kaplan (New York: New York Public Library, 1981), 7.
[79] Ibid., 87.
[80] To Forster, 20 January 1856, *Letters*, vol. 8, 33.
[81] Ibid.
[82] Dickens, 'Lying Awake', 91.

136 *Dickens and Switzerland*

means 'the whole story' which is set there. Other, sometimes earlier texts of his suggest that he had been toying with such an idea for a while. 'To Be Read at Dusk', published in 1852, is set on top of the St Bernard, and 'Lying Awake', a very personal piece which appeared in 1853, also mentions the mountain. In both texts the references to the pass fade into the background and vanish somewhat behind the plot, as if Dickens were already experimenting with the effect this particular location could create in his stories. But he never wrote a 'whole story' set on the Swiss pass. Was it because it simply would not come together? Or was it the kind of project which is so close to one's heart that it is postponed so that it never takes form at all? At any rate, Switzerland still seems to have offered an appealing escape, if only, perhaps, in Dickens's imagination, whenever times became troubled. There was, however, *The Frozen Deep*. First performed in January 1857 at Tavistock House, Dickens's home until 1860, the play dealt with the disappearance of an Arctic expedition. Dickens and Collins had certainly let themselves be inspired by their journey to Switzerland, but Fred Kaplan also claims that 'stimulated by his playing the role of Wardour, the main character and hero of Wilkie Collins's drama *The Frozen Deep*, [Dickens] was beginning to jot down ideas for *A Tale of Two Cities*'.[83] Not only are the play and the novel connected but with their implicit ties to Switzerland they may also have offered a metaphorical outlet for Dickens's wish to escape there.

Claire Tomalin considered 1858 a year from which 'You want to avert your eyes from a good deal of what happened' in Dickens's life.[84] Dickens himself chose to express his situation through allusions to mountains. It was the year in which he severed personal and professional ties, among them the marriage with his wife, Catherine. The late 1850s were truly troublesome and troubled years. He sent 'semi-confessional letters to admiring women friends' about the relationship with Ellen Ternan, and his metaphor of choice was that of a fairy tale set on a mountain:[85]

> I wish I had been born in the days of Ogres and Dragon-guarded Castles. I wish an Ogre with seven heads (and no particular evidence of brains in the whole lot of them) had taken the Princess whom I adore – you have no idea how intensely I love her! – to his stronghold on the top of a high series of Mountains, and there tied her up by the

[83] Dickens, *Memoranda*, 2.
[84] Tomalin, *Charles Dickens*, 294.
[85] Ibid.

hair. Nothing would suit me half so well this day, as climbing after her, sword in hand, and either winning her or being killed. – *There's* a state of mind for you, in 1857.[86]

Mrs Watson, to whom this letter is addressed, was among the friends Dickens had met in Lausanne. Even though Switzerland is not mentioned directly, the Ogre's stronghold which Dickens imagines 'on the top of a high series of Mountains' would inevitably trigger a range of memories which both the writer and reader shared. Their families had been on several trips together to the Alps in 1846. In a letter written at the same time, the Ogre is replaced with a number of Dragons, the narcissistic violence against the poor princess is dropped, but the climb of the mountain remains essential. Once more only this, as well as the additional excitement of saving a maiden and slaying monsters, promises satisfaction and a release from his distress:

> What am I doing? Tearing myself – My usual occupation, at most times. Wild and misty ideas of a story are floating about somewhere (I don't know where), and I am looking after them. One of the most restless of men at all times, I am at such a crisis worse than ever. Nothing would satisfy me at this present writing, but the having to go up a tremendous mountain magic spell in one hand and sword in the other, to find the girl of my heart (whom I never did find), surrounded by fifty Dragons – kill them all – and bear her off, triumphant. I might finish the story in the usual way, by settling down and living happy ever afterwards – Perhaps; I am not sure even of that.[87]

As late as 1869, Dickens longingly replied to an invitation to return to the Alps:

> Walk across the Alps? Lord bless you, I am 'going' to take up my alpenstock and cross all the Passes, and I am 'going' to Italy; I am also 'going' up the Nile to the Second Cataract, and I am 'going' to Jerusalem, and to India, and likewise to Australia. My only dimness of perception in this wise, is, that I don't know when. If I did but know when, I should be so wonderfully clear about it all! At present I can't see even so much as the Simplon, in consequence of certain Farewell Readings, and a certain new book (just begun) interposing their dwarfish shadow. But whenever (if ever) I change 'going' into 'coming', I shall come to see you.[88]

---

[86] To The Hon. Mrs. Watson, 7 December 1857, *Letters*, vol. 8, 488. Emphasis in original.
[87] To Lady Duff Gordon, 23 January 1858, *Letters*, vol. 8, 508.
[88] To Thomas Adolphus Trollope, 4 November 1869, *Letters*, vol. 12, 435.

138   *Dickens and Switzerland*

Dickens cannot see 'even so much as the Simplon', as if it was a nearby hill. Comically enough, of all the destinations he mentions here, the Swiss pass is the closest. Yet, his desire to return to Switzerland had softened somewhat by the late 1860s. In 1869 he wrote to his Swiss friend Cerjat:

> And yet I often think that if Mary were to marry (which she won't), I should sell [Gad's Hill], and go genteelly vagabondizing over the face of the earth. Then indeed I might see Lausanne again. – But I don't seem in the way of it at present; for the older I get, the more I do, and the harder I work.[89]

The Wanderer, or Letters from the 1860s

Dickens and Cerjat had been exchanging regular Christmas letters since 1846, when they met in Lausanne. Occasionally, Dickens seems to have been somewhat late with his letters, but in 1852, he wrote rather apologetically:

> Looking to the date of your last letter, I feel as if I were a perfect ruffian of a correspondent; but I really think so often of my friends in writing my books, [...] that I have a sort of stupid sense as if they served for letters[90]

The *Pilgrim* editors state in their preface to the tenth volume of Dickens's letters (1862–1864) that even towards the end of his life, the Swiss friend continued 'to be the main recipient of [Dickens's] views on public issues'.[91] It may be just the chance of manuscript survival, or a strange coincidence, then, that there seems to be no surviving 1863 Christmas letter to Cerjat. In 1862, Dickens told his friend that 'The Year would not go out naturally now, without that [Christmas] letter [from him]: so completely have I come to regard it as a necessary part of that landmark in my life'.[92] He ended by asking his friend to 'send my love to Mrs. Cerjat, and beg to enquire when it will be convenient to her to take another ride up the Great St. Bernard and discourse about Cows'.[93] This humorous remark –

---

[89] To Cerjat, 4 January 1869, *Letters*, vol. 12, 269.
[90] To Cerjat, 20 December 1852, *Letters*, vol. 6, 828.
[91] Preface to *Letters*, vol. 10, xi.
[92] To Cerjat, 16 March 1862, *Letters*, vol. 10, 52.
[93] Ibid., 55.

Uncovering Switzerland   **139**

and possibly a reference to Mrs Skewton's utterance on cows in *Dombey* – may be more sincere than it first appears.

Cerjat paid Dickens a surprise visit in July 1862 – an event which surely would have encouraged Dickens to send his friend his season's greetings, yet the otherwise regular Christmas letter is missing. There is no indication that there had not been a Christmas or New Year's letter for the season of 1862/3. In October 1864, Dickens writes Cerjat 'a limping brute of a reply to your always-welcome Christmas letter', and repeats the joke that he 'should like to go up the Great St. Bernard again, and shall be glad to know if she is open to another ascent'. He briefly wallows in reminiscences of 1846 and reminds Cerjat not to 'fail – but I know you won't in your Christmas letter'.[94] Dickens addressed his only surviving 1863 letter to Cerjat in May.[95] It suggests that there had been correspondence between them earlier, but this is lost, as Dickens replies to a comment Cerjat had made about a play which Dickens must have described to him in a previous letter. The May letter itself only survives as an extract, and its last part, where Dickens would usually recall a Swiss memory, is missing. With the exception of another apparently lost letter in 1858, when Dickens, perhaps due to his domestic troubles, may deliberately have omitted or was not in the mood to write Christmas letters, the one of 1863 interrupts a yearly chain of regular correspondence since Dickens's last known visit to Switzerland in 1853.

Cerjat must have been a reliable collector of the letters he received from Dickens, as their correspondence seems complete apart from these exceptions. The fact that at least one if not two letters are missing and that another only survives in parts – the only known letter written to Cerjat which is incomplete – suggests that the content of their conversations may have been pruned by a third party. The incomplete letter to Cerjat from 1863 appeared in the first collection of his correspondence, edited by Georgina Hogarth and Mamie Dickens.[96] Letters or passages of letters which were deemed not interesting enough or too delicate were frequently removed or made illegible by those who edited Dickens's correspondence for the general public. Among them, his sister-in-law and daughter were, understandably, among the most prominent.

There are other irregularities in Dickens's correspondence in the 1860s, but the most striking – and consistent – in terms of

---

[94] To Cerjat, 25 October 1864, *Letters*, vol. 10, 445.
[95] To Cerjat, 28 May 1863, *Letters*, vol. 10, 253.
[96] See ibid., 252.

140   *Dickens and Switzerland*

Switzerland are those around the turn of the year in 1862/3. At the time, Dickens was travelling a lot, as he was frequently on tour giving public readings. However, on some occasions, he was also intent on covering his tracks, most likely to conceal his meetings and relationship with Ellen Ternan. There are, however, hints of his whereabouts in his fiction and his letters.

In 1864, Dickens and his coauthors wrote a sequel to a Christmas Story of the previous year. *Mrs Lirriper's Legacy* appeared in the Christmas number of *All the Year Round* in December 1864.[97] The story is mainly set in Sens, a rather remote French town, which Dickens briefly travelled through twice, in 1844 and 1846.[98] There is no evidence that Dickens ever went back to it before he wrote the story, yet Michael Slater notes that the text is 'almost certainly [...] a result of Dickens having visited Sens, perhaps with Nelly', during one of his many unexplained absences.[99] Earlier in the year, Dickens had written a letter to his sub-editor, William Henry Wills, announcing a 'Mysterious Disappearance' of his, which has been linked with a possible trip to Sens.[100] The question, however, remains as to what brought Dickens back to the relatively insignificant French town he had already seen when travelling from England to Italy and from Switzerland to Paris, almost two decades earlier. In 1927, Mildred Ransom pointed out that Sens was 'situated on one of the main roads between Paris and Switzerland'.[101] Sens only ever figures twice in Dickens's letters: in 1846, when he was coming from Switzerland, and in 1864, when we do not know what took him there.

On several occasions during the 1860s, Dickens claimed to be about to travel to Switzerland. But there is no evidence that he ever did. In 1863, for example, Dickens disappears from our view twice, first 11–14 January and then for a longer spell in the same month, 21–28. The letters in which he spoke about an alleged trip to Switzerland were manifold and had been addressed to different members of his family and some of his friends.

Late in December 1862, Dickens was staying in Paris and wrote to his sister, Letitia Austin, that 'it is likely enough that I may go on from here to see some friends in Genoa – and in any case I want to

---

[97] Charles Dickens et al., 'Mrs Lirriper's Legacy', *All the Year Round*, 1 December 1864, 580.

[98] To Forster, ?14–15 July 1844, *Letters*, vol. 4, 155n1; to W. W. F. Cerjat, 27 November 1846, *Letters*, vol. 4, 662.

[99] Slater, *Charles Dickens*, 528.

[100] To W. H. Wills, 26 June 1864, *Letters*, vol. 10, 409n5 and n6.

[101] Mildred Ransom, 'Sens: A Landmark in France', *Dickensian* 23, no. 203 (1927): 202.

look about me in many odd places'.[102] These 'odd places' are not specified, nor is the route which Dickens intended to travel. From Paris, his most likely choices would have been either to travel to Marseille and from there to Genoa by ship, as he had done when he moved his household to Genoa in 1844. The other route would have led him through Switzerland and over the Simplon, as in 1845 and 1853. A short story set in Switzerland and called 'The Professor's Adventure' by Amelia Edwards had appeared early in mid-December in *All the Year Round*.[103] In a letter to Wills Dickens wrote towards the end of November that 'Miss Edwards I have done'.[104] The *Pilgrim* editors tentatively suggest that Dickens may have meant another piece, but it may also have been the story on Switzerland which he was referring to here.[105]

In a Christmas letter he sent to Thomas Beard, one of his close friends, four days later, he mentioned once more that 'It is possible that I may take the opportunity of going on to Genoa'.[106] On 1 January 1863, Dickens sent an outline of his forthcoming plans to Wilkie Collins. Despite the overall detail of the letter, he remained vague on one subject: 'On Sunday', he wrote, 'I vanish into space for a day or two'.[107] There is no indication as to where 'space' may be and whether Dickens was still thinking of going to Genoa and the 'many odd places' he had mentioned in the letter to his sister.

Six days after he had written the letter to Collins, Dickens wrote to Sir Joseph Olliffe, an Irish physician and originally a friend of a friend. After charting the same tight schedule he had already outlined in the letter to Collins, he explained that 'On Sunday morning early, I am going away to see a sick friend concerning whom I am anxious, and from whom I shall work my way round to Paris'.[108] There is no mention of Genoa here, but three days later, he declined an invitation by Chandos Wren Hoskyns, a writer on agriculture and another friend of a friend, and explained:

> it unluckily happens that I go to Paris to-morrow night – that I read at our Embassy for the benefit of an English Charity on the following Saturday – and that I have made all kinds of pledges and promises to

---

[102] To Mrs Henry Austin, 20 December 1862, *Letters*, vol. 10, 178.

[103] Amelia Edwards, 'The Professor's Adventure', *All the Year Round*, 13 December 1862, 333.

[104] To W. H. Wills, 25 November 1862, *Letters*, vol. 10, 166.

[105] Ibid., 166n3.

[106] To Thomas Beard, 24 December 1862, *Letters*, vol. 10, 181.

[107] To Wilkie Collins, 1 January 1863, *Letters*, vol. 10, 186.

[108] To Sir Joseph Olliffe, 6 January 1863, *Letters*, vol. 10, 190.

142 *Dickens and Switzerland*

> go on to Lausanne a-visiting, afterwards, and perhaps to Genoa. We only came back from Paris for Christmas, and I have made all these plans before we left.[109]

Seeing Dickens refuse an invitation is nothing out of the ordinary. By this time, Dickens had been a popular and well-established writer for many years. He had made many influential friends, led a busy life-style with endless engagements and travelled extensively whenever he could. Surprising, however, is Dickens's claim that he was going to Switzerland – Lausanne – ten years after his supposed last trip. The editors of the *Pilgrim* edition of Dickens's letters tell us that there is 'no evidence that he visited either Lausanne or Genoa' and that the plans he mentioned 'probably masked a week's holiday with Ellen Ternan'.[110] That may be true, but why would Dickens give inconsistent information and announce in three letters to family and friends that he was going to Genoa and, on one occasion, also to Lausanne? Why would he use Genoa and Lausanne, rather than other, more inconspicuous places in France or Italy to hide his travel plans? And while at least the claim that he was intending to go to Genoa is consistent, why does Dickens only speak of going to Lausanne in the letter to Hoskyns? Even more surprising are the 'pledges and promises' which Dickens claimed to have made in the letter to Hoskyns. Miraculously, he seems to have forgotten to mention them to all previous correspondents.

As he had announced, Dickens did indeed 'vanish into space' for four days in January. He reappeared in Paris on 15 January to give the reading at the Embassy. On 18 January he wrote to an acquaintance, Pierre Michel François Chevalier, in French, and told him that he could not meet him. The reason was that he, Dickens, had just received a letter which called for his immediate departure to the French countryside the next day, and to Geneva afterwards, where he would stay with a friend for two or three days. He promised to get in touch once he was back in Paris, which he was expecting to be towards the end of the next week.[111]

The same day, Dickens wrote to another letter to Olliffe, the same person he had already told nine days earlier that he was worried about a sick friend. This time, Dickens wanted to make arrangements for a meeting. He proposed to meet on the same day that Chevalier had wanted to see him and joked to Olliffe that he had

---

[109] To Chandos Wren Hoskyns, 9 January 1863, *Letters*, vol. 10, 192.
[110] Ibid., 192n3 and n4.
[111] To M. Pitre-Chevalier, 18 January 1863, *Letters*, vol. 10, 195.

put off the oyster-eyed Chevalier (under a most horribly lying pretext that I am going – I forget exactly where – I think to the East Indies – for a week), and have no other appointment for tomorrow than that my sister is coming here at eleven in the forenoon.[112]

Dickens knew very well, of course, that his 'horribly lying pretext' to meet Olliffe and avoid Pitre-Chevalier was not the East Indies but Switzerland, as he must have written the letters within hours, perhaps minutes, of each other. Yet, in the letter to Olliffe he once more repeated that he was worrying about something or someone, that there was 'some unstringing of the nerves – coupled with an anxiety not to be mentioned here'. He also confirmed he was about to leave Paris, but did not say where to. Whereas his rejection of Pitre-Chevalier's invitation was a ruse to meet Olliffe instead, the explanation he provided may not have been as 'horribly lying' as he may have wished Olliffe to believe.

On 19 January, the day on which Pitre-Chevalier had wanted to meet Dickens and was 'put off' under the 'most horribly lying pretext', Dickens sent an apologetic letter to another acquaintance, Gabriel Legouvé. In it, Dickens explains that he was unwell 'with a neuralgic attack in the face, and that I was in bed this morning' when Legouvé must have called.[113] Whether Dickens was truly ill or made up yet another excuse to meet his sister, who, as he had told Olliffe, was 'coming here at eleven in the forenoon', we do not know.[114] Dickens continued: 'I find myself engaged for to night [sic]; but as I leave Paris tomorrow and have a long journey before me, I doubt if I shall fulfil even that engagement.'[115] The engagement he mentions in the evening might be the one he had arranged with Olliffe the day before, but the information that he had 'a long journey' before him, is revealing. Within a period of less than three weeks, Dickens told his sister Letitia, his close friend Thomas Beard and Wren Hoskyns a very similar story, but only in the case of Pitre-Chevalier did his travel plans become a 'most horribly lying pretext'. In both letters Dickens had sent to Olliffe, on 6 and 18 January, he spoke of his intention to leave Paris, but avoided mentioning where exactly he was going.

[112] To Sir Joseph Oliffee, 18 January 1863, *Letters*, vol. 10, 196.
[113] To Gabriel Legouvé, 19 January 1863, *Letters*, vol. 10, 197.
[114] The editors of the *Pilgrim* edition point out that Dickens was not meeting his biological sister, but 'in fact his sister Letitia's sister-in-law, Amelia Filloneau'; see to Olliffe, 18 January 1863, *Letters*, vol. 10, 196n2.
[115] Ibid., 197.

144   *Dickens and Switzerland*

Due to the letter Dickens sent to Olliffe on 18 January, we know that he 'put off' Pitre-Chevalier, and probably met Oliffee and almost certainly his sister the next day – but to him he remained suspiciously quiet about the fact that he was going to leave the French capital around 20 January. Why would Dickens give his less intimate friends more specific information about his alleged travel destination than those he was closer to? Did he think that a clearer indication of place would trigger fewer questions from his more distant acquaintances? Did his closer friends understand where he was going when he told them that he was about to 'vanish into space', and did they know what or where 'space' was? If Dickens was simply using Switzerland as a pretext in his letters to Hoskyns and Pitre-Chevalier, why had he already told his sister and Thomas Beard the same story in December? Or did Dickens feel safe enough to share his plans with those who were not immediate friends and from whom he did not expect too many questions?

On 20 January, Dickens sent a letter to Collins, telling him that 'I had been meaning to write before now, but have been unsettled and made uncertain by "circumstances over which –" &c &c &c'.[116] Dickens is clearly enjoying the secret knowledge which he shares with Collins and continues:

> The same circumstances (generally classed under this novel description, but serious enough, as you shall know one day) take me from Paris this evening, *for a week*. But, a week hence, I shall be back here. [...] On Tuesday the 27th. Or Wednesday the 28th. I shall certainly be back. My absence is entre nous, and my domesticity all retained in the excellent little Hotel – where I have dined *better than I ever dined in Paris*.[117]

Dickens's last sentence here is ambiguous. What hotel was he referring to? Did he mean the one where he was presently staying, the Hotel Helder, in Paris? Or was he speaking of another one, outside Paris, which Collins knew about? The only hotel which Dickens once described as better than any in Paris was one in Rome. In 1853, on occasion of his trip through Switzerland and Italy with Wilkie Collins and Augustus Egg, he wrote to Catherine that 'There is no house comparable to it in Paris, and it is better than Mivarts'.[118] Even though Dickens claimed in some of the letters he sent in 1863

---

[116] To Wilkie Collins, 20 January 1863, *Letters*, vol. 10, 198.
[117] Ibid. Emphasis in original.
[118] To Catherine Dickens, 14 November 1853, *Letters*, vol. 7, 196.

that he intended to travel to Italy, there was no mention of Rome. The last known letter Dickens sent before his announced week's absence was dated on Wednesday, 21 January. It is addressed to Wills, who, like Collins, was probably in the know about Dickens's relationship with Ellen Ternan.[119] 'I am chased out of Paris by enthusiasm', Dickens confessed to him 'and shall not come back for some five days'.[120]

Logistically, a journey to Switzerland no longer required several days of travelling by 1863. It may also have offered a good stopping point for a possible continuation to Genoa or even Rome: in 1844, Dickens's journey between Paris and Strasbourg took more than 50 hours, but by 1853 this had already been reduced to a mere 11 due to a new railway line.[121] When the Dickens household moved to Switzerland in 1846, they took the train between Strasbourg and Basel, which had opened two years before. From there, Forster tells us, 'they started for Lausanne next day, in three coaches, two horses to each, taking three days for the journey'.[122] Individual travellers needed less time for the journey: Dickens told family and friends that it could be done in 24 hours.[123] Nonetheless, for an individual traveller the trip from Ostend to Lausanne would still have taken at least five days in 1846. When Dickens travelled from Paris to Strasbourg in 1853 – a journey that had taken him more than 50 hours in 1844 – the travelling time had reduced significantly. From what would seem to have been his last journey to Switzerland, he wrote to Catherine:

> We got [to Strasbourg] at 7 last night. We left Paris at a quarter past 8 in the morning, and travelled all day (the distance is nearly 300 miles) by the very best Railroad I have ever seen. We dine today at half past 2, and go on at half past 4 by the Railroad to Basle. We are due there before 10, and go on tomorrow morning early.[124]

In the 1860s, travel time from Paris to Switzerland would have been reduced again thanks to a the new railway network which had connected Basel with Lausanne and Geneva since 1859, and other even

---

[119] Tomalin, *Invisible Woman*, 143; Ackroyd, *Dickens*, 1006.
[120] To W. H. Wills, 21 January 1863, *Letters*, vol. 10, 200.
[121] To Catherine Dickens, 13 October 1853, *Letters*, vol. 7, 163.
[122] Forster, *Life of Dickens*, 411.
[123] To Jerrold, 16 June 1846 and to Frederick Dickens, 16 June 1846, *Letters*, vol. 4, 564–6.
[124] To Catherine Dickens, 13 October 1853, *Letters*, vol. 7, 163.

146 *Dickens and Switzerland*

more recent refurbishments of the public transport system.[125] An article called 'Switzerland at Three Shillings a Day', which appeared in *Bentley's Miscellany* in 1862, describes how

> Starting from Paris in the morning, the traveller arrives by railway at Mulhausen, where the train stops the same evening; and by three o'clock the next day he may be at Berne, or Zurich, or Lucerne, in the heart of Switzerland.[126]

It would therefore not have been difficult for Dickens to travel to Switzerland and onwards to Italy within the seven or eight days during which he was absent. The question is, of course, to what purpose Dickens would have wanted to travel so far and back within so little time.

Upon his return, Dickens quoted from *Dombey* in a letter to Collins: '[Frank Beard]'s reflections when the knocks come to the door, run in my head, as the river ran – excuse the reference – I have just been reading it up – in Little Dombey's mind.'[127] The quotation may have been in his mind because he was giving a public reading from the novel the next day, but *Dombey* was also the novel Dickens started writing in Switzerland and for which the 'association between the writing and the place of writing is so curiously strong in my mind'.[128] In another letter, written on the same day, Dickens tells a friend that he has 'been visiting in the country these six days', but again, 'the country' gives no indication about where he really was.[129]

It has been suggested that Ternan was the 'sick friend' and the cause for 'anxiety not to be mentioned' which Dickens keeps referring to in January 1863. Some scholars believe that she was living in Paris or Boulogne, and may have been pregnant and gave birth to a child at that time.[130] However, in *The Invisible Woman*, Claire Tomalin does not rule out the possibility that Ternan may have had a baby abroad: 'the birth and death of a baby in England, France,

---

[125] See, for example, F. W. Putzger, *Historischer Atlas zur Welt- und Schweizer Geschichte*, ed. Dr Th. Müller-Wolfer, 5th ed. (Aarau: H. R. Sauerländer & Co, 1961), viii.

[126] W. E. U., 'Switzerland at Three Shillings a Day', *Bentley's Miscellany*, July 1862, 469.

[127] To Collins, 29 January 1863, *Letters*, vol. 10, 200.

[128] Dickens, *Dombey and Son*, 834 . See also Collins and Dickens, *No Thoroughfare*, 190.

[129] To Frederic Ouvry, 29 January 1863, *Letters*, vol. 10, 201.

[130] See, for example: Tomalin, *The Invisible Woman*, 140–4; John Bowen, 'Bebelle and "His Boots": Dickens, Ellen Ternan and the Christmas Stories', *Dickensian* 96, no. 3 (2000): 197–208; and Robert R. Garnett, 'The Crisis of 1863', *Dickens Quarterly* 23, no. 3 (2006): 181–91; Michael Slater, *The Great Charles Dickens Scandal* (New Haven, CT: Yale University Press, 2012), 101.

Switzerland, Italy or indeed any other European country could have been registered under a false name or simply lost in archives subject to destruction by the hand of God or man'.[131] But Dickens describes himself as being 'chased out of Paris by enthusiasm'. Once more, his words are ambiguous. Did he mean that he was looking forward to escaping the overwhelming enthusiasm of his reading audience or was he speaking of his own anticipation of the trip? If the latter is true, enthusiasm certainly was not the word which best describes Dickens's reaction to the announcement of another child during his marriage with Catherine. Things may, though, have been different with Ellen Ternan.[132]

In 'Bebelle and "His Boots": Dickens, Ellen Ternan and the "Christmas Stories",' John Bowen confirms that 'the period of the latter half of 1862 and 1863 has been generally recognised as one of the most mysterious and troubled parts of Dickens's adult life', and points out Dickens's occupation with 'possible fates of illegitimate children' in some of the texts he wrote during the early 1860s.[133] He connects this with the idea that Dickens and Ternan may have had a child. Yet, if we find abandoned and adopted children in Dickens's fiction in France in *Somebody's Luggage*, we can certainly find them in Switzerland as well, albeit a little later. *No Thoroughfare*, the 1867 Christmas Story Dickens wrote with Wilkie Collins, features another tale of problematic parentage, doubles, mistaken identities and absent fathers. The wine merchant Walter Wilding is a foundling child, who is adopted by a mother who brought her own son to the Foundling Hospital when he was still a baby. Since there are two Walter Wildings, the original Walter (who turns out to be George Vendale) is adopted by a Mrs Jane Anne Miller, a widow and a stranger 'acting this matter for her married sister, domiciled in Switzerland' on 3 March 1836.[134] The fact that 1836 is an inversion of 1863 may be significant. The widow is to bring the child to Switzerland where it will be adopted by the couple and 'brought up in the belief that he is really our son'. The sister's husband 'is resolved to spare the child whom we make our own, any future mortification and loss of self-respect which might be caused by a discovery of his true origin'. As the couple's name is 'a very uncommon one', they ask the sister, whose name is that of 'thousands of other people' to

---

[131] Tomalin, *The Invisible Woman*, 144.
[132] Tomalin, *Charles Dickens*, 246; 248.
[133] Bowen, 'Bebelle and "His Boots"', 197; 206.
[134] Collins and Dickens, *No Thoroughfare*, 228.

148   *Dickens and Switzerland*

'appear on the Register' so that 'there need be no fear of any discoveries in that quarter'. This 'harmless little conspiracy' results in Wilding inheriting the couple's fortunes and becoming partners with Vendale, the true Walter Wilding.[135]

I Am Involved in Mystery, or More Letters from the 1860s

If the letters discussed above were puzzling and vague, the following material will be even more so. Its references to Switzerland are remote and, worse, are more disconnected than the previous ones. Yet, they nicely prepare for Dickens's treatment of Switzerland in his later fiction which, at least in part, are equally vague and unexpected.

In 1865, at the beginning of September perhaps – the exact date is lost – Dickens writes to an unknown correspondent.

> *He regrets, that he cannot see him since he is going immediately to Switzerland, having need of change and rest. He thanks him for his two interesting letters and for his book.* [...] I am not the author of the article on your system which I consult abundantly. It was written by an English gentleman resident in France.
>
> I beg you on your return to Paris to embrace my dear Dumas [Alexandre Dumas Père], and to assure him of the undiminished admiration and regard of his fellow-labourer.[136]

It is an enigmatic and remarkable letter for several reasons. First of all, its unknown correspondent is a mystery. All we know is that he was male and may have been English or French. The letter was 'cut off after [the] signature, presumably removing addressee's name'.[137] The removal of the addressee's name seems to suggest that it contained information which, for some reason or other, was not intended for public disclosure. As if this was not quite enough, there is yet another piece of doubt in this jigsaw puzzle of oddities connected to the letter. It consists both of a 'facsimile' and an 'extract', the latter of which seems to have been 'retranslated into English', supposedly from French, and its known content appeared in two auctioneer's catalogues in the late 1980s.[138] Once again, the *Pilgrim*

---

[135] Ibid.
[136] To Unknown Correspondent, ?early September 1865, *Letters*, vol. 11, 89. Emphasis in original.
[137] Introductory comments to Unknown Correspondent, ibid.
[138] Ibid.

editors note that there is 'No evidence that [Dickens] went on to Switzerland'.[139] In later letters Dickens speaks of a trip he had made to France during that time.[140] Unlike in 1863, there are no other references to Switzerland in Dickens's letters written around the same time. It is also unclear when in 1865 it was composed, which makes it difficult to look for other hints.

Dickens did indeed leave England in September 1865 – probably to take a break after completing *Our Mutual Friend*. His next letters indicate that he went to Boulogne and Paris, and that by walking 'by the sea perpetually', he got sunburnt and had some trouble with his foot.[141] There is no reason to believe that Dickens went anywhere else than to Paris and Boulogne in September 1865. But then, the fact that he asks his correspondent to 'embrace my dear Dumas' when he himself was going to Paris in just a few days and could have seen him in person seems odd. There is more evidence that Dickens did not go to Switzerland at the beginning of September 1865. On 19 September he writes that he has 'come back from France'.[142] He confirms this in another letter written five days later: 'I wrote myself neuralgic – fled to France when I had done – and have come back *un*-neuralgic.'[143] Yet what was Dickens's motivation to tell his unknown correspondent that he was going to Switzerland? A possibility, is, of course, that the letter has been misdated. Another, that it is not genuine. A third, that Dickens lied to his correspondent and used Switzerland as an excuse or a distraction. Maybe he changed his plans because of his foot. Perhaps Ellen Ternan had something to do with it. One wonders whether Switzerland became a personal in-joke of Dickens's when he did not want to meet people and needed a convincing excuse. Yet how does this relate to the earlier letters in which he claimed that he was going to Switzerland? And what about the fact that Switzerland keeps reappearing in the fiction Dickens wrote in the last decade of his life?

There is another peculiar moment in Dickens's letters concerning Switzerland and the last one I will discuss in this respect. In April 1866, he wrote a letter to Georgina Hogarth, and asked her:

> Do you remember Sir Charles Styles at Lausanne? Think of *his* turning up, as living at Bath, and inviting me to stay with him 'on

---

[139] Ibid., 89n2.
[140] To Benjamin Webster, 19 September 1865, *Letters*, vol. 11, 93.
[141] To Forster, ?mid-September 1865], *Letters*, vol. 11, 92.
[142] To Benjamin Webster, 19 September 1865, *Letters*, vol. 11, 93.
[143] To Charles Kent, 24 September 1865, *Letters*, vol. 11, 96.

150 *Dickens and Switzerland*

my approaching visit to that city to read' – which I hope there is no chance of my visiting in my life for any such purpose.[144]

At some point, someone decided that this portion of the letter contained information which was not suitable – or interesting enough – for general circulation. From the editors of the *Pilgrim* collection we learn that the passage quoted here was omitted in two earlier editions of Dickens's letters. One of these was the edition by his sister-in-law, Georgina Hogarth, and his oldest daughter, Mamie Dickens. But the editing process even affected the manuscript, as this part of the text is not only omitted in the published editions but has also been inked out in the original.[145] I suspect that the reason for this intervention was either the reference to the person Dickens mentioned or his unkind comment about Bath. Despite his hostile position, Dickens would read there on two later occasions.[146] Not much is known about Sir Charles Styles whom Dickens mentions. According to the *Pilgrim* editors, Dickens is misspelling the name and refers to Sir Thomas Charles Style (1797–1879), 8th Baronet of Wateringbury Place, Kent. Biographical information about him is extremely scarce, and Dickens did not refer to him in his letters from Lausanne in 1846, the only known journey to Switzerland in which Dickens was accompanied by Georgina.[147]

In the 1840s, Dickens was a regular and rather reliable correspondent in terms of the people he met. Since he was abroad for 'more than half of the period' between 1844 and 1846, the 'incidence of letters varies accordingly'.[148] For the scholar, it is not only the high number of letters from this time that is a blessing but also the fact that so many of them have survived. Even though Dickens did not envisage using his letters from Switzerland for a book as he had done for the *Pictures*, he frequently wrote to Forster, who, in his biography, was 'free to print as much as he wished from Dickens's letters to him, and he was liberal with his extracts'.[149] With the very odd and singular exception of Style, we seem to have a fairly comprehensive list of people Dickens met in Lausanne, no matter how brief, random or unpleasant their encounter. Style and his wife had a daughter called Emma, who died in Lausanne in 1834, but it is unclear

---

[144] To Georgina Hogarth, 17 April 1866, *Letters*, vol. 11, 185. Emphasis in original.
[145] Ibid., 185n*aa*.
[146] Ibid., 185n8.
[147] To Georgina Hogarth, 17 April 1866, *Letters*, vol. 11, 185n6.
[148] Preface to *Letters*, vol. 4, vii.
[149] Ibid., xv.

whether they were still in Lausanne in 1846 or returned later on.[150] In either case, Style's absence in Dickens's correspondence is an oddity and remains unaccounted for, unless Dickens and Georgina met him on a journey which we do not know of. This might also explain why the entire passage has been inked out, rather than just the last part which contains Dickens's unflattering remark. All of this is speculation, of course, and it may well be that Dickens never went back to Switzerland after 1853. If he did not, it is, however, an interesting coincidence that his daughter Katey travelled to Switzerland on her long honeymoon with her husband, Charles Allston Collins and that his sub-editor and indispensable 'factotum', Wills, who knew of Ellen Ternan, went to Switzerland for his 'annual holiday' in 1861.[151] Wilkie Collins, who was probably informed as well, was also repeatedly there in the 1860s.[152]

Intelligence, or Dickens's 'Swiss' Books

The 1870 *Catalogue of the Library of Charles Dickens from Gad's Hill* features some unexpected entries. No *Murray*, the travel guide most often cited by scholars in discussions on Dickens and Switzerland, was found on his shelves after his death.[153] Instead, there was a copy of *Bradshaw's Illustrated Handbook to Switzerland and the Tyrol*.[154] This would not be otherwise remarkable had this book been published before the time Dickens had last travelled to Switzerland. The first version of Bradshaw's book only appeared in 1857. No date is given for Dickens's edition, but according to the British Library Catalogue, an updated copy came out annually until 1899.[155] Dickens also owned Murray's *Knapsack Guide for Travellers in Switzerland*, a 'condensed and corrected revision' of the *Handbook for Travellers in Switzerland*, which was first published

---

[150] Henry Reed Stiles, *The Stiles Family in America* (Jersey City, NY: Doan & Pilson, 1895), 720.

[151] To Bulwer Lytton, 23 September 1861, *Letters*, vol. 9, 463; to Cerjat, 1 February 1861, *Letters*, vol. 9, 380.

[152] To Bulwer Lytton, 23 September 1861, *Letters*, vol. 9, 462; to Wilkie Collins, 4 October 1844, *Letters*, vol. 11, 251; Peter Ackroyd, *Wilkie Collins* (London: Vintage, 2013), 133.

[153] See, for example, to Forster, 24 and 25 August 1846, *Letters*, vol. 4, 611.

[154] J. H. Stonehouse, ed., *Catalogue of the Library of Charles Dickens from Gad's Hill* (London: Piccadilly Fountain Press, 1935), facsimile rpt. in Japan by Takashi Terauchi (2003), 15.

[155] Library Catalogue, British Library, s.v. 'Bradshaw, Switzerland, Tyrol'.

152 *Dickens and Switzerland*

in 1864, though Dickens's copy was from 1867 – when he wrote *No Thoroughfare* with Wilkie Collins.[156] He also owned Louis Simond's *A Tour in Italy and Sicily*, which opens with a description of Switzerland.[157] An even stranger entry from the catalogue of Dickens's bookshelves is Baedeker's *Hand-book for Travellers in Switzerland and the Adjacent Portions of Italy, Savoy, and the Tyrol*. The year given with this title is 1873, which is evidently difficult to explain as Dickens died in 1870.[158] The Harvard College Library holds a second edition of the same title from 1864, so it is not impossible that Dickens owned an earlier copy of this text and that the date is an error, given that the catalogue was only compiled as late as 1878.[159] Another possibility is that the text is among those works in the catalogue which have been classified as 'elusive'.[160] However, this still does not explain the presence of the *Bradshaw* and Murray's *Knapsack Guide*.

Slightly less odd but nonetheless unexpected finds among Dickens's remains are signed and inscribed presentation copies of John Forbes's *Physician's Holiday, or a Month in Switzerland in the Summer of 1848*, published in 1850, and of a work simply entitled *Genève*, a book about the local reformation, signed by the editor and published in 1854.[161] He also owned presentation copies of Albert Smith's *Ascent of Mont Blanc* from 1854, Madame de Staël's *Oeuvres Complètes* from 1820–1821, his friend Talfourd's *Recollections of a First Visit to the Alps, in Aug. and Sep. 1841*, printed for private circulation, the *Supplement to his 'Vacation Rambles': Recollections of a Tour through France, to Italy, and Homeward by Switzerland, in the Vacation of 1846* from 1854 and The Reverend Tagart's *Sketches of the Lives and Characters of the Leading Reformers of the Sixteenth Century: Luther, Calvin, Zwingle, Socinus, Cranmer, Knox* from 1843.[162] Among the collection of James Fenimore Cooper's novels which Dickens owned was *The Headsman*, published in 1833, a story set in Switzerland.[163] In 1837, Dickens returned a copy of Browning's poem *Paracelsus* to a friend.[164] The accompanying letter does not give away whether

[156] Stonehouse, *Catalogue of the Library of Charles Dickens*, 68.
[157] Louis Simond, *A Tour in Italy and Sicily* (London: Printed for Longman, et al., 1828).
[158] Stonehouse, *Catalogue of the Library of Charles Dickens*, 9.
[159] Ibid., ii.
[160] Ibid., iii.
[161] Ibid., 47; 50.
[162] Ibid., 102; 104; 108; 106.
[163] Ibid., 24.
[164] To Miss Ely, ?late July 1837, *Letters*, vol. 12, 558.

Dickens read the poem, but Paracelsus, born in the late fifteenth century and a Renaissance philosopher and physician, was Swiss and the place also matters. 'Basil' in the poem is Basel, and 'Zuinglius', Huldrych Zwingli, one of the leaders of the Swiss Reformation, is also mentioned.[165] Also among his collection was Dr Flügel's *Practical Dictionary of the English and German Languages* from 1856.[166] It seems odd that by the time of his death, Dickens should not – or no longer – have owned a *Murray*, nor his wife's uncle's *Two Journeys*, which he proofread when he was a young journalist, but several more recent travel books on Switzerland instead.[167]

Yet we know from previous purchase accounts that not all books Dickens purchased made it to Gad's Hill. In May 1849, Dickens bought a copy of the well-known *Swiss Family Robinson*, which does not feature among the books in the Gad's Hill catalogue.[168] Another book omitted is Maria Elizabeth Budden's *Claudine; or Humility the Basis of All the Virtues. A Swiss Tale* which Dickens bought in 1850.[169] Like *The Swiss Family Robinson*, *Claudine* was successfully translated into a play. Adapted by John Courtney, it opened at the Old Vic in 1849.[170] This collection not only underlines Dickens's own preoccupation with Switzerland, and tell of a familiarity with Swiss plots which was typical for the age he lived in, but the number of presentation copies also shows that the social circle Dickens moved in was equally interested and familiar with the country and some of its most prominent citizens.

Leon Litvak's excellent article, 'What Books Did Dickens Buy and Read?' covers a number of the books Dickens owned in or on a foreign language, but when describing Dickens's travel destinations, he effaces Switzerland entirely:

> Given the fact that the Dickens family had spent time in both France (a country for which the novelist had great affection) and Italy, it should come as no surprise that the accounts feature texts on French grammar, vocabulary, and literature [...] Italian books include [...][171]

Nor does Litvak comment on the fact that Dickens purchased all of the books belonging to this category after his first period of

---

[165] Robert Browning, *Paracelsus* (London: J. M. Dent, 1898).
[166] Stonehouse, *Catalogue of the Library of Charles Dickens*, 47.
[167] See Chapter 2, 69ff.
[168] Leon Litvak, 'What Books Did Dickens Buy and Read?', 114; see Chapter 1, 32.
[169] Litvak, 'What Books Did Dickens Buy and Read?', 117.
[170] Nicoll, *A History of English Drama 1660–1900*, vol. 4, 516.
[171] Litvak, 'What Books Did Dickens Buy and Read?', 86.

154 *Dickens and Switzerland*

travelling and living abroad in the 1840s. Only in 1854, for example, did Dickens buy *A New Practical and Easy Method of Learning the Italian Language* and *A New Method of Learning the German Language*.[172] Perhaps he needed them for his children, for inspiration with the beginning of *Little Dorrit*, or he wanted to refresh his foreign language skills after the journey to the Continent with Wilkie Collins and Augustus Egg. At any rate, Dickens owned a surprising number of books which were connected with Switzerland in some way or other.

Domestic, or a Chalet at Gad's Hill

If Switzerland's appearances in Dickens's writing in the late 1850s are present but unexpected, they become less visible in the 1860s. *No Thoroughfare* stands out, but other than that, Dickens only occasionally refers to the country in his fiction and often in oblique allusions, though he does – as we have seen – mention the country in his letters. Yet, right next to his English house which proudly boasted a Shakespearean connection, Dickens had his very own piece of domestic Switzerland to inhabit from 1865 onwards. Charles Fechter, an actor and close friend to Dickens, presented him with a Swiss chalet for Christmas. A cheaply made, artistically unsophisticated construction, it arrived 'straight from Switzerland' to Gad's Hill by water in ninety-four pieces with a set of French instructions.[173] Dickens thought that it would 'really be a pretty thing', and was 'much higher than we supposed'.[174] He was aware that it was not an architectural masterpiece, but decided to use it as a study straight away: 'in the summer (supposing it not to be blown away in the spring), the upper room will make a charming study'.[175]

The chalet became indeed his cherished writing retreat. He wrote parts of *Our Mutual Friend* in it and drafted the first plans for *No Thoroughfare* with Wilkie Collins there.[176] Malcom Morley even suggests that the inspiration for Obenreizer's Swiss house in London 'must surely have been the Swiss Chalet at Gadshill [*sic*] where

---

[172] Ibid., 124.

[173] Marcus Stone, 'Mr. Marcus Stone, R. A., and Charles Dickens', *Dickensian* 8, no. 8 (1912): 216.

[174] To Forster, 7 January 1865, *Letters*, vol. 11, 3.

[175] Ibid.

[176] Wilkie Collins, 'Wilkie Collins's Recollections of Charles Fechter', in *Charles Albert Fechter. American Actor Series*, Kate Field (Boston, MA: James R. Osgood and Co., 1882), 163.

Charles mused with Wilkie Collins when, together, they invented the plot of *No Thoroughfare*'. He adds: 'Then, too, that chalet was a gift to Dickens from Charles Fechter, the actor for whom the stage piece was contrived and who was to create the character of Jules Obenreizer.'[177] Dickens had seen Fechter for the first time in a 'rather good melodrama' called *Sang Melé* by M. E. Plouvier.[178] During the performance, Dickens found that 'One "set," where the action of a whole act is supposed to take place in the great wooden verandah of a Swiss hotel overhanging a mountain ravine, is the best piece of stage carpentering I have seen in France'.[179] *No Thoroughfare*'s Swiss passages can therefore at least partly be explained by the many ties which connect Fechter, Dickens and Collins with Switzerland.

In a well-known and often-quoted letter to a friend, Dickens describes the atmosphere in which he worked at the chalet:

> I have put five mirrors in the Swiss chalet (where I write) and they reflect and refract in all kinds of ways the leaves that are quivering at the windows, and the great fields of waving corn, and the saildotted river. My room is up among the branches of the trees; and the birds and the butterflies fly in and out, and the green branches shoot in, at the open windows, and the lights and shadows of the clouds come and go with the rest of the company. The scent of the flowers, and indeed of everything that is growing for miles and miles, is most delicious.[180]

It is the vocabulary of the idyll that Dickens deploys here. Like his omniscient and semi-omniscient narrators, Dickens sits above 'the great fields of waving corn' and the 'saildotted river', both of which suggest human activity, observing, thinking, writing. In his letter, Dickens reduces the inner space of the chalet to the 'open windows', which make fluid any sense of interior and exterior as 'the birds and the butterflies fly in and out, and the green branches shoot in', and 'the lights and shadows of the clouds come and go'.[181] Dickens himself is almost reduced to a passive subject in this description, were it not for the remarks in the first clause of the initial sentence. Peter Ackroyd also mentions that Dickens had a telescope placed in the chalet and emphasises his 'boyish delight' with the structure, comparing it to a 'fantasy of boyhood' and a 'secret place among

[177] Malcolm Morley, '*No Thoroughfare* Back Stage', *Dickensian* 50 (1954): 37.
[178] To Forster, 23 March 1856, *Letters*, vol. 8, 76.
[179] Ibid.
[180] To Mrs. J. T. Fields, 25 May 1868, vol. 12, 119.
[181] Ibid.

156   *Dickens and Switzerland*

the trees'.[182] Just as when he was in Switzerland in 1846, the chalet seems to have triggered something of the child in Dickens, only that this time, the sensation was a joyous and playful one. His study in the first floor of his chalet now allowed him to experience what he had described earlier in 'Lying Awake'. With the chalet, he could re-enact the sensation of 'up I go' whenever he fancied.[183]

Much has been made of the mirrors in Dickens's chalet and the fact that they 'reflect and refract' Dickens's writing environment. What has not been noticed yet, however, is how closely Dickens's description of the chalet resembles that of his house in Lausanne. In 1846, he writes to a friend that the Rosemont 'is surrounded by a lawn, a vineyard, a garden, a corn-field, and some other agricultural trifles, of its own – and is, at present overwhelmed in a cluster of Roses'.[184] A few days later he tells Forster that 'From a fine long broad balcony on which the windows of my little study on the first floor (where I am now writing) open, the lake is seen to wonderful advantage' and that

> Under the balcony is a stone colonnade, on which the six French windows of the drawing-room open; and quantities of plants are clustered about the pillars and seats, very prettily. One of these drawing-rooms is furnished (like a French hotel) with red velvet, and the other with green; in both, plenty of mirrors and nice white muslin curtains[185]

At Gad's Hill, he was surrounded by 'agricultural trifles' and even though there was no lake, he could – and did – observe the river when writing. Whereas Dickens had no influence over the location of the Rosemont in Lausanne, he was free to choose where to place his chalet at Gad's Hill. In the same letter to Forster from 1846, when he could not yet have had an inkling of ever owning the house with the Shakespearean connection, Dickens wrote about Lausanne: 'The green woods and green shades about here, are more like Cobham in Kent, than anything we dream of at the foot of the Alpine passes.'[186] Cobham is of course one of the villages right next to Higham, where Gad's Hill is situated.

Lillian Nayder has pointed out the similarities between Dickens's study in the chalet and the description of Maître Voigt's office in

[182] Ackroyd, *Dickens*, 956.
[183] Dickens, 'Lying Awake', 91.
[184] To Daniel Maclise, 14 June 1846, *Letters*, vol. 4, 562.
[185] To Forster, ?22 June 1846, *Letters*, vol. 4, 568.
[186] Ibid., 569.

No Thoroughfare.[187] It is indeed remarkably similar to Dickens's own workplace:

> An oddly pastoral kind of office it was, and one that would never have answered in England. It stood in a neat back yard, fenced off from a pretty flower-garden. Goats browsed in the doorway, and a cow was within half-a-dozen feet of keeping company with the clerk. Maître Voigt's room was a bright and varnished little room, with panelled walls, like a toy-chamber. According to the seasons of the year, roses, sunflowers, hollyhocks, peeped in at the windows. Maître Voigt's bees hummed through the office all the summer, in at this window and out at that, taking it frequently in their day's work, as if honey were to be made from Maître Voigt's sweet disposition.[188]

Dickens's letter about the chalet is further significant in another respect. It bears three, probably inadvertent, references to Switzerland. All of them are indirect and deal with something 'Swiss' rather than the country itself. They refer to a dog, a building and a play. Dickens opens the letter with a paragraph about his dogs, and relates how they greeted him after an absence from Gad's Hill. Whereas his Newfoundland dogs behaved 'exactly in their usual manner', 'Linda (the St. Bernard)' – according to the *Pilgrim* editors a 'daughter of one brought by Albert Smith from the Alps' – 'was greatly excited; weeping profusely, and throwing herself on her back that she might caress my foot with her great fore-paws'.[189] Beryl Gray has aptly commented on Dickens's profound interest in dogs and outlined Linda's significance as well as the meaning of her cultural heritage relating to Switzerland.[190] The next 'Swiss' reference is the description of Dickens's chalet above, and the last is to *No Thoroughfare*, which was 'very shortly coming out in Paris'.[191] The play was still running in London at the time, but 'without Fechter, who has been very ill'.[192] The references in this letter are remarkable because they effortlessly – and unconsciously – illustrate Dickens's many seemingly minor links with Switzerland in his later years. They remain unconnected except that they all fit into an autobiographical account of Dickens's preoccupations at that time and that each of them

---

[187] Nayder, *Unequal Partners*, 158.
[188] Dickens and Collins, *No Thoroughfare*, 213.
[189] To Mrs. J. T. Fields, 25 May 1868, *Letters*, vol. 12, 119; to The Hon. Mrs. Richard Watson, 7 December 1857, *Letters*, vol. 8, 489n1.
[190] Gray, *The Dog in Dickensian Imagination*, 35–66.
[191] To Mrs. J. T. Fields, 25 May 1868, *Letters*, vol. 12, 120.
[192] Ibid.

relates to Switzerland independently. The letter is not of the kind that one would identify as a 'Swiss' letter and yet all of the 'Swiss' aspects Dickens mentioned shaped his life in some form or other.

The chalet seems to have been the place where Dickens spent the majority of his last working days, continuing his work on *The Mystery of Edwin Drood*.[193] He claimed that he had 'never worked better any where' than in the chalet, an ironic remark, if we remember that in 1846, writing in Switzerland caused him 'infinite pains'.[194] In none of his letters does Dickens express surprise about Fechter's gift and, to my knowledge, no scholar has ever questioned the choice either – as if chalets were commonplace Victorian Christmas presents. As we have seen at the beginning of Chapter 1, they were popular and decorative objects in nineteenth-century Britain, but I have been unable to find any other presentee of an assembly kit chalet – Victorian or otherwise. Why could Fechter assume that Dickens would develop a 'boyish delight'? And is the fact that it was a Swiss chalet (rather than, say, a French or an Austrian one) significant?

Return, or Fictional Journeys

But the chalet is only one of the objects linking Gad's Hill with Switzerland. Another one is a story. Dickens wrote 'Travelling Abroad' in 1860 as a part of his *Uncommercial Traveller* series. He had purchased Gad's Hill in 1856 after his father had allegedly told him that 'he might himself live in it or in some such house when he came to be a man, if he would only work hard enough'.[195] The journey which the narrator seems to undertake in the piece traces his encounters with several grotesque characters. Yet, it turns out to be a daydream only, mixing recollections of trips Dickens had indeed undertaken earlier in his life. There is no obvious link between Gad's Hill and Switzerland other than that they stand at the beginning and the end, respectively, of the same mental journey undertaken in the story. The connection exists but in the narrator's mind. Chronology is distorted, as Dickens never – as far as we know – undertook a trip in the way it is presented here. Gad's Hill would only be '*my* house' to Dickens ten years after he met the rifle-shooting and 'more than

---

[193] Forster, *Life of Dickens*, 943.
[194] To Fechter, 21 July 1865, *Letters*, vol. 11, 75; to Forster, 30 August 1846, *Letters*, vol. 4, 612.
[195] Forster, *Life of Dickens*, 6.

usually accomplished and amiable country man' in Lausanne, for example.[196]

Yet both Gad's Hill and the narrator's adventures in Switzerland bear connections with Dickens's childhood. 'I had', we learn at the opening of the story, 'no idea where I was going (which was delightful), except that I was going abroad'.[197] The way 'abroad' leads past his own house, where he meets a younger version of himself. Yet, he refuses to 'halt there' for long and 'soon dropped the very queer small boy and went on', as if he was trying to discard the memory of his childhood.[198]

The trip, reminiscent of a picaresque adventure, is nothing less than a continuous flow of recollections of childhood stories with a childlike narrator who has an insatiable urge to see plots everywhere. It is both an autobiographical account and a castle in the air, as the journey is an imaginary one. After crossing France, the narrator rattles towards Switzerland in his German chariot, where 'the nursery rhyme about Banbury Cross and the venerable lady who rode in state there, was always in my ears'.[199] He feels 'like a new Gesler in a Canton of Tells' and 'like Don Quixote on the back of the wooden horse'.[200] The 'idiot lying on a wood-pile who sunned himself and nursed his goître' utters a howl 'like a young giant on espying a traveller – in other words, something to eat'.[201] One night,

> the stove within, and the cold outside, awakened childish associations long forgotten, and I dreamed I was in Russia – the identical serf out of a picture-book I had, before I could read it for myself – and that I was going to be knouted by a noble personage in a fur cap, boots, and earrings, who, I think, must have come out of some melodrama.[202]

Switzerland seems to trigger an abundance of – English – childhood memories, once again confirming Dickens's close association of certain aspects of Switzerland with Britain.[203] The narrator's imagination becomes so overshadowed that the place itself almost disappears behind this screen of 'childish associations'. Italy, where

---

[196] Dickens, 'Travelling Abroad', 94; on the 'amiable countryman', i.e. Lord Vernon, see to Forster, ?15–17 August 1846, *Letters*, vol. 4, 605.

[197] Dickens, 'Travelling Abroad', 85.

[198] Ibid., 86.

[199] Ibid., 94.

[200] Ibid.

[201] Ibid., 95.

[202] Ibid.

[203] See Chapter 2, 72.

160 *Dickens and Switzerland*

Dickens lived for a whole year, surprisingly does not find a place in this story, as it ends on the 'Lausanne shore of the Lake of Geneva' where the narrator suddenly awakes from his dream, and we learn that the narrator was daydreaming but had, in fact, a commission to buy a chariot 'for a friend who was going abroad'.[204] The biographical and narrative pasts and presents form an odd convolution of time:

> I stood looking at the bright blue water, the flushed white mountains opposite and the boats at my feet with their furled Mediterranean sails, showing like enormous magnifications of this goose-quill pen that is now in my hand.
>
> The sky became overcast without any notice; a wind very like the March east wind of England, blew across me; and a voice said, 'How do you like it? Will it do?'[205]

The journey tempts the narrator into extravagant musings, but it is in Switzerland that he awakes from his dream.

David Copperfield experiences a similar dreamlike state and awakening in Switzerland, but his is decidedly more romantic. However, no second Agnes, but a – presumably male – seller is involved in the awakening in 'Travelling Abroad'. Dickens's letters offer no hint as to whether his visit to the 'Carriage Department of the London Pantechnicon' sprang from an actual event or is the product of imagination.

Little Dorrit's experience of Switzerland is a similar one and bears remarkable parallels to the narrator's awakening in 'Travelling Abroad' – only that in the novel it is an expression of Amy Dorrit's disbelieving and de-realised perception of the recent events. As the Dorrits reach Martigny, Amy is unable to accept her fate as real:

> Her present existence was a dream. All that she saw was new and wonderful, but it was not real; it seemed to her as if those visions of mountains and picturesque countries might melt away at any moment, and the carriage, turning some abrupt corner, bring up with a jolt at the old Marshalsea gate.[206]

In both narratives, it is the process of travelling in a carriage which distances the character from the present reality – Switzerland in Amy Dorrit's case, England in the Uncommercial Traveller's.

---

[204] Dickens, 'Travelling Abroad', 95.
[205] Ibid.
[206] Dickens, *Little Dorrit*, 451.

A more subtle reference to Switzerland appears in 'Shy Neighbourhoods', another piece from the *Uncommercial Traveller* series. It opens with the narrator outlining that 'much of my travelling is done by foot' and telling of his 'last special feat' which was 'turning out of bed at two, after a hard day, pedestrian and otherwise, and walking thirty miles into the country to breakfast'.[207] As if he were still asleep and dreaming, he relates how he was 'without the slightest sense of exertion, dozing heavily and dreaming constantly'.[208] In another parallel to *Little Dorrit*, where the second book opens 'In the autumn of the year', our Uncommercial Traveller notices how

> The day broke mistily (it was autumn time), and I could not disembarrass myself of the idea that I had to climb those heights and banks of clouds, and that there was an Alpine Convent somewhere behind the sun, where I was going to breakfast.[209]

Similarly, great emphasis is put on the cloud on top of the mountain in *Little Dorrit*, yet here the clouds sit on top of the pass, rather than below it: 'up here in the clouds, everything was seen through cloud, and seemed dissolving into cloud'.[210] Switzerland, or the memory of the St Bernard, rather, forces itself upon the narrator in 'Shy Neighbourhoods' and overshadows the English countryside:

> This sleepy notion was so much stronger than such substantial objects as villages and haystacks, that, after the sun was up and bright, and when I was sufficiently awake to have a sense of pleasure in the prospect, I still occasionally caught myself looking about for wooden arms to point the right track up the mountain, and wondering there was no snow yet.[211]

As shown in Chapter 2, Dickens also used a very similar yet more gruesome ghostly personification of trees in the form of pointing arms in *Little Dorrit*.[212]

[207] Dickens, 'Shy Neighbourhoods', 118.
[208] Ibid.
[209] Dickens, *Little Dorrit*, 419; Dickens, 'Shy Neighbourhoods', 118.
[210] Dickens, *Little Dorrit*, 420.
[211] Dickens, 'Shy Neighbourhoods', 118.
[212] See Chapter 2, 103; Dickens, *Little Dorrit*, 420.

162   *Dickens and Switzerland*

Another Retrospect, or Switzerland in *Our Mutual Friend*

Some of the most surprising allusions to Switzerland in Dickens's later fiction are those in *Our Mutual Friend*. The most subtle perhaps is Boffin's 'Decline-And-Fall-Off-The-Rooshan Empire'. It is a text, we learn, that comes in 'Eight wollumes. Red and gold. Purple ribbon in every wollume, to keep the place where you leave off'.[213] There are two interesting connections between Dickens and Edward Gibbon: not only was 'Gibbon, like Dickens, [...] steeped in the Arabian Nights when a child' but both lived in Lausanne for a while though Gibbon's stay lasted much longer with five years than Dickens's own of five months. Both found an intellectually stimulating environment in the Swiss town and were working towards some of their most successful texts there. When Dickens and his family arrived in Lausanne in 1846, the best-known hotel was the 'Gibbon', where they stayed before renting the 'Rosemont'. The hotel was named after Gibbon, who completed his *Decline and Fall of the Roman Empire* while living in a building called 'La Grotte' which previously stood on the site.[214] Dickens would have known of Gibbon's stay in Lausanne and was conscious of the connection. By the time of his death, Dickens owned a copy of Gibbon's *Decline and Fall*, which came, 'like Boffin's, in eight volumes'.[215]

In *Our Mutual Friend*, Boffin's Bower is 'as difficult to find, as Fair Rosamond's without the clue'.[216] Adrian Poole and Michael Cotsell point out the reference to Henry II in this passage, yet Dickens may also play a clever game of double entendre.[217] After just two days of house-hunting, Dickens found a suitable property to house his family in. The name of the house was Rosemont and he described it in a letter as 'secluded', but at the same time 'not at all lonely' and 'beautifully situated on the hill that rises from the lake, within ten minutes' walk of this hotel'.[218] While I am not suggesting that Boffin's Bower is, in fact, a reproduction of Dickens's Lausanne

---

[213] Dickens, *Our Mutual Friend*, ed. Adrian Poole (London: Penguin, 1997), 59.

[214] To Forster, ?13 or 14 June 1846, *Letters*, vol. 4, 560; also see n1, though the name of the house is wrongly given as 'Le Grotto', rather than 'La Grotte'.

[215] Michael Cotsell, *The Companion to* Our Mutual Friend (London: Allen & Unwin, 1986), 58; also, see Stonehouse, *Catalogue of the Library of Charles Dickens*, 50.

[216] Dickens, *Our Mutual Friend*, 61.

[217] Ibid., 808; Cotsell, *Companion to* Our Mutual Friend, 59.

[218] To Forster, ?13–14 June 1846, *Letters*, vol. 4, 560.

Rosemont, it may be a conscious or unconscious play on words which reminded Dickens of his time in Lausanne.

It was during his stay at the Rosemont when it crossed Dickens's mind that 'a great deal of money might possibly be made [...] by one's having Readings of one's own books. It would be an *odd* thing. I think it would take immensely. What do you say?'[219] Forster presents this moment as the very starting point, or, 'the prelude to his public readings', as the *Pilgrim* editors would have it, even though Forster never seemed too keen on the idea himself.[220] In *Our Mutual Friend*, Silas Wegg becomes, like Dickens, a professional reader – albeit a less faithful one. Just like Dickens, he understands that reading 'was an opportunity to be improved, and that here might be money to be got beyond present calculation', but unlike his creator, Wegg is neither acquainted with the material he is to read – 'Mr. Wegg would even have picked a handsome quarrel with any one who should have challenged his deep acquaintance with those aforesaid eight volumes of Decline and Fall' – nor does he read out of a noble motive.[221] Unlike Dickens, who planned his reading career carefully, Wegg becomes a professional reader by accident.

When Mortimer Lightwood, Eugene Wrayburn, Gaffer Hexham and Charley visit the Night-Inspector, they find him busy 'with a pen and ink, and ruler, posting up his books in a whitewashed office as studiously as if he were in a monastery on top of a mountain'.[222] The simile of the Night-Inspector as 'the quiet Abbot of that Monastery' continues through the rest of the scene.[223] There is no geographical specificity, but the only two monasteries 'on top of a mountain' which Dickens visited were those on the Simplon and the St Bernard. The Night-Inspector appears as a monk in charge of the dead, but also as a personification of Dickens's 1854 wish of 'going above the snow-line in Switzerland, and living in some astonishing convent'.[224] Just as Dickens imagined himself about ten years earlier, when he told Forster that he had 'visions of living for half a year or so, in all sorts of inaccessible places, and opening a new book therein', the Night-Inspector too seems to spend his time with books:

[219] To Forster, 11 October 1846, *Letters*, vol. 4, 631.
[220] Forster, *Life of Dickens*, 450; Preface to *Letters*, vol. 4, xii.
[221] Dickens, *Our Mutual Friend*, 61.
[222] Ibid., 33.
[223] Ibid., 35.
[224] To Forster, ?29 September 1854, *Letters*, vol. 7, 428.

164   *Dickens and Switzerland*

> With the same air of a recluse much given to study, he desisted from
> his books to bestow a distrustful nod of recognition upon Gaffer [...].
> Then, he finished ruling the work he had in hand (it might have been
> illuminating a missal, he was so calm)[225]

Once he decides that their conversation has come to an end, the
Night-Inspector, 'becoming once again the quiet Abbot of that
Monastery, dipped his pen in his ink and resumed his book'.[226]

The passage echoes some of the key themes in *No Thoroughfare*
and the second volume of *Little Dorrit*. There are questions of
unsolved and masked identities: in *Little Dorrit*, the travellers are
only identified by name at the end of the chapter. Rigaud changes his
name to Blandois on top of the mountain, and Pet Meagles appears
as Mrs Gowan for the first time in the narrative. Vendale in *No
Thoroughfare* is the true Mr Wilding. In *Our Mutual Friend*, identities are problematic throughout and the case of Harmon/Rokesmith/
Handford is only solved towards the end. In this passage, Hexam,
Lightwood and Wrayburn visit the Night-Inspector about the uni-
dentified body. Yet the Night-Inspector's identity itself seems to float
between that of a policeman and an abbot. In all three texts, water –
in any state of matter – becomes the number one threat to health or
life in general.

I Observe, or Water, Death, Sound and Solitude

As Vybarr Cregan-Reid has pointed out in 'Bodies, Boundaries and
Queer Waters', *David Copperfield* and *Our Mutual Friend* 'both take
the trope of drowning as their focal rhetoric'.[227] In *No Thoroughfare*
the place where the first Walter Wilding sets up his wine business
already suggests – and foreshadows – violence in relation to water:

> Years before the year one thousand eight hundred and sixty-one,
> people had left off taking boat at Break-Neck-Stairs, and watermen
> had ceased to ply there. The slimy little causeway had dropped into
> the river by a slow process of suicide, and two or three stumps of
> piles and a rusty iron mooring-ring were all that remained of the
> departed Break-Neck glories.[228]

---

[225] Dickens, *Our Mutual Friend*, 33.
[226] Ibid., 35.
[227] Vybarr Cregan-Reid, 'Bodies, Boundaries and Queer Waters: Drowning and
Prosopopoeia in Later Dickens', *Critical Survey* 17, no. 2 (2005), 20.
[228] Dickens, *No Thoroughfare*, 113.

As another prefiguration of what is to come, Vendale, 'following it with his eyes', observes in Obenreizer's house – which is a manifestation of 'domestic Switzerland' – that 'Mimic water was dropping off a mill-wheel under the clock'.[229] What appears as picturesque in England is in fact an eternal reminder of Obenreizer's own 'sordid childhood'.[230] Obenreizer remembers telling Vendale about his youth 'that evening in the boat upon the lake, floating among the reflections of the mountains and valleys, the crags and pine-woods, which were my earliest remembrance'.[231]

Flowing water becomes important again when Vendale and Obenreizer reach Basel. The sound of the running Rhine seems to drive Obenreizer into an obsessive frenzy:

> 'Where shall I rob him, if I can? Where shall I murder him, if I must?'
> So as he paced the room, ran the river, ran the river, ran the river.
>
> The burden seemed to him at last, to be growing so plain that he stopped; thinking it as well to suggest another burden to his companion.
>
> 'The Rhine sounds tonight,' he said with a smile, 'like the old waterfall at home. That waterfall which my mother showed to travellers (I told you of it once). The sound of it changed with the weather, as does the sound of all falling waters and flowing waters. When I was a pupil of the watch-maker, I remembered it as sometimes saying to me for whole days, "Who are you, my little wretch? Who are you my little wretch?" I remembered it as saying, other times, when its sound was hollow, and storm was coming up the Pass: "Boom, boom, boom. Beat him, beat him, beat him." Like my mother enraged – if she was my mother.'[232]

Flowing water once more triggers questions of identity, but its uniform sound also brings back memories of childhood trauma. Obenreizer cannot let go of his infancy and environmental triggers perpetuate his repetitive obsession with it. The sound of the waterfall turns into the voice of his enraged mother, brings forth questions of identity and sexual adultery. In turn, the same sound kindles in Obenreizer the wish to kill Vendale – his own, more successful rival and double with an equally unresolved identity and a passion for the same woman. Obenreizer and Vendale's fight happens in the snow, an 'interminable waste of deathly white', frozen, but water

---

[229] Ibid., 137.
[230] Ibid., 138.
[231] Ibid.
[232] Ibid., 191.

166   *Dickens and Switzerland*

nonetheless. How closely connected water, obsession and violence were for Dickens becomes clear in his letter to Annie Fields, the same in which he so affectingly describes his working environment in the chalet. He tells his friend about his ideas for the stage version of the story:

> I particularly want the drugging and attempted robbing in the bedroom scene at the Swiss inn to be done to the sound of a waterfall rising and falling with the wind. Although in the very opening of that scene they speak of the waterfall and listen to it, nobody thought of its mysterious music.[233]

Dickens's style is often perceived as visual, and even cinematic. Yet here, he is particularly interested in the auditive dimension of the scene. Dickens remains silent on the intended symbolism of the effect, but another letter makes it clear that he was especially intent on getting this scene right:

> I have an idea about the bedroom act, which I should certainly have suggested if I had been at our 'repetitions' here. I want it done to the sound of the Waterfall. I want the sound of the Waterfall louder and softer as the wind rises and falls, to be spoken through – like the music. I want the Waterfall listened to when spoken of, and not looked out at. The mystery and gloom of the scene would be greatly helped by this, and it would be new and picturesquely fanciful.[234]

Dickens's argument that 'the mystery and gloom of the scene would be greatly helped' by the sound of a waterfall and that it would be 'new and picturesquely fanciful' appears like a suggestion, but his obstinate repetition of 'I want' makes it clear that this is nothing less than a demand.

In *Little Dorrit*, it is vaporised water, cloud and snow which connect the living and the dead: 'silently assembled in a grated house, half a dozen paces removed, with the same cloud enfolding them, and the same snow flakes drifting in upon them, were the dead travellers found upon the mountain'.[235] The house of the dead is just another cell in this novel of prisons, yet it also stands as a symbol of a parallel world of the dead, unnoticed by the living. Morgues held an irresistible attraction to Dickens, as he admits in 'Travelling Abroad': 'Whenever I am at Paris, I am dragged by invisible force

---

[233] To Mrs. J. T. Fields, 25 May 1868, *Letters*, vol. 12, 120.
[234] To Charles Fechter, 22 May 1868, *Letters*, vol. 12, 116.
[235] Dickens, *Little Dorrit*, 421.

into the Morgue. I never want to go there, but am always pulled there.'[236] Others have already commented on Dickens's obsession with the Paris morgue, but only few critics seem to have noticed the parallels to the morgue on top of the Alpine pass.[237] On the pass, the Parisian 'children in arms with little pointing fingers' can be paralleled to the 'Blackened skeleton arms of wood' pointing 'upward to the convent, as if the ghosts of former travellers overwhelmed by the snow, haunted the scene of their distress'.[238]

In *David Copperfield*, water and death bear another memory of Switzerland. Back in England, the protagonist contemplates the sea:

> Out at sea, beyond my window, the wind blew ruggedly from the north. I had been thinking of it, sweeping over those mountain wastes of snow in Switzerland, then inaccessible to any human foot; and had been speculating which was the lonelier, those solitary regions, or a deserted ocean.[239]

Solitude also appears to be the key attraction in Fascination Fledgeby and Jenny Wren's exchange on the rooftop in London, which becomes a metaphorical rather than an actual elevation. Fledgeby's refusal to accept Jenny's statement that it is the 'quiet, and the air' which allows them some rest from the city below, triggers another explanation:

> 'Ah!' said Jenny. 'But it's so high. And you see the clouds rushing on above the narrow streets, not minding them, and you see the golden arrows pointing at the mountains in the sky from which the wind comes, and you feel as if you were dead'.

In *Our Mutual Friend*, the pointing skeleton arms have been replaced with golden arrows whereas Alpine peaks have found their urban equivalent in the 'mountains in the sky'. As in *David Copperfield*, the wind is the unaltered link, connecting metaphorical and actual mountain space. It was on the St Bernard that Dickens 'thought for a moment I had died in the night and passed into the unknown world'.[240]

In the 1850s, Dickens had repeatedly told Forster that he wanted to get away and live 'in all sorts of inaccessible places' and continue

---

[236] Dickens, 'Travelling Abroad', 89.
[237] See, for example, Stone, *Night Side of Dickens*, 88 ff; Carey, *The Violent Effigy*, 80ff.
[238] Dickens, 'Railway Dreaming', in *Dent Uniform Edition of Dickens' Journalism*, vol. 3, 375.
[239] Dickens, *David Copperfield*, 734.
[240] To Forster, ?6 September 1846, *Letters*, vol. 4, 618.

his work on some 'remote elevation above the level of the sea'.[241] He contemplated going to Switzerland and living among the monks, the dogs and, perhaps, the dead he had seen in the Alps. It was, perhaps, the same solitude, loneliness, detachment and escape that Dickens sought when he was complaining of the 'restlessness' which had got hold of him. In his later fiction, Switzerland comes to the fore in lonely offices, on solitary morning walks, in daydreaming fancies and identity-seeking business trips. Its treatment is more earnest and equally unexpected as in earlier fiction. Yet, the sudden appearance of Switzerland is no longer comic or humorous, as it often was in the 1840s and occasionally in the 1850s. It is now often unsettling and contemplates the boundaries between life and death. If Dickens did not return to Switzerland in or around January 1863 – or later in the 1860s – the reason for claiming that he was going to in some of his letters may not just have been a pretext but also an indicator of where he would have liked to find some recreation and rest. The cluster of claims in January 1863 also show that, to Dickens's family and friends, it seemed a credible and likely place for him to go. If Switzerland featured in connection with popular entertainment in early Dickens, he seems to have reimagined it as somewhat of a retreat in his later work. 'Swiss' space promised to be a productive haven, whether it was in Switzerland itself or in his garden chalet at Gad's Hill.

[241] To Forster, ?29 September 1854, *Letters*, vol. 4, 428.

More Perspectives on Dickens and Switzerland: A Conclusion

If I have not gone to foreign countries, young man, foreign countries have come to me.

The Mystery of Edwin Drood, Chapter 4

Both at Their Best, or Dickens and Switzerland

In November 1846, Dickens's departure to Paris was imminent after five months in Lausanne. In one of the last letters he sent from Switzerland he confessed to Forster:

> I have no doubt that constant change, too, is indispensable to me when I am at work: and at times something more than a doubt will force itself upon me whether there is not something in a Swiss valley that disagrees with me. Certainly, whenever I live in Switzerland again, it shall be on the hill-top. Something of the *goître* and *crétin* influence seems to settle on my spirits sometimes, on the lower ground. How sorry, ah yes! how sorry I shall be to leave the little society nevertheless. We have been thoroughly good-humoured and agreeable together, and I'll always give a hurrah for the Swiss and Switzerland.[1]

The passage nicely summarises Dickens's complex and ambivalent fascination with the country. It demonstrates both his appreciation ('I'll always give a hurrah for the Swiss and Switzerland') as well as his difficulties and doubts ('whether there is not something in a Swiss valley that disagrees with me'). Dickens does not elaborate

---

[1] To Forster, 13 November 1846, *Letters*, vol. 4, 656.

on the 'something' which seems to disagree with him and in what way it does – another characteristic of Dickens's attitude towards the country. As outlined in Chapter 2, goitres and 'cretinism' were attributed to a valley's supposed static air and confined water, yet Dickens's claim that 'Something of the *goître* and *crétin* influence' which seems to 'settle on my spirits sometimes' sounds rather as if Dickens was discussing a strictly personal rather than general phenomenon.[2] The frequent goitres in Dickens's most explicit texts on Switzerland may be a fictionalised symptom of this concern. Oddly enough, despite the 'something' which disagrees with him, Dickens never questioned his decision to live in Switzerland. Nor does there seem to have been any doubt as to whether he was going to live in Switzerland again. He writes 'whenever', rather than 'if ever' he will 'live in Switzerland again' he was going to do so on the hilltop, rather than in the valley. In Chapter 3 we saw that Dickens did indeed dream of returning to Switzerland in the 1850s. Interestingly enough, his urge to return sprang up precisely in those moments when life became difficult and 'something' disagreed with him.

More Confidences than One, or Dickens and the St Bernard Monastery

Dickens was deeply suspicious of Switzerland's Catholic cantons, even though he found the most spectacular scenes of 'awful beauty that is most sublime' in the Valais and the Ticino.[3] He wrote to Forster:

> On the Protestant side, neatness; cheerfulness; industry; education; continual aspiration, at least, after better things. On the Catholic side, dirt, disease, ignorance, squalor, and misery. I have so constantly observed the like of this, since I first came abroad, that I have a sad misgiving that the religion of Ireland lies as deep at the root of all its sorrows, even as English misgovernment and Tory villainy.[4]

Despite this anti-Catholic attitude, he was 'beset by my former notions of a book whereof the whole story shall be on top of the Great St. Bernard'.[5] He wanted to spend 'a whole winter' with these

---

[2] See Chapter 2, 113ff.
[3] To Forster, 15 June 1846, *Letters*, vol. 4, 320.
[4] To Forster, 24 and 25 August 1846, *Letters*, vol. 4, 611. See Chapter 2, 110 for the first part of this excerpt.
[5] To Forster, 20 January 1856, *Letters*, vol. 8, 33.

More Perspectives on Dickens and Switzerland: A Conclusion   **171**

Catholic 'Monks and the Dogs' on the pass, imagining himself – and his new story – 'among the blinding snows that fall about that monastery' at various points in time during 1850s.[6] In this respect, 'To Be Read at Dusk', the story set on top of the St Bernard Pass bears the preliminary, tentative feel of a first attempt or draft for such a plot. This is further emphasised by the story's brevity. In this light, the Swiss opening of the second book in *Little Dorrit* seems to be just another such experiment, as if it were a further study of whether and how such a story could be told.

It appears that it could not, or at least not in the time before Dickens's premature death in 1870. However, *The Mystery of Edwin Drood* may have some remainders of Dickens's fascination with the monastery on top of the mountain. The story is set in a 'city of another and a bygone time' and the plot takes place in and around a former convent and monastery.[7] John Jasper complains of the 'cramped monotony of [his] existence' which grinds him 'away by the grain'. He continues:

> The echoes of my own voice among the arches seem to mock me with my daily grudging round. No wretched monk who droned his life away in that gloomy place, before me, can have been more tired of it than I am. He could take for relief (and did take) to carving demons out of the stalls and seats and desks. What shall I do? Must I take to carving them out of my heart?[8]

There are no longer any monks in Cloisterham, but nuns instead, of whom the narrator wonders 'whether they were ever walled up alive in odd angles and jutting gables of the building', like the dead travellers Dickens found in the morgue on top the St Bernard.[9] Durdles, the stonemason, 'goes continually sounding and tapping all about and about the Cathedral', looking for dead bodies and stone coffins in the walls.[10] He also seems to find an attraction in getting 'stoned' himself, as he hires Deputy, the 'hideous small boy' to throw stones at him.[11] There is an ancient vineyard, 'belonging to what was once the Monastery'.[12] Wine, as we have seen, is part of the Swiss

---

[6] Ibid.

[7] Charles Dickens, *The Mystery of Edwin Drood*, ed. Margaret Cardwell (Oxford: Clarendon Press, 1972), 14.

[8] Ibid., 11.

[9] Ibid., 15.

[10] Ibid., 29.

[11] Ibid., 32.

[12] Ibid., 36.

172   *Dickens and Switzerland*

descriptions in *Little Dorrit* and also plays an important role in *No Thoroughfare*. The imagery of wine or blood appears in other Swiss narratives as well and is particularly strong in 'To Be Read at Dusk'.

A more straightforward connection is Dickens's recycling of an idea in *The Mystery of Edwin Drood* which he had already used in *The Battle of Life*, the Christmas Story he wrote in Lausanne in 1846. In 'Oral Dickens', Ian Watt points out that in Dickens's second 'gastric phase', which he places between 1844 and 1857, 'there is less simple celebration of the pleasures of the table, while the appetites are presented in a much larger psychological and social perspective'.[13] He introduces an uncomfortable, sometimes even uncanny dimension to eating and the act of consumption. As outlined in Chapter 2, in *The Battle of Life*, a grotesque, cannibalistic link is established between the dead bodies rotting on and into the soil where the bloody battle was fought and the people living on and from the crops of this land up to the time when the story is set. Nourishment and death go hand in hand in this location. Cloisterham is not too dissimilar to this description, as it is

> A monotonous, silent city, deriving an earthy flavour throughout from its Cathedral crypt, and so abounding in vestiges of monastic graves, that the Cloisterham children grow small salad in the dust of abbots and abbesses, and make dirt-pies of nuns and friars; while every ploughman in its outlying fields renders to once puissant Lord Treasurers, Archbishops, Bishops, and such-like, the attention which the Ogre in the story-book desired to render to his unbidden visitor, and grinds their bones to make his bread.[14]

Cannibalism is a frequent theme in Dickens's writing and not specific to 'Swiss' texts, of course.[15] What is specific, however, is the connection of an old guilt being passed on to the next generations through the soil fertilised with the bones and blood of dead bodies by indirect cannibalism. Most explicit in *The Battle of Life*, but oddly present in various texts implicitly or explicitly dealing with Catholicism, is Dickens's depiction of a cannibalistic tradition being passed on from generation to generation. The generations following the one causing or experiencing some sort of 'lapse' quite literally feed from the dead bodies of their forefathers, perpetuating thus a particular form of guilt. What characterises Durdles, the stonemason of Cloisterham, is

---

[13] Watt, 'Oral Dickens', 167.
[14] Dickens, *The Mystery of Edwin Drood*, 14.
[15] See, for example: Carey, *The Violent Effigy*, 22ff; Stone, *Night Side of Dickens*, 3ff.

More Perspectives on Dickens and Switzerland: A Conclusion   **173**

that he 'leads a hazy, gipsy sort of life, carrying his dinner about with him in a small bundle, and sitting on all manner of tombstones to dine'.[16] Dickens's strange fascination with this idea is also reflected in his *Memoranda*, where he once noted:

> 'There is some virtue in him too.'
> 'Virtue! Yes. So there is in any grain of seed in a seedsman's shop – but you must put it in the ground before you can get any good out of it.'
> 'Do you mean that *he* must be put in the ground before any good comes of *him*?'
> 'Indeed I do. You may call it burying him or you may call it sowing him, but as you like. You must set him in the earth, before you get any good of him.'[17]

This is an odd passage and stands as an isolated entry in Dickens's notes. The idea is one that he used several times in his writing, never finding a moment to include this particular quote though.

More metaphorically, this cannibalistic tradition is also present in *Little Dorrit*, where, during vintage time, 'Grapes, spilt and crushed under foot, lay about everywhere'.[18] The Valais, where the St Bernard stands, is the Catholic canton which Dickens knew best and which, in his letters, served as the prime example for his criticism of the faith in Switzerland. From the child 'carried in a sling by the laden peasant-woman' to the 'idiot sunning his big goître' and the cows and goats whose breath was 'redolent of leaves and stalks of grapes', everyone is partaking in a carnivalesque feast which causes a grotesque breakdown of class and animal–human distinctions. That there is an unhealthy dimension to this event becomes evident in the last sentence of the paragraph: 'A pity that no ripe touch of this generous abundance could be given to the thin, hard, stoney wine, which after all was made from the grapes!'[19] As discussed in Chapter 2, there is a reflection of this scene in *A Tale of Two Cities*, where a cask of wine breaks which causes a similar breakdown of boundaries.[20] In the novel's passage, the link between wine and blood is made explicit and unsurprisingly, the scene once more occurs in a Catholic location. The 'idiot', the goitre-ridden 'crétin' and the mother or nurse suckling a child are

[16] Dickens, *The Mystery of Edwin Drood*, 29.
[17] Dickens, *Memoranda*, 4. Emphasis in original.
[18] Dickens, *Little Dorrit*, 419.
[19] Ibid.
[20] See Chapter 2, 109.

174   *Dickens and Switzerland*

characters which also appear often when Dickens writes about Catholicism.

There is more evidence that his 1846 stay in Switzerland prompted Dickens to reflect on religious differences. When Dickens was in Lausanne, the first conflicts between Catholics and Protestants started to emerge. It was the only 'revolution' Dickens witnessed almost first-hand. He told Forster:

> And if I were a Swiss with a hundred thousand pounds, I would be as steady against the Catholic cantons and the propagation of Jesuitism as any radical among 'em: believing the dissemination of Catholicity to be the most horrible means of political and social degradation left in the world. Which these people, thoroughly well educated, know perfectly ... The boys of Geneva were very useful in bringing materials for the construction of the barricades on the bridges; and the enclosed song may amuse you. They sing it to a tune that dates from the great French revolution – a very good one.[21]

The song, which Dickens enclosed to Forster, since it dates from the 'great French revolution', provides further support for the biographer's claim that some of the mental work Dickens had done during the five months in Switzerland eventually became material for *A Tale of Two Cities*.[22]

In Lausanne, Dickens was also inspired to write his own version of the New Testament for his children, *The Life of Our Lord*. He expected his offspring to take the text seriously, as a letter to one of his sons, Henry Fielding Dickens, who was nineteen years old in 1868 when the letter was written, illustrates:

> As your brothers have gone away one by one, I have written to each of them what I am now going to write to you. You know that you have never been hampered with religious forms of restraint, and that with mere unmeaning forms I have no sympathy. But I most strongly and affectionately impress upon you the priceless value of the New Testament, and the study of that book as the one unfailing guide in Life. Deeply respecting it, and bowing down before the character of Our Saviour, as separated from the vain constructions and inventions of men, you cannot go very wrong and will always preserve at heart a true spirit of veneration and humility. Similarly, I impress upon you the habit of saying a Christian prayer every night and morning. These things have stood by me all through my life, and you remember that

---

[21] To Forster, 20 October 1846, *Letters*, vol. 4, 639.
[22] See Chapter 2, 83.

More Perspectives on Dickens and Switzerland: A Conclusion **175**

I tried to render the New Testament intelligible to you and loveable by you when you were a mere baby.[23]

The Life of Our Lord was written for the Dickens children as part of their educational canon. It was a personal piece, too personal for publication: 'In the last year of his life, when asked by Georgina to consider having it privately printed, CD reread the MS and took "a week or two to consider" before deciding against it'.[24] More than eighty years after it had been written, the *Life* was finally released for publication.

Philanthropy in Minor Canon Corner, or Dickens and Swiss Institutions

Dickens's own emotional response and attitude to Switzerland was similarly private. His engagement with Switzerland touched upon both his private life and authorship. Even though these had many points of contact, they were by no means identical. Many of Dickens's personal 'Swiss' concerns and interests are not directly or only very implicitly reflected in his 'Swiss' fiction. The political and religious dimensions have already been mentioned, but Dickens also took great interest in Swiss institutions – as he had already done in the USA and elsewhere.[25] He was particularly fascinated with prisons and as we have seen in Chapter 2, it was in Switzerland that he came up with the idea that 'good Christmas characters might be grown out of the idea of a man imprisoned for ten or fifteen years'.[26] Prisons and long imprisonments became one of the central motifs in *Little Dorrit* and *A Tale of Two Cities*, texts which feature other links to Switzerland as well. Prisons were of interest to him long before Dickens came to Switzerland, but it was from here, only a week or so after he had moved his entire household to Lausanne, that he wrote to Lord Morpeth:

I wish to confide to you, a very earnest desire of mine, and to leave it entirely to your discretion and inclination, whether it shall remain a point in confidence between yourself and me, or whether you shall communicate it, at your own time, to anyone else.

---

[23] To Henry Dickens, 15 October 1868, *Letters*, vol. 12, 202.
[24] To Forster, ?28 June 1846, *Letters*, vol. 4, 573n2.
[25] See, for example, to Forster, 25–26 July 1846, *Letters*, vol. 4, 590.
[26] To Forster, 25–26 July 1846, *Letters*, vol. 4, 590.

176   *Dickens and Switzerland*

> I have an ambition for some public employment – some Commissionership, or Inspectorship, or the like, connected with any of those subjects in which I take a deep interest, and in respect of which the Public are generally disposed to treat me with confidence and regard. On any questions connected with the Education of the People, the elevation of their character, the improvement of their dwellings, their greater protection against disease and vice – or with the treatment of Criminals, or the administration of Prison Discipline, which I have long observed closely – I think I could do good service, and I am sure I should enter with my whole heart. I have hoped, for years, that I may become at last a Police Magistrate, and turn my social knowledge to good practical account from day to day; and I have the strongest hope that in any such position as I have glanced at, I could prove my fitness for improving the execution of that trust. It is not a very towering ambition perhaps; but never was a man's ambition so peculiarly associated with his constant sympathies – and, as I fancy, with his capabilities – as this of mine.[27]

It is a remarkable letter, as for once we do not see Dickens in charge, but asking for a favour. In essence, the passage is both a confession and an application for something which is 'not a very towering ambition perhaps', but one for which Dickens not only expresses 'deep interest' but also a talent, having the 'strongest hope' that in such a position he could prove his 'fitness for improving the execution of that trust'.

However, this extract is not only interesting in terms of how Dickens, in his ongoing fascination with prisons, phrased a text which hovers between being a 'confidence' and a request. It is also significant in relation to his last completed novel, *Our Mutual Friend*. In it, we meet a Night-Inspector who is likened to a monk, 'posting up his books in a whitewashed office, as studiously as if he were in a monastery on top of a mountain, and no howling fury of a drunken woman were banging herself against a cell-door in the back-yard at his elbow'.[28] Dickens's 'ambition for some public employment – some Commissionership, or Inspectorship, or the like', his interest in public institutions, his fascination with deviant, violent and even criminal characters, as well as his preference for seemingly unprovoked references to Switzerland all come together here. In the light of what I have discussed above, they suddenly 'make sense' and acquire a meaning beyond the fictional. It is as if almost twenty years after Dickens mentioned this 'point in confidence', a shadow, or a ghost

[27] To Lord Morpeth, 20 June 1846, *Letters*, vol. 4, 566–7.
[28] Dickens, *Our Mutual Friend*, 33.

More Perspectives on Dickens and Switzerland: A Conclusion   **177**

of his old self resurfaced as one of his characters. His former wish to live among the monks and the dogs on top of the St Bernard had still not materialised beyond the stage of a simile or a metaphor, and yet, creating the figure of the Night-Inspector allowed him to embody this character with visions of an *alter ego* he had imagined for himself. Since nothing came out of his wish for public employment with Lord Morpeth, Dickens found another, similar project to turn to. With the support of his wealthy and influential friend, the heiress Angela Burdett Coutts, Dickens founded Urania Cottage, a home for so-called fallen women.[29]

Even though such a project had been on his mind before he moved to Switzerland, some of his closest friends in Lausanne showed Dickens how such a philanthropical institution could be managed and run.[30] Frédéric Recordon (who does not figure in Dickens's letters and whom he might not have known), William Haldimand and Miss Elisabeth de Cerjat founded the 'Asile des Aveugles', the Asylum for the Blind, in 1843.[31] Dickens was a frequent visitor and took great interest in some of the inmates, describing them and their progress to Forster in great detail. He visited the institution again in 1853, when he was travelling in the country with Wilkie Collins and Augustus Egg. Yet, unlike the St Bernard monastery, his interest in the Asile does not seem to have found entry into his fiction, but was redirected towards his own project at Urania Cottage.

Philanthropy, Professional and Unprofessional, or Mesmerism and Switzerland

Just as Dickens's interest in the Asylum for the Blind in Lausanne was not discussed in depth in any of the chapters of this book, there are other subjects which, due to their more theoretical or broad contextual implications, have not been exhausted or mentioned. One of them is Dickens and education in relation to Switzerland. He had found the Swiss well educated and mentions this on occasion in his letters, but had probably come in contact with at least one other Swiss influence. Malcolm Andrews has outlined how strongly Jean-Jacques Rousseau had influenced Victorian 'morality', an aspect of culture Dickens

[29] On this subject, see Jenny Hartley, *Charles Dickens and the House of Fallen Women* (London: Methuen, 2008).
[30] See to Miss Burdett Coutts, 26 May 1846, *Letters*, vol. 4, 552.
[31] See to Forster, ?28 June 1846, *Letters*, vol. 4, 574n2. Recordon is not mentioned here, however.

certainly had not been able to avoid.[32] In a letter, Dickens also quotes Rousseau as a source for a passage in *A Tale of Two Cities*.[33]

There are also Swiss links in the room-dividing screen which Macready and Dickens created together at Sherbourne House in Dorchester. Decorated with prints cut out from periodicals, there are several images relating to Switzerland: there are various pictures of alpine scenes with mountains and waterfalls. Many of them come from a book called *Illustrations of the Passes of the Alps by which Italy communicates with France, Switzerland and Germany* by William Brockedon.[34] Most of the images are picturesque landscape and architectural scenes or portraits of famous personalities, or refer to moments in literature and drama. Some are reproductions of antique art. Depending on when the screen was made, Brockedon was another early source about Switzerland for Dickens before he travelled there. On the screen, we also find a portrait of Calvin, the French Protestant reformer who lived in Geneva, for example, and an image entitled 'The Swiss Peasant Girl', which seems to be an illustration to a short story by Mary Shelley.[35] There is 'The Rhine Falls with Schloss Laufen' in Switzerland, 'The Witch of the Alps' from Byron's poem 'Manfred' and the 'Colonne de Joux, and Hospice of the Little Saint Bernard'.[36]

Another subject which has remained unexplored is Dickens's involvement with, his belief in and occasional practice of two pseudosciences, physiognomy and mesmerism. Johann Kaspar Lavater, born in Zurich in 1741, is generally seen as the founder of physiognomy and its redevelopment into phrenology. He made some influential friends in Germany such as Goethe. His works found 'several translators in England', among them Henry Fuseli, the Swiss painter.[37] Michael Hollington speaks of Lavater's studies as 'a major Swiss intellectual influence in [Dickens's] fiction', which is 'ubiquitous throughout his work'.[38] Hollington might be somewhat optimistic in this claim, but there certainly are a great number of references to physical traits in Dickens's work. Lavater was left

---

[32] Andrews in Schlicke, *Oxford Reader's Companion to Dickens*, 90.

[33] To Bulwer Lytton, 5 June 1860, *Letters*, vol. 4, 259.

[34] William Brockedon, *Illustrations of the Passes of the Alps by which Italy communicates with France, Switzerland and Germany* (London: Rodwell et al., 1829).

[35] Images 4.44 and 2.34 on the University of Kent's website are dedicated to the screen, accessed 31 January 2024: www.kent.ac.uk/macready/macready-screen.html

[36] Ibid., images 2.72; 3.54; 4.59.

[37] Dinah Birch, ed., *The Oxford Companion to English Literature*, 7th ed. (Oxford: Oxford University Press, 2009), 576.

[38] Hollington, in Schlicke, *Oxford Reader's Companion to Dickens*, 559.

More Perspectives on Dickens and Switzerland: A Conclusion **179**

undiscussed here because his nationality was irrelevant to his influence. The same is true for Franz (or Friedrich) Anton Mesmer, who was born and died in Germany, had studied in Vienna but also acquired Swiss citizenship.[39] He is often referred to as German, but the *Oxford Illustrated Companion to Medicine* calls him Swiss.[40] In *Dickens and Mesmerism*, Fred Kaplan points out that

> early in the 1820's [*sic*] phrenology, whose fortunes were soon to be closely allied with those of mesmerism, came to England as part of the larger interest in the relationship between mind and matter. Dickens' friend, John Elliotson, the Englishman most responsible for the 'mesmeric mania' in England, founded and became the first president of the London Phrenological Society in 1824.[41]

Elliotson was not just Dickens's friend, but also his family doctor. It was he who introduced Dickens to Townshend on the occasion of a dinner in 1840.[42] Townshend had published his *Facts in Mesmerism* the same year, which became one of the movement's key texts. The *Pilgrim* editors state that 'Dickens was clearly very fond of Townshend: he had dedicated *Great Expectations* to him and given him the MS'.[43] Kaplan asserts that 'Townshend was aggressive in his courting of Dickens' in that he presented to him 'a sonnet addressed to "Man of the genial mind!"'[44] Kaplan's choice of the word 'courting' may be deliberately ambiguous. Townshend, a 'self-confessed hypochondriac', was married between 1826 and 1843, but separated from his wife in 1845 due to 'unhappy differences'.[45] There were no children and in descriptions, his physical appeal is hinted at suspiciously frequently, at least pointing at sexual ambivalence. Bulwer Lytton, who went to school with him, said of Townshend that 'His beauty of Countenance was remarkable at that time. Those who knew Byron said it was Byron with bloom and health. He grew plain in later life – an accomplished man – but effeminate and mildly selfish [...] an "amiable sybarite"'.[46]

---

[39] *Historisches Lexikon der Schweiz*, online version, s.v. 'Mesmer, Franz Anton'.

[40] Stephen Lock, et al., *The Oxford Illustrated Companion to Medicine* (Oxford: Oxford University Press, 2001), 487.

[41] Fred Kaplan, *Dickens and Mesmerism. The Hidden Springs of Fiction* (Princeton, NJ: Princeton University Press, 1975), 13.

[42] Ibid., 58.

[43] Storey, Preface to *Letters*, vol. 12, xvin1.

[44] Ibid., 59.

[45] *Oxford Dictionary of National Biography*, s.v. 'Townshend, Chauncy Hare'.

[46] Edward Bulwer Lytton, qtd. in Leslie Mitchell, *Bulwer Lytton, The Rise and Fall of a Victorian Man of Letters* (London: Hambledon and London, 2003), 98.

180 *Dickens and Switzerland*

Indeed, Kaplan confirms that Dickens 'could not have been unaware of Townshend's predilection for male relationships'.[47] A closer analysis of *No Thoroughfare* might even discern an echo of Townshend's character in Jules Obenreizer, the 'robustly made, well proportioned' male with 'handsome features' who renders Vendale a rather queer visit one night in Switzerland.[48] Kaplan points out that 'Evil has its own dynamic in the Dickens world, inseparable from sexual needs'.[49] Even though Obenreizer is in love with Marguerite, the object of his violent passion is Vendale. The two characters are in Basel when Obenreizer enters Vendale's room in the middle of the night, telling him about 'a bad dream about you'.[50] This is followed by a short but remarkable conversation revolving around the topic of dressing and undressing. Obenreizer asks: 'How is it that I see you up and dressed?' and Vendale answers: 'My good fellow, I may as well ask you how it is that I see *you* up and undressed?'[51] Obenreizer repeats that he has had a bad dream and speaks of a restlessness which prevents him from going back to sleep. His appearance is ruffled, as if he had been in a fight, and great emphasis is put on the body parts which are naked:

> His feet were bare; his red-flannel shirt was thrown back at the throat, and its sleeves were rolled above the elbows; his only other garment, a pair of under pantaloons or drawers, reaching to the ankles, fitted him close and tight.[52]

Exposed throats, arms and ankles are body parts which were – and perhaps still are – traditionally seen as erotic, as these were the only parts where mid-Victorian garments would allow glimpses of the wearer's skin. These eroticised parts of the body are frequently of importance in terms of female beauty.

Obenreizer confesses that his dream was about Vendale and that it also involved a fight: 'If there had been a wrestle with a robber, as I dreamed,' said Obenreizer, 'you see, I was stripped for it.'[53] Vendale's role in this dream remains unclear and poses the question of whether Obenreizer was protecting him from an anonymous robber or if, in fact, it was a struggle between the two of them. Immediately after

---

[47] Kaplan, *Dickens and Mesmerism*, 198.
[48] Collins and Dickens, *No Thoroughfare*, 139.
[49] Kaplan, *Dickens and Mesmerism*, 191.
[50] Collins and Dickens, *No Thoroughfare*, 194.
[51] Ibid., 194.
[52] Ibid., 195.
[53] Ibid.

More Perspectives on Dickens and Switzerland: A Conclusion   181

this, the conversation moves to even more explicitly eroticising references. Vendale, 'glancing at [Obenreizer's] girdle', notices that his opponent is 'armed, too', namely with a traveller's dagger, to which the Swiss, while 'half drawing it from its sheath with his left hand, and putting it back again', replies: 'Do you carry no such thing?' Vendale confirms twice that he carries 'Nothing of the kind'.[54] The Englishman has neither weapons nor candles, as his has 'burnt out', which induces Obenreizer, who still has 'a whole one in my room' to go and fetch his. Every object mentioned in the two men's conversation at this point is conspicuously phallic, with Obenreizer keeping the upper hand throughout the scene. Combined with the allusions to Obenreizer's ruffled clothes, his relative nakedness in symbolically charged parts of the body and his agitated state, the passage has a queer undertone to it. Once the dialogue on carrying weapons is over, Obenreizer admits that 'my fire has gone the way of your candle'.[55] In other words: it has burnt out too, after the Swiss villain discovers that Vendale is unable to stand up to him.

The *Oxford Dictionary of National Biography* claims that Townshend is now mainly remembered as a collector of precious stones and 'Swiss coins, cameos, photographs, drawings, and engravings'.[56] A great number of paintings by Swiss artists in the Victoria and Albert Museum are the bequest of Townshend, as he spent long periods of time living in Lausanne. When Townshend died in 1868, he had appointed Dickens as his 'literary executor' in his will, asking him to 'edit his religious opinions'. This was 'Not a particularly congenial task', the *Pilgrim* editors note, as these opinions were 'dispersed and fragmentary'.[57] Dickens was in America when the news of his friend's death reached him and he wrote from Buffalo: 'It is not a light thing to lose such a friend, and I truly loved him. [...] I never, never, never, never was better loved by man than I was by him, I am sure. Poor dear fellow, good affectionate gentle creature.'[58]

There is yet another 'Swiss' connection in Dickens's interest in mesmerism. In 1844, when Dickens moved to Genoa, he met the de la Rues, a Swiss banker and his English-born wife. Kaplan dramatically states that 'Even before the Dickens entourage arrived in Italy, the de la Rues were part of their fate'.[59] Emile de La Rue was an intimate of

[54] Ibid.
[55] Ibid., 195.
[56] *Oxford Dictionary of National Biography*, s.v. 'Townshend, Chauncy Hare'.
[57] Storey, Preface to *Letters*, vol. 12, xvi and xvin1.
[58] To Georgina Hogarth, 12 March 1868, *Letters*, vol. 12, 72.
[59] Kaplan, *Dickens and Mesmerism*, 74.

182   *Dickens and Switzerland*

Cavour, and 'had contacts among the authorities at Turin; he knew the country and the language as if it were his own; he had the authority and reputation of a prominent banking firm of which he was the chief representative in Italy'.[60] Augusta de la Rue, on the other hand was 'something of an invalid during the 1830 and 1840s', suffering from 'a number of neurasthenic symptoms, including a nervous tic, convulsions, headaches, and insomnia'.[61] Eventually, 'Dickens and Madame de la Rue were deeply involved' in what Kaplan describes as 'a relationship of intensive mutual need that had suddenly broken the boundaries of normal rules of proportion'.[62] As with Lavater and Mesmer, the de la Rue's 'Swissness' did not seem to play a role in Dickens's approach or understanding of mesmerism though. Once more, the 'Swiss' links seem incidental, and yet there are too many to be ignored, even though they only offer loose ends. When Dickens was in Lausanne in 1846 he also seems to have 'magnetized a man at Lausanne among unbelievers, and stretched him on the dining-room floor'.[63] Nothing more is known of this event though and the episode appears as just another random occurrence. It highlights that despite the wealth of biographical evidence which Dickens's letters offer, they are by no means exhaustive as a source and are only a partial representation of Dickens's involvement with a particular issue.

A Gritty State of Things Comes On, or How Loose Ends Come Together

As the 'loose ends' discussed above indicate, Switzerland seems to connect different aspects of Dickens's interest in mesmerism. On a first glance they appear as entirely irrelevant. It is as if Switzerland had become some sort of setting for different scenes through which mesmerism and the role of 'Dickens the Mesmerist' are performed. The country has become a lens to discuss the topic of mesmerism and relate it to Dickens's life. In this book, unexpectedly frequent appearances of loose 'Swiss' threads have been put in perspective to nineteenth-century culture, Dickens's texts and biography. The result of this surprisingly rewarding search for 'Swiss' needles

---

[60] Ibid.

[61] To Forster, 17 and 18 November 1844, *Letters*, vol. 4, 223n2; 'mesmerism', Logan Delano Browning in Schlicke, *Oxford Reader's Companion to Dickens*, 383.

[62] Kaplan, *Dickens and Mesmerism*, 78.

[63] To Emile de la Rue, 24 March 1847, *Letters*, vol. 5, 43; see also to Douglas Jerrold, 24 October 1846, *Letters*, vol. 4, 645.

More Perspectives on Dickens and Switzerland: A Conclusion   **183**

in English haystacks is, as I have been hoping to show, not only greater but more substantial and more fascinating than the mere sum of its parts. 'Switzerland' and 'Swissness' – understood in the broadest terms as 'relating to Switzerland' – were integral parts of nineteenth-century popular culture associations, emotions and expectations.

Chapter 1 outlined how Dickens, like many other Victorians of the middle and upper classes who could afford and had been educated to appreciate the theatre, was introduced to a wide range of Swiss characters and plots in his childhood and youth. Dickens used terms connected to 'Swissness' even before he had set foot on Swiss soil for the first time in 1844. On the one hand, Dickens's references prior to his first visit to the country stem from this culturally modelled source of generic associations. Both the 'Swiss maid' and the 'Swiss peasant' were character types with particular functions on the stages of early nineteenth-century melodrama. Dickens had also met Swiss characters as comic sidekicks in the novels he read as a child. On the other hand, his knowledge also came from first-hand accounts, such as that of his wife's uncle, for whom he proofread *Two Journeys through Italy and Switzerland*.[64] To Dickens himself Switzerland also offered a sort of stage. It was the place where he began a new novel, wrote a Christmas Story and where he came up with a tremendous amount of new, creative material which he used later. In Lausanne, he also thought of writing an autobiography and going on public reading tours. His stay became a platform for self-discovery or at least a thorough reassessment of his own identity. Interestingly, in the 1858 preface he wrote for *Dombey* and in which he admits that he 'yet confusedly' imagines 'Captain Cuttle as secluding himself from Mrs. Mac Stinger among the mountains of Switzerland', he also describes Dombey as going through a development which is both similar and yet entirely opposite to that which he experienced in Lausanne himself:

> Mr. Dombey undergoes no violent internal change, either in this book, or in life. A sense of his injustice is within him all along. The more he represses it, the more unjust he necessarily is. Internal shame and external circumstances may bring the contest to the surface in a week, or a day; but it has been a contest for years, and is only fought out then, after a long balance of victory.[65]

---

[64] See Chapter 2, 70.
[65] Dickens, *Dombey and Son*, 834.

184 *Dickens and Switzerland*

It was in Switzerland where Dickens thought about his childhood and asked Forster whether he wanted to be his biographer. 'Internal shame', his experiences at the Blacking Factory and 'external circumstances', a particular walk in Geneva, had caused a crisis within himself as well. Switzerland therefore often figures as a stage for great emotional feeling and challenges identity. This is the case for some of the texts Dickens wrote in Switzerland, *Dombey* and *The Battle of Life*, but also whenever fiction relocates there, such as in *David Copperfield*, *Little Dorrit*, 'Lying Awake' and *The Uncommercial Traveller*'s 'Travelling Abroad', for example. As moments of self-discovery are limited to particular situations, this might also explain why Dickens never succeeded in – or decided against – setting a whole book in Switzerland. Just as in the books he read as a child, the theatricals he saw on stage as well as his own journeys, his references to Switzerland remain incidental and episodic. Switzerland offers a stage on which the main action can take place and develop, but in Dickens's fiction it is not an active part of the plot itself. Mrs General's introduction on top of the St Bernard in *Little Dorrit* is an example of this and outlines how this character cannot and will not develop, no matter whether she is taken 'to the top of the Alps and the bottom of Herculaneum'.[66] Switzerland offers a backdrop against which a particular set of stories progress, but the country itself is not problematised and explored. Switzerland never takes on the importance of France in *A Tale of Two Cities* or the United States in *Martin Chuzzlewit* because it seems to be a much less suitable setting in which to set a whole novel for Dickens. By contrast, Switzerland seemed to promise restoration, seclusion and resolution, both in fiction and real life.

Dickens's involvement with Switzerland was deeply personal. In terms of his own journeys, there is no evidence that he ever considered them in the light of the distinction between the 'tourist' and the traveller', which James Buzard outlines in *The Beaten Track*.[67] Dickens was aware of the difference, of course, however, and provides some examples in his fiction. The Dorrit family's continental journey in *Little Dorrit* as well as the character in 'Our Bore' are used to discuss their view of themselves as 'travellers' as opposed to others seeing them as mere 'tourists'. It does not seem to have been of any consequence to his experience of the country whether

---

[66] Dickens, *Little Dorrit*, 438.
[67] James Buzard, *The Beaten Track, European Tourism, Literature and the Ways to Culture, 1800–1918* (Oxford: Clarendon, 1993), 18ff.

More Perspectives on Dickens and Switzerland: A Conclusion   **185**

or not Switzerland was a popular destination for the English. He did comment on English acquaintances when he lived in Lausanne and mocked the 'preposterous, insolent little aristocracy of Geneva', but he did not mention many of his fellow travellers when he crossed the Simplon in 1844 and 1845, making it sound as if he had been on the trip on his own.[68] His journeys appear as highly individualistic, personal experiences in which he does not see himself as partaking in a mass phenomenon. The 'mass' are the Mrs Generals of this world, but not Dickens nor his feeling, sensitive protagonists. Switzerland offered Dickens a resource of lifelong inspiration of which the chalet at Gad's Hill as well as Linda, the St Bernard dog, were only the most obvious and visible symbols present at the time of his death. Switzerland had also been a physical, biographical experience through the performative acts of travelling and living there on at least four occasions. It became a personal memory and an abundant resource and playground for his imagination.

In this book I have attempted a *rethinking* of Switzerland in terms of Dickens. For the first time, this study looks at the major influences of Switzerland in Dickens's fiction, journalism and letters. It does not limit itself to Dickens's own encounters, but also takes into account the wider cultural perspective in which the country was represented in nineteenth-century England. Yet, this book has attempted to stay as biographical in its literary connections between Dickens and Switzerland as was necessary in such a first attempt. Most importantly, Switzerland was not merely an episode in Dickens's life between 1844 and 1853, but his interest and points of contact reach far beyond the few days and months he actually spent there. Even though his references to the country may appear incidental on the whole, there was deep psychological investment in the country, its people and his experiences there. So profound was this investment that it attained a peculiar perpetuity in the memory of Dickens.

[68] To John Forster, 11 October 1846, *Letters*, vol. 4, 633.

Bibliography

Primary Sources

Collins, Wilkie and Charles Dickens. *No Thoroughfare*. London: Chapman and Hall, 1890.

Dickens, Charles. *American Notes*. Ed. Patricia Ingham. London: Penguin, 2000.

—. *Barnaby Rudge*. Ed. John Bowen. London: Penguin, 2003.

—. *Bleak House*. Ed. Nicola Bradbury. London: Penguin, 2003.

—. *Charles Dickens' Book of Memoranda*. Ed. Fred Kaplan. New York: New York Public Library, 1981.

—. *Charles Dickens's Uncollected Writings from* Household Words, *1850–1859*. Ed. Harry Stone. Bloomington, IN: Indiana University Press, 1968, vol. 1.

—. *A Child's History of England* in *Master Humphrey's Clock and A Child's History of England*. London: Oxford University Press, 1963.

—. *The Christmas Books. Vol. 2: The Cricket on the Hearth, The Battle of Life, The Haunted Man*. Ed. Michael Slater. London: Penguin, 1971.

—. *A Christmas Carol, and Other Christmas Writings*. Ed. Michael Slater. London: Penguin, 2003.

—. *David Copperfield*. Ed. Nina Burgis. Oxford: Clarendon Press, 1981.

—. *Dickens in Europe*. Ed. Rosalind Vallance. London: Folio, 1975.

—. *Dombey and Son*. Ed. Alan Horsman. Oxford: Clarendon Press, 1974.

—. *Great Expectations*. Ed. Edgar Rosenberg. New York: Norton, 1999.

—. *Hard Times*. Ed. Kate Flint. London: Penguin, 2003.

—. *The Dent Uniform Edition of Dickens's Journalism. Vol. 2: The Amusements of the People and Other Papers: Reports, Essays and Reviews, 1834–51*. Ed. Michael Slater. London: J. M. Dent, 1996.

—. *The Dent Uniform Edition of Dickens's Journalism. Vol. 3: 'Gone Astray' and Other Papers from* Household Words *1851–59*. Ed. Michael Slater. London: J. M. Dent, 1998.

—. *The Dent Uniform Edition of Dickens' Journalism. Vol. 4: 'The Uncommercial Traveller' and Other Papers, 1859–70*. Ed. Michael Slater and John Drew. London: J. M. Dent, 2000.

—. *The Letters of Charles Dickens*. Ed. Madeline House, Graham Storey, Kathleen Tillotson et al. The Pilgrim Edition. 12 vols. Oxford: Clarendon Press, 1965–2002.

—. *The Life of our Lord*. New York: Simon & Schuster, 1934.

—. *Little Dorrit*. Ed. Harvey Peter Sucksmith. Oxford: Clarendon Press, 1979.

—. *Martin Chuzzlewit*. Ed. Margaret Cardwell. Oxford: Clarendon Press, 1982.

—. *Memoirs of Joseph Grimaldi. Edited by 'Boz'. A New Edition with Notes and Additions, Revised by Charles Whitehead*. London: Routledge & Co., 1853.

—. *Mudfog Papers*. Gloucester: Alan Sutton, 1987.

—. *The Mystery of Edwin Drood*. Ed. Margaret Cardwell. Oxford: Clarendon Press, 1972.

—. *Nicholas Nickleby*. Ed. Mark Ford. London: Penguin, 1999.

—. *The Old Curiosity Shop*. Ed. Elizabeth M. Brennan. Oxford: Clarendon Press, 1997.

—. *Oliver Twist*. Ed. Kathleen Tillotson. Oxford: Oxford University Press, 1982.

—. *Our Mutual Friend*. Ed. Adrian Poole. London: Penguin, 1997.

—. *The Pickwick Papers*. Ed. James Kinsley. Oxford: Oxford University Press, 2008.

—. *Pictures from Italy*. Ed. Kate Flint. London: Penguin, 1998.

—. *Selected Short Fiction*. Ed. Deborah A. Thomas. London: Penguin, 1985.

—. *Sketches by Boz*. Ed. Dennis Walder. London: Penguin, 1995.

—. *A Tale of Two Cities*. Oxford: Oxford University Press, 2008.

—. *The Uncommercial Traveller*. Ed. Daniel Tyler. Oxford: Oxford University Press, 2015.

Forster, John. *The Life of Charles Dickens*. The Fireside Edition. London: Chapman & Hall, Ltd.; and Henry Frowde, *c*.1904 [undated].

—. *The Life of Charles Dickens*. London: Chapman and Hall, 1873, vol. 2.

Stonehouse, J. H., ed. *Catalogue of the Library of Charles Dickens from Gad's Hill*. London: Piccadilly Fountain Press, 1935. Facsimile reprint in Japan by Takashi Terauchi, 2003.

Online Resources

Dickens Journals Online. Ed. John Drew et al. *Household Words* and *All the Year Round*. www.djo.org.uk/

Historisches Lexikon der Schweiz. https://hls-dhs-dss.ch/

The Victorian Literary Studies Archive, Hyper-Concordance, Graduate School of Languages and Cultures, Nagoya University, Japan. http://victorian-studies.net/concordance/dickens/

The Charles Dickens Letters Project. Ed. Leon Litvack, Emily Bell, Lydia Craig and Jeremy Parrott (London: Dickens Fellowship). https://dickensletters.com/project-team

Secondary Sources

Ackroyd, Peter. *Dickens*. London: Sinclair-Stevenson, 1990.
—. *Wilkie Collins*. London: Vintage, 2013.
Adler, Judith. 'Travel as Performed Art'. *American Journal of Sociology* 94, no. 6 (1989): 1366–91.
Alexander, William Lindsay. *Switzerland and Swiss Churches*. Glasgow: James Maclehose, 1846.
Allen, Michael. *Charles Dickens and the Blacking Factory*. Oxford: Oxford Stockley, 2011.
Altick, Richard. *The Shows of London*. Cambridge, MA: Belknap, 1978.
Andrews, Malcolm. *Charles Dickens and His Performing Selves: Dickens and the Public Readings*. Oxford: Oxford University Press, 2006.
—. *Dickensian Laughter: Essays on Dickens and Humour*. Oxford: Oxford University Press, 2013.
—. *The Picturesque*. Mountfield: Helm Information, 1994.
Anon. *Dialogue, & c. in the Grand, Romantic, Domestic, Tragi-Comic Christmas Pantomime, Entitled Harlequin and William Tell*. London: S. G. Fairbrother, 1842.
Armstrong, Nancy. *Fiction in the Age of Photography*. Cambridge, MA: Harvard University Press, 1999.
Auerbach, Nina. *Private Theatricals*. Cambridge, MA: Harvard University Press, 1990.
Axton, William. *Circle of Fire: Dickens's Vision and Style and the Popular Victorian Theatre*. Lexington: University of Kentucky Press, 1966.
Beattie, Andrew. *The Alps. A Cultural History*. Oxford: Oxford University Press, 2006.
Beavan, Darren. 'Mountain Thoroughfares: Charles Dickens and the Alps'. *Dickens Quarterly* 29, no. 2 (2012): 151–61.
—. *Cultural Climbs: John Ruskin, Albert Smith and the Alpine Aesthetic*. Saarbrücken: VDM Verlag Dr. Müller, 2010.
Benjamin, Walter. *The Arcades Project*. Ed. Rolf Tiedemann. Cambridge, MA: Belknap, 1999.
Bentley, Nicolas et al. *The Dickens Index*. Oxford: Oxford University Press, 1988.
Berard, Jane H. *Studies in Nineteenth-Century British Literature. Vol. 16: Dickens and Landscape Discourse*. New York: Lang, 2006.
Birch, Dinah, ed. *The Oxford Companion to English Literature*. 7th ed. Oxford: Oxford University Press, 2009.
Bodenheimer, Rosemarie. *Knowing Dickens*. Ithaca, NY: Cornell University Press, 2007.

Booth, Michael R. et al. *The Revels History of Drama in English*. Vol. 6: *1750–1880*. London: Methuen & Co. Ltd., 1975.

—. *Theatre in the Victorian Age*. Cambridge: Cambridge University Press, 1991.

Bowen, John, 'Bebelle and "His Boots": Dickens, Ellen Ternan and the Christmas Stories'. *Dickensian* 96, no. 3 (2000): 197–208.

—. *Other Dickens*. Oxford: Oxford University Press, 2000.

—. and Robert L. Patten, eds. *Palgrave Advances in Charles Dickens Studies*. Basingstoke: Palgrave Macmillan, 2006.

Bradshaw, George. *Bradshaw's Illustrated Hand-Book to Switzerland and the Tyrol*. London: W. J. Adams, 1863.

Brockedon, William. *Illustrations of the Passes of the Alps by which Italy Communicates with France, Switzerland and Germany*. London: Rodwell et al., 1829.

Brontë, Charlotte. *The Professor*. Ed. Heather Glen. London: Penguin, 1989.

—. *Villette*. Ed. Helen Cooper. London: Penguin, 2004.

Brookes Cross, A. E. 'Albert Smith, Charles Dickens and "Christopher Tadpole"'. *Dickensian* 34, no. 247 (1938): 157–63.

Brooks, Peter. *The Melodramatic Imagination: Balzac, Henry James, Melodrama, and the Mode of Excess*. New Haven, CT: Yale University Press, 1976.

Browning, Robert. *Paracelsus*. London: J. M. Dent, 1898.

Burgan, William. '"Little Dorrit" in Italy'. *Nineteenth-Century Fiction* 29, no. 4 (1975): 393–411.

Burke, Edmund. *A Philosophical Enquiry into the Origin of our Ideas of the Sublime and Beautiful*. Oxford: Oxford University Press, 1998.

Burwick, Frederick et al., eds. *The Encyclopedia of Romantic Literature*. Oxford: Blackwell Publishing, 2012.

—. *Playing to the Crowd: London Popular Theatre, 1789–1830*. Basingstoke: Palgrave Macmillan, 2011.

Butler, Amy. 'Dickens's Swiss Chalet'. *Dickensian* 73, no. 383 (1977): 147–8.

Butt, John and Kathleen Tillotson. *Dickens at Work on 'Dombey and Son'*. London: Methuen, 1951.

Buzard, James. *The Beaten Track, European Tourism, Literature and the Ways to Culture, 1800–1918*. Oxford: Clarendon, 1993.

—. *Disorienting Fiction: the Autoethnographic Work of Nineteenth-Century British Novels*. Princeton, NJ: Princeton University Press, 2005.

Byerly, Alison. '"A Prodigious Map Beneath His Feet": Virtual Travel and The Panoramic Perspective'. *Nineteenth-Century Contexts* 29, no. 2–3 (2007): 151–68.

Carey, John. *The Violent Effigy*. London: Faber, 1973.

Chandler, David. '"Above all natural affections": Sacrifice, Sentiment and Farce in *The Battle of Life*'. *Dickensian* 106, no. 2 (2010): 139–51.

Chesterton, G. K. *Chesterton on Dickens*. London: Everyman, 1992.

—. *Charles Dickens*. London: Methuen, 1906.

Clemm, Sabine. *Dickens, Journalism, and Nationhood. Mapping the World in* Household Words. New York: Routledge, 2009.

Coleman, Simon and Mike Crang. *Tourism: Between Place and Performance*. New York: Berghahn Books, 2002.

Colley, Ann C. *The Victorians in the Mountains. Sinking the Sublime*. Farnham: Ashgate, 2010.

Collins, Philip. 'Dickens's Reading'. *Dickensian* 60, no. 344 (1964): 136–42.

—. *Dickens and Crime*. London: Macmillan, 1964.

—. *Dickens and Education*. London: Macmillan, 1963.

—. *The Public Readings*. Oxford: Clarendon Press, 1975.

Collins, Wilkie. 'Wilkie Collins's Recollections of Charles Fechter'. In *Charles Albert Fechter. American Actor Series*, Kate Field. Boston, MA: James R. Osgood and Co., 1882, 145–76.

—. *The Woman in White*. Ed. Matthew Sweet. London: Penguin, 2003.

Comment, Bernard. *The Panorama*. London: Reaktion Books, 1999.

Coolidge, W. A. B. *Swiss Travel and Swiss Guide-Books*. London: Longmans, Green and Co., 1889.

Cotsell, Michael. *The Companion to* Our Mutual Friend. London: Allen & Unwin, 1986.

Cregan-Reid, Vybarr. 'Bodies, Boundaries and Queer Waters: Drowning and Prosopopoeia in Later Dickens'. *Critical Survey* 17, no. 2 (2005): 20–33.

Cruikshank, R. J. *Charles Dickens and Early Victorian England*. London: Pitman, 1949.

Davies, James. 'John Forster at the Mannings' Execution'. *Dickensian* 67, no. 363 (1971): 12–15.

Davis, Jim, ed. *Victorian Pantomime. A Collection of Critical Essays*. Basingstoke: Palgrave Macmillan, 2010.

Davis, Tracy C. and Peter Holland. *The Performing Century. Nineteenth-Century Theatre's History*. Basingstoke: Palgrave Macmillan, 2007.

de Beer, Gavin. *Travellers in Switzerland*. Oxford: Oxford University Press, 1949.

Dever, Carolyn. *Death and the Mother from Dickens to Freud: Victorian Fiction and the Anxiety of Origins*. Cambridge: Cambridge University Press, 1998.

Dickens, Mamie. *Charles Dickens*. London: Cassell, 1885.

—. *My Father As I Recall Him*. Westminster: Roxburghe Press, 1902.

Disher, M. Willson, *Greatest Show on Earth*. London: G. Bell and Sons, 1937.

—. *Blood and Thunder: Mid-Victorian Melodrama and its Origins*. London: Muller, 1949.

—. *Clowns & Pantomimes*. New York: B. Blom, 1968.

—. *Fairs, Circuses and Music Halls*. London: William Collins, 1942.

—. *Melodrama: Plots that Thrilled*. London: Rockliff, 1954.

Bibliography 191

Duncan, Ian. *Modern Romance and Transformations of the Novel: The Gothic, Scott, Dickens*. Cambridge: Cambridge University Press, 1992.

Ebel, Johann Gottfried. *The Traveller's Guide through Switzerland: In Four Parts*. London: Printed for Samuel Leigh, 1820.

Eberli, Henry. *Switzerland: Poetical and Pictorial*. Zurich: Art Institut Orell Füssli, 1893.

Edgecombe, Rodney Stenning. 'Theatrical Dance in Dickens'. *Dickens Studies Annual* 41 (2010): 1–23.

Edmondson, John. *Dickens on France*. Oxford: Signal, 2006.

Edwards, Owen Dudley. *Burke and Hare*. 3rd ed. Edinburgh: Birlinn, Ltd., 2014.

Edwards, Simon. 'Anorexia Nervosa versus the Fleshpots of London: Rose and Nancy in Oliver Twist'. *Dickens Studies Annual* 19 (1990): 49–64.

Eigner, Edwin. *The Dickens Pantomime*. Berkeley, CA: University of California Press, 1989.

Eisenstein, Sergei. 'Dickens, Griffith, and the Film To-Day'. In *Film Form*, ed. and transl. Jay Leyda. Orlando, FL: Harcourt, 1977, 195–255.

Fenner, Theodore. *Opera in London. Views of the Press, 1785–1830*. Carbondale, IL: Southern Illinois University Press, 1994.

Fitzsimons, Raymund. *Garish Lights. The Public Reading Tours of Charles Dickens*. Philadelphia, PA: J. B. Lippincott Co., 1970.

Flaad, Paul. *England und die Schweiz: 1848–1852*. Bäretswil: Graph. Werkstätte, 1935.

Flint, Kate. *Dickens*. Brighton: Harvester Press, 1986.

Fontaney, Pierre. 'Ruskin and Paradise Regained'. *Victorian Studies* 12, no. 3 (1969). 347–56.

Freud, Sigmund. *Psychologische Schriften*. Ed. Alexander Mitscherlich et al. Study edition. Frankfurt am Main: S. Fischer, 1970, vol. 4.

Fuss, Diana. *The Sense of an Interior: Four Writers and the Rooms that Shaped Them*. London: Routledge, 2004.

Garnett, Robert R. 'The Crisis of 1863'. *Dickens Quarterly* 23, no. 3 (2006): 181–91.

Gearing, Nigel. *Dickens in America*. London: Oberon, 1998.

Gibbon, Edward. *Private Letters of Edward Gibbon, 1753–1794*. Ed. Rowland E. Prothero. 2 vols. London: John Murray, 1896.

Gibson, Frank A. 'Nature's Possible: A Reconsideration of *The Battle of Life*'. *Dickensian* 58 (1962): 43 6.

Gitter, Elisabeth. *The Imprisoned Guest: Samuel Howe and Laura Bridgman, the Original Deaf-Blind Girl*. New York: Farrar, Straus & Giroux, 2001.

Glancy, Ruth. 'To Be Read at Dusk'. *Dickensian* 83, no. 441 (1987): 40–50.

Goldberg, Michael. *Carlyle and Dickens*. Athens, GA: University of Georgia Press, 1972.

Gray, Beryl. *The Dog in the Dickensian Imagination*. Farngate: Ashgate, 2014.

—. 'A Home of Their Own'. *Dickensian* 107, no. 484 (2011): 151–2.

Grossman, Jonathan H. *Charles Dickens's Networks*. Oxford: Oxford University Press, 2012.

Hale, Philip. 'Hortense and the Mannings'. *Dickensian* 1, no. 19 (1923): 22–3.

Hanna, Robert. 'Selection Guide to Dickens's Amateur Theatricals – Part 2'. *Dickensian* 108, no. 486 (2012): 33–46.

Hansen, Peter H. 'Albert Smith, the Alpine Club, and the Invention of Mountaineering in Mid-Victorian Britain'. *Journal of British Studies* 34, no 3. *Victorian Subjects* (1995): 300–24.

Hanssen, Beatrice. *Walter Benjamin and* The Arcades Project. London: Continuum, 2006.

Hartley, Jenny. *Charles Dickens and the House of Fallen Women*. London: Methuen, 2008.

Hartnoll, Phyllis and Peter Found. *The Concise Oxford Companion to the Theatre*. 2nd ed. Oxford University Press, 1996.

Harvey, William. *The Peasants of Chamouni. Containing an Attempt to Reach the Summit of Mont Blanc, and a Delineation of the Scenery among the Alps*. 2nd ed. London: Printed for Baldwin, et al., 1826.

Hawksley, Lucinda. *Katey: The Life and Loves of Dickens's Artist Daughter*. London: Doubleday, 2006.

Hayman, John. *John Ruskin and Switzerland*. Waterloo, Ontario: Wilfrid Laurier University Press, 1990.

Healey, Edna. *Lady Unknown: The Life of Angela Burdett-Coutts*. London: Sidgwick and Jackson, 1978.

Hennelly, Mark M. Jr. 'Victorian Carnivalesque'. *Victorian Literature and Culture* 30, no. 1 (2002): 365–81.

—. '"Playing at Leap-Frog with the Tombstones": the "Danse Macabre" Motif in Dickens'. *Essays in Literature* 22, no. 2 (1995): 227–44.

Henson, Louise et al., eds. *Culture and Science in the Nineteenth-Century Media*. Aldershot: Ashgate, 2004.

Herbert, David, ed. *Heritage, Tourism and Society*. London: Picador, 1995.

Hibbert, Christopher. *Queen Victoria: A Personal History*. London: HarperCollins, 2001.

—. *The Making of Charles Dickens*. New York: Harper & Row, 1967.

Hippisley-Coxe, Antony. *A Seat at the Circus*. Hamden, CT: Archon Books, 1980.

Hobsbaum, Philip. *A Reader's Guide to Charles Dickens*. New York: Farrar, Straus and Giroux, 1972.

Holbein, Hans. *The Dance of Death*. Ed. Francis Douce. London: William Pickering, 1833.

Hollington, Michael, 'Dickens and the Dance of Death'. *Dickensian* 76 (1980): 67–76.

—. 'Dickens the Flâneur'. *Dickensian* 77, no. 394 (1981): 71–87.

—. *Dickens and the Grotesque*. London: Croom Helm, 1984.

—. ed. *The Reception of Charles Dickens in Europe*. 2 vols. London: Bloomsbury, 2013.

—. and Francesca Orestano, eds. *Dickens and Italy:* Little Dorrit *and* Pictures from Italy. Newcastle upon Tyne: Cambridge Scholars, 2009.

Hornback, Bert G. *Noah's Arkitecture. A Study of Dickens's Mythology*. Athens, OH: Ohio University Press, 1972.

Huish, Robert. *The Progress of Crime, or The Authentic Memoirs of Maria Manning*. London: M'Gowan & Co., 1849.

Hulme, Peter and Tim Youngs, eds. *The Cambridge Companion to Travel Writing*. Cambridge: Cambridge University Press, 2002.

Hyde, Ralph. *Panoramania! The Art and Entertainment of the 'All-Embracing View'*. London: Trefoil in association with Barbican Art Gallery, 1988.

Imlah, Ann. *Britain and Switzerland, 1845–60. A Study of Anglo-Swiss Relations during some Critical Years for Swiss Neutrality*. Hamden, CT: Archon Books, 1966.

Ireland, Kenneth R. 'Urban Perspectives: Fantasy and Reality in Hoffmann and Dickens'. *Comparative Literature* 30, no. 2 (1978): 133–56.

Isba, Anne. *Dickens's Women. His Great Expectations*. London: Continuum, 2011.

John, Juliet. *Dickens's Villains: Melodrama, Character, Popular Culture*. Oxford: Oxford University Press, 2001.

Johnson, Celia. 'Pedestrian Adventures'. *Poets & Writers* 42, no. 1 (2014): 50–2.

Johnson, Edgar. *Charles Dickens: His Tragedy and Triumph*. London: Allen Lane, 1977.

Jones, Colin, Josephine McDonagh and Jon Mee, eds. *Charles Dickens, A Tale of Two Cities and the French Revolution*. Basingstoke: Palgrave Macmillan, 2009.

Jones, Harry. *The Regular Swiss Round. In Three Trips*. London: Alexander Strahan, 1865.

Jordan, John and Nirshan Perera, eds. *Global Dickens*. Farnham: Ashgate, 2012.

Kaplan, Fred. *Dickens. A Biography*. New York: William Morrow & Co., 1988.

—. *Dickens and Mesmerism. The Hidden Springs of Fiction*. Princeton, NJ: Princeton University Press, 1975.

Kennedy, Dennis, ed. *The Oxford Companion to Theatre and Performance*. Oxford: Oxford University Press, 2010.

Knoepflmacher, U. C. et al., eds. *Nature and the Victorian Imagination*. Berkeley, CA: University of California Press, 1977.

Knowles, James Sheridan. *William Tell. A Play in Five Acts*. London: Thomas Dolby, 1825.

Koshar, Rudy. *Histories of Leisure*. Oxford: Berg, 2002.

Kucich, John. *Repression in Victorian Fiction: Charlotte Brontë, George Eliot, and Charles Dickens*. Berkeley, CA: University of California Press, 1987.

Kucich, John. *Excess and Restraint in the Novels of Charles Dickens.* Athens, GA: University of Georgia Press, 1981.

Kunst- und Ausstellungshalle der Bundesrepublik Deutschland, ed. *Sehnsucht: Das Panorama als Massenunterhaltung des 19. Jahrhunderts.* Frankfurt and Basel: Stroemfeld/Roter Stern, 1993.

Leavis, F. R. and Q. D Leavis. *Dickens, the Novelist.* Harmondsworth: Pelican, 1980.

Ledger, Sally and Holly Furneaux, eds. *Charles Dickens in Context.* Cambridge: Cambridge University Press, 2011.

Leman, Thomas Rede. *The Road to the Stage.* London: Joseph Smith, 1827.

Lemon, Mark. *Arnold of Winkelried; or, The Fight of Sempach!* London: J. Duncombe & Co., 1825.

Lennartz, Norbert. 'Charles Dickens Abroad: The Victorian Smelfungus and the Genre of the Unsentimental Journey'. *Dickens Quarterly* 25, no. 3 (2008): 145–59.

Leroy, Maxime. *Charles Dickens and Europe.* Newcastle: Cambridge Scholars, 2013.

Lippard, Lucy R. *On the Beaten Track: Tourism, Art, and Place.* New York: New Press, 1999.

Litvak, Joseph. *Caught in the Act: Theatricality in the Nineteenth-Century English Novel.* Berkeley, CA: University of California Press, 1992.

Litvak, Leon. 'What Books Did Dickens Buy and Read? Evidence from the Book Accounts with his Publishers'. *Dickensian* 94, no. 445 (1998): 85–130.

Lock, Stephen et al. *The Oxford Illustrated Companion to Medicine.* Oxford: Oxford University Press, 2001.

Löhrer, Hans. *Die Schweiz im Spiegel englischer Literatur 1849–1875.* Zurich: Juris Verlag, 1952.

Lokin, Jan. 'Realism and Reality in Dickens's Characters: Dickens Seen through the Eyes of Dutch Writers'. *Dickensian* 105, no. 477 (2009): 21–32.

Longfellow, Henry Wadsworth, ed. *Poems of Places. An Anthology in 31 Volumes.* Boston, MA: James R. Osgood & Co., 1876–79.

Louttit, Chris. *Dickens's Secular Gospel: Work, Gender, and Personality.* New York: Routledge, 2009.

Lunn, Arnold. *Switzerland and the English.* London: Eyre & Spottiswoode, 1944.

—. *Switzerland in English Prose and Poetry.* London: Eyre & Spottiswoode, 1947.

Macready, William Charles. *The Diaries of William Charles Macready, 1833–1851.* Ed. by William Toynbee. 2 vols. New York: G. P. Putnam's Sons, 1912.

Marchbanks, Paul. 'From Caricature to Character: the Intellectually Disabled in Dickens's Novels'. *Dickens Quarterly* 23, part I no. 1 (2006): 3–13; part II no. 2 (2006): 67–84; part III no. 3 (2006): 169–80.

Marcus, Steven. *Dickens. From Pickwick to Dombey*. New York: Basic Books, 1965.

Mathews, Mrs. *Mémoirs of Charles Mathews, Comedian*. London: Richard Bentley, 1839, vol. 4.

—. *The Life and Correspondence of Charles Mathews, the Elder. Comedian*. Ed. Edmund Yates. London: Routledge, Warne, and Routledge, 1860.

McCalman, Iain et al., eds. *An Oxford Companion to the Romantic Age: British Culture, 1776–1832*. Oxford: Oxford University Press, 1999.

Miller, J. Hillis *Topographies*. Stanford, CA: Stanford University Press, 1995.

Minca, Claudio and Tim Oakes. *Travels in Paradox: Remapping Tourism*. Lanham, MD: Rowman & Littlefield Publishers, 2006.

Mitchell, Leslie. *Bulwer Lytton, The Rise and Fall of a Victorian Man of Letters*. London: Hambledon and London, 2003.

Moody, Jane. *Illegitimate Theatre in London, 1770–1840*. Cambridge: Cambridge University Press, 2000.

Moretti, Franco. *Atlas of the European Novel 1800–1900*. London: Verso, 1998.

Morgentaler, Goldie. 'Dickens and Dance in the 1840s'. *Partial Answers 9*, no. 2 (2011): 253–66.

—. 'The Doppelgänger Effect: Dickens, Heredity, and the Double in *The Battle of Life*'. *Dickens Studies Annual 42*, no. 1 (2011): 159–75.

Morley, Malcolm. 'No *Thoroughfare* Back Stage'. *Dickensian 50* (1954): 37–42.

—. '*The Battle of Life* in the Theatre'. *Dickensian 48* (1952): 76–81.

Murray, John. *Murray's Handbook for Travellers in Switzerland 1838*. The Victorian Library. Leicester: Leicester University Press, 1970.

Naville, René. *Charles Dickens (1812–1870): seine Besuche in der Schweiz*. Zurich: Pro Helvetia, 1973.

Nayder, Lillian. *The Other Dickens: A Life of Catherine Hogarth*. Ithaca, NY: Cornell University Press, 2011.

—. *Unequal Partners. Charles Dickens, Wilkie Collins, and Victorian Authorship*. Ithaca, NY: Cornell University Press, 2001.

Neate, Jill. *Mountaineering Literature – A Bibliography*. Milnthorpe, Cumbria: Cicerone Press, 1986.

Nicoll, Allardyce. *A History of English Drama 1660–1900. Vol. 4: Early Nineteenth-Century Drama*. Cambridge: Cambridge University Press, 1955.

—. *A History of English Drama 1660–1900. Vol. 5: Late Nineteenth-Century Drama*. Cambridge: Cambridge University Press, 1962.

Nisbet, Ada. *Dickens and Ellen Ternan*. Berkeley, CA: University of California Press, 1952.

Oettermann, Stephan. *The Panorama. History of a Mass Medium*. New York: Zone Books, 1997.

Orford, Peter. 'An Italian Dream and a Castle in the Air: The Significance of Venice in *Little Dorrit*'. *Dickensian 103*, no. 472 (2007): 157–65.

Ortiz-Robles, Mario. 'Dickens Performs Dickens'. *ELH* 78 (2011): 457–78.

Page, Norman. *A Dickens Chronology*. Boston, MA: G. K. Hall, 1988.

Paroissien, David, ed. *A Companion to Charles Dickens*. Oxford: Blackwell, 2008.

Parrinder, Patrick. *Nation & Novel: The English Novel from its Origins to the Present Day*. Oxford: Oxford University Press, 2008.

Patten, Robert L. *Charles Dickens and 'Boz': The Birth of the Industrial-Age Author*. Cambridge: Cambridge University Press, 2012.

Pelham, Camden. *The Chronicles of Crime; or, The New Newgate Calendar*. London: Bradbury and Evans, 1841, vol. 2.

Philpotts, Trey. *The Companion to* Little Dorrit. The Banks, Mountfield: Helm Information Ltd., 2003.

Piggott, Gillian. *Dickens and Benjamin: Moments of Revelation, Fragments of Modernity*. Burlington, VT: Ashgate, 2012.

Pope-Hennessey, Una. *Charles Dickens: 1812–1870*. London: Chatto Windus, 1945.

Powell, Kerry, ed. *The Cambridge Companion to Victorian and Edwardian Theatre*. Cambridge: Cambridge University Press, 2004.

Putzger, F. W. *Historischer Atlas zur Welt- und Schweizer Geschichte*. Ed. Dr. Th. Müller-Wolfer. 5th ed. Aarau: H. R. Sauerländer & Co, 1961.

Ransom, Mildred. 'Sens: A Landmark in France'. *Dickensian* 23, no. 203 (1927): 202.

Rapin, René. 'Lausanne and some English Writers'. *Etudes de Lettres* 2, no. 3 (1959): 92–121.

Reed Stiles, Henry. *The Stiles Family in America*. Jersey City, NY: Doan & Pilson.

Remak, Joachim. *A Very Civil War. The Swiss Sonderbund War of 1847*. Boulder, CO: Westview Press, 1993.

Richards, Kenneth and Peter Thomson. *Essays on Nineteenth Century British Theatre*. London: Methuen & Co. Ltd., 1971.

Richardson, Ruth. *Dickens and the Workhouse. Oliver Twist and the London Poor*. Oxford: Oxford University Press, 2012.

Ring, Jim. *How the English Made the Alps*. London: John Murray, 2000.

Robb, Graham. *Strangers: Homosexual Love in the 19th Century*. London: Picador, 2004.

Robinson, Peter Frederick. *Village Architecture: Being a Series of Picturesque Designs for the Inn, the Schoolhouse, Almshouses, Markethouse, Shambles, Workhouse, Parsonage, Townhall, and Church. Forming a Sequel to a Work on Rural Architecture*. 4th ed. London: Henry G. Bohn, 1838.

Rossi-Wilcox, Susan. *Dinner for Dickens. The Culinary History of Mrs Charles Dickens' Menu Books. Including a Transcript of* What Shall We Have For Dinner? *by 'Lady Maria Clutterbuck'*. Trowbridge: Prospect Books, 2005.

Sadrin, Annie, ed. *Dickens, Europe, and the New Worlds*. Basingstoke: Palgrave Macmillan, 1999.

Sanders, Andrew. *Authors in Context: Charles Dickens*. Oxford: Oxford University Press, 2003.

Saxon, A. H. *Enter Foot and Horse. A History of Hippodrama in England and France*. New Haven, CT: Yale University Press, 1968.

—. *Life and Art of Ducrow and the Romantic Age of the English Circus*. Hamden, CT: Archon Books, 1979.

Schazmann, Paul-Emile. *Charles Dickens in Switzerland*. Trans. H. P. B. Betlem. Lausanne: Swiss National Tourist Office, 1972.

Schindler, Johannes. *Das Bild des Engländers in der Kunst- und Volksliteratur der deutschen Schweiz von 1798–1848*. Zurich: Juris Verlag, 1950.

Schirmer, Gustav. 'Charles Dickens und die Schweiz'. Offprint from *Neue Zürcher Zeitung*, 1912.

—. *Die Schweiz im Spiegel englischer und amerikanischer Literatur bis 1848*. Zurich: Orell Füssli, 1929.

—. *Edward Gibbon und die Schweiz*. Zurich: Zürcher & Furrer, 1910.

—. 'Über James Sheridan Knowles' William Tell'. *Anglia* 12 (1889): 1–12.

Schlicke, Paul. *Dickens and Popular Entertainment*. London: Allen & Unwin, 1985.

—. *The Oxford Companion to Charles Dickens*. Oxford: Oxford University Press, 2011.

—. *The Oxford Reader's Companion to Dickens*. Oxford: Oxford University Press, 2000.

Scott, Walter. *Anne of Geierstein*. Ed. J. H. Alexander. Edinburgh: Edinburgh University Press, 2000.

Sedgwick, Eve Kosofsky. *Between Men: English Literature and Male Homosocial Desire*. New York: Columbia University Press, 1985.

—. *Epistemology of the Closet*. Berkeley, CA: University of California Press, 1990.

Shattock, Joanne, ed. *Cambridge Bibliography of English Literature*. 3rd ed. Cambridge: Cambridge University Press, 1999, vol. 4.

Shaw, Philip. *The Sublime*. London: Routledge, 2006.

Shore, W. Teignmouth. *Charles Dickens and His Friends*. London and New York: Cassell and Company, Ltd., 1909.

Simond, Louis. *A Tour in Italy and Sicily*. London: Printed for Longman et al., 1828.

Simpson, Margaret. *The Companion to Hard Times. The Dickens Companions*. Westport, CT: Greenwood Press, 1997.

Slater, Michael. *Charles Dickens*. New Haven, CT: Yale University Press, 2009.

—. *Dickens and Women*. London: J. M. Dent, 1983.

—. *Dickens on America and the Americans*. Austin, TX: University of Texas Press, 1978.

—. *The Catalogue of the Suzannet Charles Dickens Collection*. London: Sotheby in association with the Trustees of the Dickens House, 1975.

—. *The Great Charles Dickens Scandal*. New Haven, CT: Yale University Press, 2012.

Smith, Albert. *Mont Blanc*. London: Ward, Lock and Tyler, 1871.

—. *The Story of Mont Blanc*. London: David Bogue, 1853.

Smith, Grahame. *Dickens and the Dream of Cinema*. Manchester: Manchester University Press, 2003.

Smollett, Tobias. *The Expedition of Humphry Clinker*. London: Harrison and Co., 1785.

Staples, Leslie C. 'Sidelight on a Great Friendship'. *Dickensian* 47, no. 297 (1950): 16–21.

—. 'A Great Dickensian. Count de Suzannet'. *Dickensian* 47, no. 298 (1951): 64–6.

Steinberg, Jonathan. *Why Switzerland?* Cambridge: Cambridge University Press, 1976.

Stewart, Susan. *On Longing: Narratives of the Miniature, the Gigantic, the Souvenir, the Collection*. Durham, NC: Duke University Press, 1993.

Stoddart, Helen. *Rings of Desire: Circus History and Representation*. Manchester: Manchester University Press, 2000.

Stone, Harry. *Dickens and the Invisible World: Fairy Tales, Fantasy, and Novel-Making*. London: Macmillan, 1980.

—. *The Night Side of Dickens. Cannibalism, Passion, Necessity*. Columbus, OH: Ohio State University Press, 1994.

Stone, Marcus. 'Mr. Marcus Stone, R. A., and Charles Dickens'. *Dickensian* 8, no. 8 (1912): 216–17.

Storey, Gladys. *Dickens and Daughter*. London: Frederick Muller Ltd., 1939.

Straumann, Heinrich. *Contexts of Literature: An Anglo-Swiss Approach. Vol. 75: Schweizer Anglistische Arbeiten*. Bern: Francke Verlag, 1973.

Sullivan, Jill A. *The Politics of the Pantomime: Regional Identity in the Theatre, 1860–1900*. Hatfield: University of Hertfordshire Press, 2001.

Thalmann, Lieselotte. *Zürcher Beiträge zur vergleichenden Literaturgeschichte, Bd. [Vol.] 6: Charles Dickens in seinen Beziehungen zum Ausland*. Zurich: Juris-Verlag, 1956.

Thomas, Ronald R. 'Dickens's Sublime Artefact'. *Browning Institute Studies* 14, The Victorian Threshold (1986): 71–95.

Thomson, William. *Two Journeys through Italy and Switzerland*. London: John Macrone, 1835.

Thorington, James Monroe. *Mont Blanc Sideshow: The Life and Times of Albert Smith*. Philadelphia, PA: J.C. Winston, 1934.

Tissot, Laurent. *Construction d'une Industrie Touristique aux 19e et 20e Siècles*. Neuchâtel: Alphil, 2003.

—. *Naissance d'une Industrie Touristique: Les Anglais et la Suisse au XIXe Siècle*. Lausanne: Payot, 2000.

Tolstoy, Leo. 'Cossacks'. In *Tales of Army Life*, trans. Louise and Aylmer Maude. London: Oxford University Press, 1932.

Tomalin, Claire. *Charles Dickens. A Life*. London: Penguin, 2012.

—. *The Invisible Woman*. London: Penguin, 1991.

Toole-Stott, Raymond. *Circus and the Allied Arts*. 4 vols. Derby: Harpur, 1958–1971.

Trumpener, Katie and Tim Barringer, eds. *On the Viewing Platform. The Panorama between Canvas and Screen*. New Haven, CT and London: Yale University Press, 2020.

Tschumi, Raymond. 'Dickens and Switzerland'. *English Studies* 60, no. 4 (1979): 443–62.

Tucker, Herbert F. *A Companion to Victorian Literature and Culture*. Malden, MA: Blackwell, 1999.

Urry, John. *The Tourist Gaze*. 2nd ed. London: Sage Publications, 2002.

Vanden Bossche, Chris R. 'Cookery, not Rookery: Family and Class in David Copperfield'. *Dickens Studies Annual* 15 (1986): 89–109.

Vanfasse, Nathalie. *La Plume et la route. Charles Dickens, écrivain-voyageur*. Aix-en-Provence: Provence University Press, 2017.

Vincent, Patrick. *La Suisse Vue par les Ecrivains de Langue Anglaise*. Lausanne: Le Savoir Suisse, 2009.

Vlock, Deborah. *Dickens, Novel Reading, and the Victorian Popular Theatre*. Cambridge: Cambridge University Press, 1998.

Wäber, Adolf. *Landes- und Reisebeschreibungen. Ein Beitrag zur Bibliographie der schweizerischen Reiseliteratur, 1479–1890*. 2 vols. Bern: K. J. Wyss, 1899–1909.

Wagner, Leopold. *Names and Their Meanings: A Book for the Curious*. London: T. Fisher Unwin, 1897.

Waters, Catherine. *Commodity Culture in Dickens's* Household Words: *The Social Life of Goods*. Aldershot: Ashgate, 2008.

Watson, Nicola J., ed. *Literary Tourism and Nineteenth-Century Culture*. Basingstoke: Palgrave Macmillan, 2009.

Watt, Ian. 'Oral Dickens'. *Dickens Studies Annual* 3 (1979): 165–81.

Wilt, Judith. *Secret Leaves. The Novels of Walter Scott*. Chicago, IL: University of Chicago Press, 1985.

Wordsworth, William. *The Prelude. A Parallel Text*. Ed. J. C. Maxwell. Harmondsworth: Penguin, 1971.

Wraight, John. *The Swiss and the British*. Wilton, Salisbury: Michael Russell Ltd., 1987.

Wylie, Neville. *Britain, Switzerland, and the Second World War*. Oxford: Oxford University Press, 2003.

Wynne, Catherine. 'Christiana Weller Thompson's Unpublished Journal (1845–6): Sidelights on Dickens'. *Notes and Queries* 61, no. 4 (2014): 548–53.

Wyss, Johann. *The Swiss Family Robinson*. Ed. John Seelye. Oxford: Oxford University Press, 1991.

Yung, Emile. *Le Sommeil Normal et le Sommeil Pathologique. Magnétisme Animal, Hypnotisme, Névrose Hysterique*. Paris: Octave Doin, 1883.

—. *Zermatt and the Valley of the Viège*. Trans. Wharton Robinson. London: J. R. Gotz, 1894.

Zimmer, Oliver. *A Contested Nation: History, Memory and Nationalism in Switzerland. 1761–1891*. Cambridge: Cambridge University Press, 2003.

Index

Aarau, 24
Abendberg, Asylum of the, 115
accidents, 22
accommodation *see* Swiss
    accommodation
Ackroyd, Peter, 155
acting, 96
activity, 101
actors and actresses, 46, 35–62, 52, 56,
    58, 126, 154
Adler, Judith, 84, 106
adventure, 15, 70
aesthetic, 80, 102, 105, 110
aggressiveness, 101
air, 113, 170
Asile des Aveugles *see* Asylum for the
    Blind
Alberti, Sophie Verena, 5
All the Year Round, 11, 14, 31, 48, 53,
    92, 120, 121, 127, 140, 141
allegory, 108
Alpine Club, 10
Alps, 9, 52, 65, 69, 98, 103, 104,
    108, 111, 114, 134, 137, 156,
    157, 167–8, 178, 184; *see also*
    mountains
Altdorf, 45
alter ego *see* alternative self
alternative self, 84, 102, 177
Altick, Richard, 20
America *see* USA; South America
American Notes, 2, 69, 70
Americans, 12
anarchy, 102
Andrews, Malcolm, 177
    *Charles Dickens and His Performing
      Selves*, 28
animal magnetism, 121, 181–2
animalistic, 107, 109, 114, 129, 173
animate, 103
anti-intellectualism, 89, 93, 95
anxiety, 66, 73–4, 79, 80, 81, 86–7, 88,

99, 111, 115, 133, 134–5, 143,
    146
apophasis, 71
apples, 45, 46–7, 51, 53, 62
Arabian Nights, 162
architecture, 17
Arctic, 9, 136
art, 89
ascending *see* rising
Astley's Amphitheatre, 35–43, 48, 50,
    62, 120
    Battle of Waterloo, 36 48
    Mazeppa, 36, 48
    Timour the Tartar, 36
    see also Swiss performances
Asylum for the Blind, 12, 73, 78–9, 114,
    177
asylum, 99, 114, 115
Athenaeum, 36, 39
audience, 54, 62, 89, 126, 128
aunts, 59, 61
Austin, née Dickens, Letitia, 140–4
Australia, 137
Austria, 44
authority, 106, 110
automatons, 21
avalanches, 10, 100
awe, 96

babies, 22, 34, 102, 105, 109, 146, 147
Baedecker, Karl, *Hand-book for
    Travellers in Switzerland and the
    Adjacent Portions of Italy, Savoy,
    and the Tyrol*, 152
balance, 97
ballet, 19, 36
balloons, 132
barbarism, 11
Barker and Burford panorama, 19, 20
Barnaby Rudge, 18, 64, 90, 124
Barrow, Thomas, 23
Basel, 24, 77, 145, 153, 165, 180

202 *Dickens and Switzerland*

Bath, 149, 150
Battersea Dogs Home, 2
Battle of Life, 18, 64, 66, 73–5, 79, 82,
    83, 112, 133, 172, 183, 184
Battle of Waterloo, 48
Beadnell, Maria, 86
Beard, Frank, 146
Beard, Thomas, 141, 143, 144
beastly *see* animalistic
beauty, 80, 91–3, 97, 102, 105, 114, 122,
    127–30, 170, 179
beds, 102, 143, 166
beginnings, 103–4
beheading, 124–6; *see also* executions
Belgium, 127
bells, 33, 93, 99, 112
Bentley's Miscellany, 25, 146
Berlepsch, 12
Berne, 146
Best Authority, 56, 57
Bible, 102, 174–5; *see also* Life of Our
    Lord
Bird Keeper's Cottage, 16
Bishop, Henry Rowley, 44
biting, 79
Bleak House, 47, 48, 90, 120, 127,
    128–9, 133
blood, 107–11, 112, 172, 173
Boarding House, 35
boats *see* ships
Bodenheimer, Rosemarie, 76
    Knowing Dickens, 86
bodies, 113–16, 127, 178–9
   dead, 34–5, 54, 79, 92, 104, 106, 111,
      112, 116, 130–2, 163, 164, 166,
      168, 171, 172
   disproportionate, 50, 51, 65, 76, 100,
      106, 109, 113, 115, 116, 136
body parts, 94, 103, 109, 110, 112–14,
    125, 131, 136, 161, 169, 170, 180;
    see also goitres
Bonaparte, Napoleon, 42, 44
books, 101, 108, 151, 163–4, 170
Booth, Michael R., 46
Boulogne, 146, 149
boundaries, 104, 113, 168, 173, 182
Bowen, John, 17–18, 95, 147
   Dickens and the Force of Writing, 95
   Other Dickens, 17–18
Boyle, Mary Louisa, 57–8
Braddon, Mary, *Lady Audley's Secret*, 25
Bradshaw, George, *Bradshaw's Illustrated*
    Handbook to Switzerland and the
    Tyrol, 151
bravery, 45–7

breastfeeding, 34–5, 109, 112–13
Brenner pass, 36
bridges, 95, 100
Britannia, 50, 51, 53, 57
British
   army, 48
   citizens, 57, 127, 128
   navy, 50
Brittany, 69
Broadstairs, 63, 80, 86, 99
Brockedon, William, 178
Brough, Robert Barnabas, 60
   William Tell, 60
Brune, Guillaume, 43
Buckingham Palace, 16
Budden, Maria Elizabeth, *Claudine;*
    or Humility the Basis of All the
    Virtues, 153
Burke, Edmund, 93
   Philosophical Enquiry into the Origin
    of our Ideas of the Sublime and
    Beautiful, 90, 91, 94
Burke, William, 92–3
burking, 92
burlesque, 50, 51, 53
Burwick, Frederick, 46
Butt, John, 64
butter, 22, 102
Buzard, James, 184
Byron, Lord, 20, 38, 178, 179
   Manfred, 20, 178

'Calamity-Mongering', 127
Calvin, Jean, 178
Cambridge, 98
cannibalism, 111–13, 115, 159, 172–3
capital punishment, 111, 122–32
Carey, John, 56, 82, 101, 107, 111, 124
caricature, 90
carnivalesque, 50, 65, 102, 107, 109, 173
castles, 103, 136
Catalogue of the Library of Charles
    Dickens from Gad's Hill, 151
catharsis, 32, 106
Catholicism, 7–8, 35, 76, 108–11, 113,
    134, 170–4
Cavour, Camillo, 182
chalet, CD's Swiss at Gad's Hill, 16,
    154–8, 166, 168, 185
chalets, 16, 47, 54, 100, 101, 102, 105,
    111, 114, 115, 116, 154–8, 166,
    168, 185
chamois, 19, 20
Chamonix, 93
chance, 103

Index   203

chaos, 105, 107
chapels, 33
character, 100, 102, 129, 169
characters, 63, 76, 78, 83, 101, 102,
    103–5, 109, 135, 175, 177, 183,
    184
  marginalised or secondary, 18, 25
Charlotte Brontë
  The Professor, 25
  Villette, 14
chemistry, 113–14
Chevalier, Pierre Michel François, 142–4
Child's History of England, 7, 120
childhood, 32–3, 35, 52, 75, 84, 85–7,
    88–9, 98, 112, 116–17, 118, 130,
    156, 159, 162, 165, 184
children, 43, 46, 59–60, 76, 84, 85–7,
    102, 105, 106, 107, 111, 113, 115,
    116–17, 146–7, 172, 173, 174
Chimes, The, 63
Christmas Books and Stories, 18, 73–4,
    75, 81, 83, 140, 147, 172, 175,
    183
chronology, 53, 130, 158, 160
churches, 131, 171, 172
cinematic, 100, 166
circus, 18, 21, 35–42, 62
cities, 63, 75, 80, 88–9, 105
cleanliness, 12, 71
climbing *see* mountaineering
clocks *see* watches and clocks
clothing, 26, 36–7, 52, 58–62, 110, 113,
    127–30, 132, 180
clouds, 76, 90, 103–4, 108, 111, 125,
    155, 161, 166, 167
clowns, 18, 39–40, 52, 109
Cobden, Richard, 39
coherency, 65
collapse, 73, 102
Collins, Charles Allston, 151
Collins, Philip
  Dickens's Reading, 98
  Dickens and Crime, 124, 127
Collins, Wilkie, 7, 9, 24, 52, 119, 136,
    141, 144–5, 146, 147, 151, 152,
    154, 177
  Woman in White, 25, 27, 127
Columbine, 39
comedy, 22, 25, 40, 46–7, 48–53, 55, 56,
    57, 62, 65, 90–3, 95–6, 111, 113,
    116, 117, 129, 136–8, 138, 168
compulsion, 65, 80, 117, 161, 165–6,
    167; *see also* obsession
conflict, 58, 100, 102, 110, 174, 180–1
consciousness, 71, 77, 78, 88–9, 118

contradictions, 89, 116
contrasts, 76, 100, 191, 102, 116, 121
control, 80, 132
convents *see* monasteries
coping mechanisms, 80
corpses *see* bodies
Courvoisier, François Benjamin, 23, 122,
    123–6
Coutts, Angela Burdett, 96, 177
cows, 25, 31, 52, 75, 105, 107, 116, 138
creativity *see* imagination
Cregan-Reid, Vybarr, 164
cretinism, 113–17, 169, 170, 173; *see also*
    idiots
crétins, 13, 169, 170, 173
criminals, 176; *see also* murder and
    murderers
crisis, 64, 133, 134–8, 184
Cromwell, Oliver, 7–8
crowds, 63, 76, 88–9, 105, 109, 124,
    126, 129, 184–5
crying *see* weeping
curiosity, 89

Daily News, 70, 81, 124
dairies, 54, 111
dancing, 109
danger, 10, 22, 34, 46, 54, 56, 77, 80, 81,
    94–5, 100–3, 105, 180–1
darkness, 33, 95, 104, 105
David Copperfield, 6, 10, 14, 17, 26,
    31–5, 52, 61, 64, 66, 77, 80, 84,
    86, 87, 96–9, 102, 108, 120, 122,
    135, 160, 164, 167, 184
Davies, James, 130
daydreaming *see* dreaming
De Beer, Gavin, 3
de Cerjat, William Woodley Frederick, 4,
    80, 99, 138–9
  de Cerjat, Elisabeth, 177
de Florian, Jean-Pierre Claris, 43
de la Rue, Augusta, 72, 181–2
  de la Rue, Emile, 181–2
deafness, 55, 96
death sentence, 123–32
death, 21, 32–5, 64, 65, 75, 76, 77, 78,
    79, 80, 83, 85–6, 92, 97, 98, 104,
    111–13, 117, 118, 122–32, 137,
    146, 163, 166–7, 168, 171, 172,
    181
decay, 79
Defoe, Daniel, *Robinson Crusoe*, 20
deformation, 65, 106, 115
degeneration, 12, 66, 76, 104, 106–7,
    110, 114, 172

Degex, Jean François, 12
degradation *see* degeneration
'Demeanour of Murderers', 126
democracy, 110
democrats, 51
demons, 50, 51, 171
descent, 94, 97
desire, 87, 101, 133, 134, 138
desolation, 96, 103
despair, 73–4, 81
destruction, 102
'Detective Police Party', 127
diabolism, 129
dialogue, 43
diary, 70, 134; *see also Memoranda*
Dickens Universe conference, 2
Dickens, Catherine, 4, 7, 14, 26, 56, 65,
    69, 70, 72, 86–7, 89, 99, 136, 144,
    145, 147
  separation from, 56, 136
  What shall we have for Dinner?, 7, 65
Dickens, Charles
  acting, 18
  adulthood *see* maturity
  amateur theatricals, 18, 58, 59–60,
    136
  autobiography, 4, 14, 33, 55, 59, 75,
    84, 85–6, 88, 112, 118, 135, 157,
    159, 183
  biography, 5, 6, 33, 55, 59, 66, 75, 81,
    83, 85–6, 89, 112, 133, 135, 150,
    160, 174, 182, 184, 185
  books read, 17, 21, 24, 25, 69, 92, 108,
    117, 151–4, 162, 183, 184
  childhood, 15, 17, 23, 25, 31, 36, 52,
    69, 75, 84, 85–7, 88–9, 112, 118,
    130, 156, 159, 162, 184
  children, 50–60, 84, 174–5
  daughters, 56
  difficulties with writing in Switzerland,
    8, 63–4, 66, 73–82, 87–8, 158,
    169
  digitisation of Dickens's writings, 5
  dogs, 20, 31, 131, 135, 157, 168, 171,
    177, 185
  enthusiasm for Switzerland, 11–14, 15,
    63, 72–3, 80–1, 169–70
  family, 56, 59, 88, 134, 140
  letters, 4, 5, 6, 58, 66, 72, 90, 94, 99,
    110, 114, 124, 125, 129, 132–51,
    154, 182
  maturity, 85, 86
  memory, 5, 54, 71, 75–6, 78, 79, 80,
    81, 85, 86, 87, 112, 118, 119, 124,
    130–2, 137, 139, 185

performativity of writing, 22, 57, 65,
    80, 84
personal trouble in England, 134–5,
    136, 136, 139, 147
personal trouble in Switzerland, 9,
    63–4, 73–4, 80–1, 82, 85, 86,
    87–8, 168, 170, 184
productivity in Switzerland, 81–2, 84,
    87–8, 117–18, 135, 158, 168, 171,
    174
self-portrayal, 4, 65, 80, 83, 84, 85, 99,
    176, 183
sons, 56
theatrical ideas, 23, 166
walking, 4, 8, 63, 69, 73, 76, 77, 80,
    86–9, 99, 134, 137, 149, 161
Dickens, Charley, 59, 60
Dickens, Dora, 99
Dickens, Harry, 59
Dickens, Henry Fielding, 84, 174
Dickens, Kate, 59, 151
Dickens, Marie, 84
Dickens, Mary 'Mamie', 59, 81, 84,
    138–9, 150
  My Father as I Recall Him, 81
Dickensian, 127
didactics, 41, 174–5
diorama, 18, 20
disappearing *see* vanishing
disease, 110, 113–17, 170
disguise, 121
disgust, 126
disorder, 107, 110
disorientation, 82
displacement behaviour, 80
Disraeli, Benjamin, 39
  Young Duke, 25
distortion, 106, 109, 116
dogs, 20, 31, 131, 135, 157, 168, 171,
    177, 185
Dombey and Son, 8, 9, 25, 52, 61, 64,
    65, 66, 69, 73–5, 79, 82, 84, 85,
    94, 111–12, 120, 133, 139, 146,
    183, 184
domestication, 12
domesticity, 10, 28, 30, 46–7, 51, 53, 54,
    56, 58, 62, 71, 81, 100–2, 117,
    144, 154–8, 165
Don Quixote, 159
Douce, Francis, *Dance of Death*, 24,
    108–9
Downing Street, 16
dragons, 96, 136, 137
dreaming, 54, 65, 77–9, 82, 130, 131,
    158–61, 168, 170, 180

Index

drinking, 96, 105, 111–17
drowning, 80, 164–8
drugging, 166
Drury Lane, 45, 50, 51
Duck Island Cottage, 16
Ducrow, Andrew and John, 36–7, 39
Dumas, Alexandre Dumas père, 148
dusk *see* sunset
dwarves, 101

East Indies, 143
echoes, 55, 97, 109, 171
Edinburgh, 92
editing, 57, 139, 150
Edmondson, John, 2
education, 84, 110, 123, 170, 174, 175,
    176, 177
Edwards, Amelia, 141
    The Professor's Adventure, 141
Edwards, Owen Dudley, 92
Egg, Augustus, 9, 119, 144, 154, 177
Egyptian Hall, 20
Eigner, Edwin, *The Dickens Pantomime*,
    39, 52, 104
Elliotson, John, 121, 179
emotions, 65
empathy, 102
Enlightenment, 39
episodic appearance of Switzerland, 52,
    53, 62, 64, 82, 88, 118, 121, 131,
    148, 158, 182, 184, 185
equestrian drama *see* Astley's
    Amphitheatre
escape, 65, 80, 87, 133, 136, 140–5,
    167–8
Eton, 59
Europe, 53
excess, 21, 92, 102
executions, 23, 46, 122–32
exoticism *see* foreignness
experience, 89
extremes, 76
exuberance, 109
eyes, 66, 87

fables, 43
Fairburn, John, 92
fairy tales, 103, 136–8
family, 61, 88, 165, 172
fantasy *see* imagination
fathers, 39–41, 43, 51, 52, 60, 61, 147
Fechter, Charles, 154–5, 157, 158
female travellers, 14
femininity, 22, 26–7, 61, 102, 128–30,
    179–80

Few Conventionalities, 19, 66
fiction, 55, 80, 84, 117–18
Fields, Annie, 166
fire, 102
fir-trees, 10, 100, 103, 131, 161, 167
flags, 43, 55
flâneur, 54, 63, 77, 80, 133, 134
flight, 65
Flint, Kate, 39, 41
flirtations, 58, 86, 120, 128, 136, 182
Foltinek, Herbert 2, 3
food and eating, 22, 31, 54, 65, 101,
    105–8, 109, 111–17, 129, 161,
    172–3
'Foolish Fashion', 127
force, 101, 102
foreignness, 31, 51, 53, 71, 104, 111,
    124, 127–9, 159
forgetting, 31–3, 42, 80
Forster, John, 1, 3, 4, 8, 45, 55, 63, 66,
    69, 71, 77, 78, 81, 82, 84–9, 92,
    98, 101, 102, 119, 125, 129,
    131, 133, 134, 135, 150, 156,
    163, 167, 169, 170, 174, 177,
    184
    Life of Charles Dickens, 3, 17
Forsyth, Neil, 6
Fox, Charles James, 39
Fra Diavolo, 21
fragments, 64–5
France, 2, 5, 37, 54, 69, 71, 72, 75, 93,
    109, 129, 134, 140–2, 147, 149,
    153, 159, 166–7, 184
Franklin expedition, 9
Franklin, John, Sir, 9
Franz Kafka
freedom, 42, 48, 50, 53, 60, 76, 106
French citizens, 12, 128–9
French revolution, 43, 174
Freud, Sigmund, 65
Fribourg, 101, 102
friends, 90, 131, 134, 136, 137, 140–2,
    144, 150, 160, 169, 177, 182, 185
Frozen Deep, 9, 24, 136
Fuseli, Henry, 178
Füssli, Henry *see* Fuseli, Henry

Gad's Hill, 16, 20, 80, 138, 154–8, 159,
    166, 168, 185
Gearing, Nigel, 2
Geneva, 3, 14, 44, 72, 75, 82, 85–9, 99,
    101, 110, 120, 142, 145, 152, 174,
    178, 184, 185
    perfume of, 25
genius, 88, 89

206 *Dickens and Switzerland*

Genoa, 63, 71, 72, 81, 140, 141–2, 145, 181–2
genre, 65, 71, 103
Gerrard Street, 24
Gesler, 46, 47, 51, 52, 54, 56, 57, 59, 62, 159
ghosts, 65, 76, 79, 80, 82, 83, 89, 103, 104, 167
giants, 101, 102, 103, 115, 136–7, 159
Gibbon, Edward, 21, 162–3
gigantic, 101, 102
glaciers, 96
Glencoe, 90, 93
gluttony, 52
Goethe, 25, 39
goitres, 13, 76, 105, 107, 113–16, 159, 169, 170, 173
Gondo, gorge of, 95–6
Good Fairy, 40
gorges, 10, 54, 55, 77, 91, 95, 100
Gotthard pass, 11, 91, 94, 100
Grand Tour, 11, 29, 38–9
Grandfather Blacktooth, 11
grapes, 105–10, 117, 173
graveyards, 131, 172, 173
Gray, Beryl, 157
Great Expectations, 24, 90, 179
Great Saint Bernard pass, 11, 33–5, 52, 64, 77, 79–80, 87, 101, 103–4, 106, 108, 109, 111, 131, 132, 134, 135, 136, 138–9, 161, 163, 166–7, 170–1, 173, 177, 184
greatness, 100–1; *see also* gigantic
greed, 109
grief, 31–4, 52, 120, 126, 131
Grimaldi, Joseph, 18
Grisons, 12
grotesque, 22, 34–5, 50, 52, 65, 66, 76, 90, 100–11, 105, 106, 109, 111, 113–18, 131, 158, 172, 173
guestbooks, 122
Guggenbühl, Johann Jakob, 115
guidebooks *see* travel writing
guilt, 56, 172

habits, 87
Haggard, Rider, 10
Haldimand, William, 73, 114, 177
Hamlet, 45
hanging, 124, 126–32; *see also* executions
happiness, 134–5, 137
happy ending, 41
Hard Times, 20, 38, 39–42, 66, 120
Hare, William, 92
Harlequin, 40, 49–62

harlequinade, 40, 53
harmony, 102
hats, 43, 51, 57, 58–62
Haunted Man, 83
headache, 66, 143
healing *see* recovery
health, 21, 87
heat, 81
helplessness, 102
Helvetian Republic, 42
Hennard Dutheil de la Rochère, Martine, 6
Herculaneum, 52, 184
heritage, 43
heroism, 137
hiding, 140
hierarchy, 106
Highgate, 99
Highlands, 90
hippodrama, 35–42
historical accuracy, 42, 51
history, 7, 51
Hofer, Andreas, 44
Hogarth, George, 26
Hogarth, Georgina, 4, 59, 86, 139, 149, 150–1, 175
Holbein, Hans, *Dance of Death*, 24, 108–9
holidays, 82
Hollington, Michael, 2, 6, 109, 120, 178
   Dickens and the Grotesque, 105, 112
Holly-Tree Inn, 52, 66, 101, 124, 125
Homer, 11
homesickness, 31
homosexuality, 179–81
honesty, 45–6
Hood, Robin, 48
horseback riding, 35–42, 43, 138
Horsemonger Lane Jail, 132
horses, 94, 145
Hoskyns, Chandos Wren, 141, 143–4
hotels *see* Swiss accommodation
Household Narrative, 98
Household Words, 7, 19, 44, 48, 56, 57, 113, 120, 121, 126, 130, 134
houses, 54, 56, 58, 69, 79, 90, 100–2, 105, 111, 114, 115, 116, 154–8, 162, 165
Huguenots *see* Protestantism
humiliation, 88–9
humility *see* modesty
humour *see* comedy
Hurdy-Gurdy, 51
hyperbole, 55, 73, 90, 91, 94, 102, 113

Index **207**

hypnosis *see* mesmerism; animal
   magnetism

ice, 96, 97, 100, 114
identity, 4, 54, 65, 83–4, 107, 108, 122,
   124, 147–8, 164, 165, 177, 183–4
'Idiots', 66, 114
idiots, 66, 76, 99, 105, 106, 109, 113–17,
   159, 173
idyll, 155, 156
ignorance, 110, 170
illegitimacy, 59
imagination, 41, 51, 52, 54, 55, 63–5,
   75, 77, 79, 80, 81–4, 87, 89, 93,
   97, 105, 109, 117–18, 120, 130,
   131, 132, 133, 135, 136, 137, 155,
   159–60, 163, 168, 169, 174, 175,
   177, 183, 185
imitation book covers, 92–3
impulse, 69, 71, 101, 124
inanimate, 103
India, 137
industrialisation, 41, 105
innocence, 46, 98, 102
Inns *see* Swiss accommodation
inspiration *see* imagination
instability, 102
interlude, 41
introspection, 65, 81, 118, 134–5
invention, 117
iodine, 113–14
Ireland, 170
irony, 41, 50, 52, 53, 71, 82, 90, 108,
   158
Italian population, 12
Italy, 2, 5, 29, 30, 38, 52, 58, 69, 70, 71,
   72, 77, 104, 105, 106, 110, 121,
   137, 140, 141, 144–6, 147, 153,
   160, 181–2

Jerrold, Douglas, 92
Jerusalem 137
Jesuits, 13
John, Juliet, *Dickens's Villains*, 56
Jordan, John, 1
Jura mountains, 82

Kant, Immanuel, 92, 93
Kaplan, Fred, 123, 135, 136, 179, 180,
   181, 182
Kemble, Charles, 21
Kent, 80, 156; *see also* Gad's Hill
keys, 101
knights, 112, 137
Knowles, James Sheridan, 45, 49, 56, 57

Lake Geneva, 34, 72, 75, 80, 104, 155,
   160, 162
Lake Moosseedorf, 11
Lamert, James, 18
landscape *see* Swiss landscape
languages, 95, 148
   foreign, 14, 31, 77, 99, 129, 153–4,
   182
'Last Cab-Driver, and the First Omnibus
   Cad', 38
Lausanne, 3, 8–9, 13, 30, 33, 55, 63,
   66–9, 72, 75, 76, 78, 80–4, 88, 99,
   118, 137, 138, 142, 145, 150, 156,
   159, 160, 162–4, 169, 172, 174,
   175, 177, 181, 182, 183, 185
   absence of streets, 8, 63–4, 74–5, 76,
   78, 80, 82, 88, 118, 133, 158
Lavater, Johann Kaspar, 42, 178, 182
Le Mierre, Antoine-Marin, 43
Leech, John, 129
legends, 42, 47, 51; *see also* myth
Legouvé, Gabriel, 143
Leicester Square, 20
Lemon, Mark, 10
letters, 4, 5, 6, 58, 66, 70, 81, 94, 110,
   124, 125, 129, 132–51, 154, 182
lies, 56, 79, 143
Life of Our Lord, also *The Children's
   New Testament*, 83–4, 174–5
life, 83–4, 85–6, 104, 118, 131, 138
Linton, Eliza Lynn, 113
Little Dorrit, 2, 6, 18, 25, 34–5, 52, 64,
   66, 69, 76, 77, 80, 83, 90, 93, 97,
   101, 103–9, 111, 113, 117, 120,
   122, 124, 129, 131, 135, 154, 160,
   161, 164, 166, 171, 172, 173, 175,
   184
Litvak, Leon, 98, 153
llamas, 31
London Historic Parks and Gardens
   Trust, 16
London, 12, 16, 63, 69, 83, 106, 107,
   121, 123, 126
loneliness, 88, 94, 97, 133, 134, 167,
   168
longing *see* nostalgia
love affairs, 56, 61, 86, 120–1, 128, 136,
   137, 140, 145, 146, 165; *see also*
   flirtations
love, 26–7, 31–3, 37–42, 46, 97, 102,
   120, 136–8, 165, 181
Lucerne, 7–8, 146
Lying Awake, 65, 66, 77, 80, 87, 103,
   122, 130, 131, 136, 156, 184
Lytton, Edward Bulwer, 58, 129, 179

208 *Dickens and Switzerland*

macabre, 110
Maclise, Daniel, 44, 99
Macready, William Charles, 45, 51, 178
Madame Tussaud's, 23, 92
magic lantern, 63
magnetism *see* animal magnetism
mania, 82
manliness, 9–10, 26, 45–7, 48, 60
Manning, Maria, 23, 122, 126–32
Manning, Frederick, 122, 126–32
manuscripts, 85–6, 138, 150, 175, 179
Marguerite, 26
marriage, 26, 33, 40–2, 64, 87, 113, 117,
    121, 127, 137, 138, 151, 179
Marseille, 71, 141
Marshalsea prison, 64, 77, 97, 135, 160
Martigny, 52, 103, 104–6, 122, 160
Martin Chuzzlewit, 2, 25, 66, 90, 103,
    184
masculinity *see* manliness
mass, 109
Mathews, Charles, 28–30, 38, 46
mazes, 103
Mediterranean sea, 71, 160
melancholia, 31, 134
melodrama, 22, 35–8, 43, 46–7, 155, 159
Memoranda, 134, 173
memory, 31–2, 48, 53–4, 71, 75–6, 78,
    81, 85, 87, 97, 112, 113, 118, 119,
    124, 130–2, 137, 139, 159, 161,
    165, 167, 185
mental illness, 181–2
Mer de Glace, 93
Mesmer, Anton Franz, 179, 182
mesmerism, 121, 178–9, 181
'Message from the Sea', 52, 66, 78, 103,
    120
Middlemarch, 25
Milan, 72
mind, 56, 80, 83, 86–9, 97, 114, 133,
    134, 158, 163, 169, 179
miniatures, 50, 93, 101
minuscule *see* miniatures
mirrors, 155, 156
misery, 110, 170
mist, 76, 90, 103
modesty, 27, 54, 60, 91, 97, 174
monasteries, 79, 103, 104, 108, 111, 131,
    132, 134, 135, 161, 163–4, 167,
    171–2
money, 69, 75, 102, 115–16, 117, 121,
    122, 123, 128, 163, 177
monks, 33, 134, 135, 163, 168, 171, 176,
    177
monsters, 136–7

Mont Blanc, 14, 93,133
morgues, 34–5, 54, 79, 104, 106, 111,
    116, 131, 166–8, 171
Morley, Henry, 44
Morning Chronicle, 124
Morning Post, 50
mothers and the maternal, 31–5, 60, 61,
    76, 97, 109, 112–13, 115–16, 147,
    165, 173
mountaineering, 9–10, 31, 34, 69, 77, 79,
    87, 91, 95, 101, 131, 134, 137,
    139, 161
mountaineers, 14, 19, 23, 34, 41, 45, 47,
    91, 108
mountains, 10, 31, 51, 65, 75, 76, 77, 78,
    79, 80, 87, 91, 94, 100–1, 102,
    103–4, 106, 111, 131, 133, 134,
    136–8, 160, 163, 164, 165, 167–8,
    178, 183, 184
Mrs Lirriper's Legacy, 140
Mudfog Papers, 90
mules, 93
Mulhouse, 146
murder, 92, 122–32, 165
murderers, 92, 122–32
Murray, John, 12
    Handbook for Travellers in
        Switzerland, 12, 70, 114, 151
    Knapsack Guide for Travellers in
        Switzerland, 151
music, 21, 32, 80, 93, 103, 166
'My Mahogany Friend', 56, 57–62, 66
Mystery of Edwin Drood, 120, 158,
    171–2
myth, 43, 80, 103

narcissism *see* vanity
narration, 64, 103, 131
nation, 51, 128
Nature, 96–7, 98, 155
Nayder, Lillian, 9–14, 156
nervousness, 73–5, 81–3, 86–7, 99, 133,
    134–5, 143, 168
Neuchâtel, 72, 107
neuralgia, 143, 149
Newgate, 46
Newgate Calendar, 124
Nice, 72
Nicholas Nickleby, 18
night, 33, 64, 76, 78, 79, 88–9, 91, 95,
    99, 104, 105, 112, 131, 133, 167,
    180
nightmares *see* dreaming
Nile, 137
Nirshan Perera, 1

Nisbet, Ada, 58
No Thoroughfare, 7, 9, 21, 23, 26–7, 47,
61, 66, 69, 76, 77, 78, 80, 107–8,
111, 116–17, 120, 122, 146n128,
147–8, 152, 154–5, 157, 164–6,
172, 180
nonsense, 95
Normandy, 69
North Pole Pub, 24
nostalgia, 31–2, 48, 80, 87
novels, 66
Victorian, 14, 25
projects, 69
nuns, 171

observation, 55, 94, 124, 155
obsession, 74, 76, 80, 87, 89, 117, 118,
165–6, 167
ogres *see* giants
Old Curiosity Shop, 90
Oliver Twist, 25, 64
Olliffe, Sir Joseph, 141, 142–4
omniscience, 155
oppression, 59
orality and the oral, 31–5, 66, 93, 97,
105, 107, 111–17, 172
order, 12, 71, 86, 102, 106, 107, 110,
121, 170
ordinariness, 89
Orestano, Francesca, 2
Orford, Peter, 77
organs, 33
orphans, 147
Ostend, 145
'Our Bore', 66, 184
Our Mutual Friend, 66, 80, 90, 120, 149,
154, 162–4, 167, 176

pain, 46, 47, 66, 73, 80, 81, 87, 149
panorama, 18, 21, 105
A View of Mont Blanc, 19
A View of the Bernese Alps, 19
Panorama of Geneva and its Lake, 19
Pantaloon, 40–2, 52
pantomime, 22, 35, 39–41, 43, 46–7,
48–53, 62, 100, 109
Paracelsus, 152
paralipsis, 71, 121
paratext, 75, 118
Paris, 21, 37, 54, 69, 72, 82, 83, 106,
109, 116, 133, 140, 141–7, 149,
157, 166–7, 169
Parliament, 95
passivity, 100, 126
passports, 133

past, 87, 102, 110, 118, 135
pastoral, 98
pastures, 100
patriarchy, 40, 60
patriotism, 34, 36, 43, 47, 48, 50, 51,
53, 57
Patten, Robert L., 4
peace, 65, 76, 80, 97, 122, 135
peaks, 14, 94, 101, 103–4, 106, 108, 116,
122, 131–2, 134, 135, 136–7, 167,
169, 170, 184
pens, 101, 160
perspectives, 65, 106, 117
'Pet Prisoners', 126
philosophy, 95
phrenology, 178–9
physical strength, 26–7, 101
physiognomy, 58, 100, 128–9, 178
picaresque, 159
Piccadilly, 21
Pickwick Papers, 64, 92
Pictures from Italy, 2, 66, 69, 70, 71, 91,
95–6, 102, 110, 121, 125, 150
picturesque, 25, 52, 65, 71, 76, 90, 105,
106, 115, 117, 155, 160, 165, 166,
178
pirates, 50
pity, 126
Planché, James Robinson, 44, 47
playwrights, 54
plurality, 65
pointing, 103, 104
police, 176
politics, 170, 175
Pompeii, 11
popular culture, 52, 62, 70, 71, 89, 117,
168, 183, 185
praying and prayers, 174
precipice, 22, 95, 96, 97
preterition, 71
Prince Albert, 20
Prince Consort *see* Prince Albert
Prince Wales Hotel (London), 12
princesses, 136, 137
prisons, 12, 73, 77, 83, 97, 123, 126,
131–2, 135, 166, 175
'Private Theatres', 35
productivity, 107
proofreading, 70
protection, 101
Protestantism, 7–8, 24, 44, 76, 110–11,
153, 170, 174, 178
pseudonyms, 124, 147
psyche *see* mind
public employment, 176

public readings, 10, 29, 75, 137, 140, 142, 146, 163, 183
punctuality, 12
punishment, 79
purity, 102
Pyrenees, 134

Queen Victoria, 16
    chalet on Isle of Wight, 17
queerness, 179–81

'Railway Thoughts', 127
railway, 53
Rambler's Magazine, 36
Ransom, Mildred, 140
Rapin, René, 75
realism, 90
reality, 53–5, 77, 84–5, 87, 105, 106, 124, 160
reconciliation, 41
Recordon, Frédéric, 177
recovery, 96, 120
Rede, Leman Thomas, *Road to the Stage*, 28
redemption, 104
regression *see* degeneration
release, 65, 109, 137
relics, 110
religion, 7–8, 24, 35, 93, 109–11, 152–3, 170–5, 178, 181
Remak, Joachim, *A Very Civil War*, 110
remembrance, 33, 81
repentance, 87
repulsion, 89
resting, 79, 108, 134, 148, 168
restlessness, 31, 66, 73–5, 79, 81–3, 86–7, 99, 133, 134–8, 168, 180
restraint, 21, 102
retrospective, 99
revolution and rebellion, 8, 43, 59, 65, 110, 174
Rhine, 165, 178
rifles, 55
    rifle-matches, 55, 158
Righi, 36
rising, 95, 101, 103–4, 105, 131, 139, 156, 167, 169
rivers, 95–6, 97, 100, 112, 146, 155, 164, 165
rocks, 96–7, 100, 171
Romantic movement, 39, 89, 98, 105
romanticism, 53, 71, 105, 160
Rome, 69, 125, 144–5
Rosemont, 72, 75, 99, 156, 162–3
Rosset, Roger, 4

Rossini, Gioachino Antonio, 44
Rossi-Wilcox, Susan, 7
Rousseau, Jean-Jacques, 21, 177–8
ruins, 101, 103
'Rule, Britannia!', 57
Ruskin, John, 18, 38
Russell, Lord John, 123
Russia, 159

Sadrin, Annie, 1
safety, 101, 137
sailors, 50
Saint Bernard pass *see* Great Saint Bernard pass
Sala, George Augustus, 31
satire, 100
savages, 12, 95
savagery, 9, 11, 95
Savoyards *see* Swiss performances
Saxon, Andrew, 37
Schazmann, Paul-Emile, 3, 6
Schiller, Johann Christoph Friedrich, 44
Schirmer, Gustav, 3, 6–7, 122
Schlicke, Paul, *Dickens and Popular Entertainment*, 39
Schramm, Jan-Melissa, 122
science, 113–15, 121
Scotland, 90, 92
Scott, Sir Walter, 25–7
    Battle of Sempach, 26
    Anne of Geierstein or, The Maiden of the Mist, 26–7, 108
sea, 51, 80, 86, 113–14, 149, 167, 168
secrets, 56, 87, 88–9, 140–51
self-development, 33, 65, 75, 83, 176, 183, 184
self-discovery, 65, 71, 83, 84, 117, 134–5, 147, 183, 184
self-examination, 99, 134–5, 176, 183
Sens (France), 140
serenity, 96, 134–5
servants, 69, 122–32
sexuality, 130, 137, 165, 179–81
shadows, 91, 176
Shakespeare, 154, 162
    Macbeth, 28
Shaw, John 'Jack', 48
Shaw, Philip, 89
Shelley, Percy Bysshe, 38
    Shelley, Mary, 178
shepherds, 32, 37, 97
Sherbourne House, 178
ships, 101, 141, 160
shooting, 43, 45, 46, 48, 53, 54–5, 158
short stories, 66

'Shy Neighbourhoods', 65, 77, 103, 111, 120, 161
sickness, 66, 113–17, 133, 141, 143, 170, 176, 182; *see also* disease
silence, 95
Simplon pass, 11, 77, 80, 91, 93, 94, 101, 110, 134, 137–8, 141, 163, 185
singing, 30–4, 53, 97, 174
skeletons, 103, 104, 110, 131, 167
Sketches by Boz, 37, 38, 50, 66
skulls, 79
Slater, Michael, 2, 57, 58, 64, 140
slavery, 50, 51, 53, 57
Sleary, Josephine, 20, 120
sleeping, 33, 65, 77–9, 86, 87, 99, 102, 112, 130, 133, 158–60, 180
sleeplessness, 77–8, 86, 99, 130, 133, 180, 182
smallness, 100–2
Smith, Albert, 10, 121, 152, 157
    Ascent of Mont Blanc see Swiss performances
    Guy Fawkes, 60
    Rogue's Walk, 127
Smith, Arthur, 10
Smollett, Tobias
    Humphry Clinker, 17
    Peregrine Pickle, 17
snow, 10, 34, 76, 79, 82, 91, 93, 94, 96, 97, 100, 103, 104, 108, 113, 134, 135, 161, 163, 165, 166, 167, 171
social services *see* public employment
Soho, 23–4
solitude, 97, 133, 134, 167, 168
Somebody's Luggage, 147
Sonderbund War, 8, 110, 174
sons, 52
sounds, 87, 95, 96, 165–6
South America, 14
special effects, 43
spectres *see* ghosts
spirituality, 99, 102
spoons, 55
stairs, 101, 103
Stanfield, Clarkson, 18
stereotypes, 71, 183
Stone, Harry, 58, 59, 88
    Night Side of Dickens, 88, 112
storytelling *see* writing
Strasbourg, 54, 145
streets, absence of and need for, 8–9, 63–4, 72, 74–5, 76, 78, 80, 82, 88, 118, 133, 158
Stroud, 134

study, 154–8, 166
style, 100, 117
Style, Sir Thomas Charles, 149–51
subjectivity, 92
sublime, 15, 39, 65, 66, 71, 76, 80, 89–99, 105, 114, 117, 170
subordination, 61
success, 87
sucking, 31, 107, 173
suffering, 80, 81, 88–9, 115, 117
suicide, 164
summer, 81
summits *see* peaks
sunset, 91, 108
supernatural, 21, 33, 65, 76, 79, 83, 100, 167
suppression, 80, 121, 183
Sweden, 127
swimming, 86
Swiss
    accommodation, 22, 54, 78, 94, 100–2, 108, 111, 155, 162, 166
    architecture, 16, 17
    arrows, 51, 167
    characters, 17, 22, 23, 26, 28, 34–5, 42–62, 76, 105–8, 173–4, 183
    charitable institutions, 12, 115, 175, 177
    children, 12, 34–5, 76, 106–7, 116–17, 146–7, 173
    churches, 24, 33, 101
    citizens, 12–14, 17, 23–4, 30, 45–6, 63, 76, 110, 122–32, 169
    cleanliness, 12, 27, 71
    cottages, 17, 56, 100, 101, 102
    criminal system, 73
    culture, 23, 28–30, 169, 170
    dress, 22, 26–7, 36, 126–30, 132
    education system, 12–13, 25, 73, 76, 110, 123, 170, 174, 177–8
    Examiner, 49
    festivals, 30, 55
    folklore, 16, 23, 28–9, 55
    friends, 13, 14, 58, 63, 73, 75, 131, 137, 138–9, 142, 150, 169, 179–80, 181–2, 185
        wives of, 14, 58, 137, 138
    heroines and heroes, 26, 46, 52, 130; *see also* Tell, William
    homes, 13, 46, 54, 56, 81, 100, 114, 115, 116, 165
    iconography, 17
    independence of character, 13, 76, 110, 174
    insanity, 21, 113–17, 169

212   *Dickens and Switzerland*

Swiss (*cont.*)
lakes, 11, 14, 34, 72, 80, 101, 104, 155, 160, 162, 165
landscape, 9, 76, 77, 80, 88, 89, 91, 94–9, 100–3, 108, 114, 116–17, 122, 133, 135: gendered, 9–11, 100; in popular British culture, 18, 31, 37, 51, 56, 117, 155, 183
literature, 24
lowlands, 13
maids, 19, 23, 25–7, 36–7, 183
manners, 12–13, 27, 129
modesty, 27
Morton, John Madison, 49
nature, 21, 32, 88, 93, 95–6, 100, 103, 114
order, 12, 110, 121, 170
parody, 49
passes, 11, 14, 34, 103, 134, 156, 165
peasants, 19, 34, 38, 43, 55, 60, 105, 106, 109, 113–17, 173, 183
performances, 12, 18, 28, 48, 56, 117, 122, 183, 184: 'All Round My Hat', 51; *Amazon Sisters* see *The Sisters; or, The Heroines of Switzerland; Ascent of Mont Blanc*, 20; 'At Homes', 28–30, 38, 46; Battle of Zurich, 21; *Flower of Lucerne*, 19; *Geneviève, the Maid of Switzerland*, 19; *Harlequin and William Tell; or, The Genius of the Ribstone Pippin*, 49–53; *Hofer; or, The Tell of the Tyrol*, 44; *Judith of Geneva*, 19; *Julian and Agnes; or The Monks of the Great St. Bernard*, 19; *Linda and Gertrude; or, The Swiss Chalet*, 19; *Linda of Chamouni*, 19; *Lover and the Avenger*, 19; *Mariette; or, the Maid of Switzerland*, 19; 'Merry Swiss Boy', 21, 28; *Nathalie; or, the Swiss Milkmaid*, 19; *Outcast of Lausanne; or, Claudine of Switzerland*, 19, 153; *Pauvrette; or, Under the Snow*, 19; Ranz des Vaches, 31; Savoyards, 28; *Sisters; or, The Heroines of Switzerland*, 19, 36; *Swiss Cottage; or, Why don't She Marry Him?* 19; *Swiss Girl; or, The Parricide*, 19; *Swiss Maid and her Tyrolean Lover*, 36–42, 62, 120; *Tereza Tomkins; or, The Fruits of Geneva*, 19; *Thérèse, the Orphan of Geneva*, 18; *Tyrolean Shepherd and*

Swiss Milkmaid, 36–42, 62, 120; *William Tell* by Robert Barnabas Brough, 60; *William Tell or, A Telling Version of an Old Tell-Tale*, 49; *William Tell or, The Arrow; the Apple and the Agony* 49; *William Tell or, the Strike of the Cantons*, 49; *William Tell with a Vengeance or, the Pet, the Patriot and the Pippin*, 49; *William Tell, The Hero of Switzerland*, 43, 49
poverty, 35, 113–17, 165, 170
prisons, 12, 73, 175–6
prizes, 55
propriety, 27, 129, 130
pudding, 7
punctuality, 12
sanity, 21, 113–17, 169
scenery *see* landscape
schools, 12–13, 73, 76
servants, 12–13, 17, 22–5, 122–32
sickness, 21, 113–17, 169, 182
theatrical plots *see* performances
towns, 101
traditions, 11, 16, 17, 23
valleys, 14, 32, 76, 97, 100, 104, 108, 110–11, 113, 114, 135, 165, 169, 170
vegetation, 10
villages, 10, 46, 97, 100–2, 105–7, 161
women, 22, 23, 26–7, 34–5, 105, 106, 115, 116, 126–32, 181–2, 183
work ethic, 12, 81, 83, 110, 116, 170
Swiss Cottage (London), 16
Swiss Tavern, 16
Switzerland
absence of streets *see* Switzerland: need for streets; streets, absence of and need for
alleged trip in 1856, 3
compared to the USA, 12–13, 17
creative crisis in, 64, 81–3, 133, 169
desire to visit and return (CD), 4, 69, 82, 99, 119, 132–51, 163, 168, 169–70, 177
in British popular culture, 15, 22, 28–30, 38, 43–62, 70, 117, 158, 168, 183, 185
lack of critical studies on CD and Switzerland, 8
need for streets, 8–9, 63–4, 72, 74–5, 76, 78, 80, 82, 88, 118, 133, 158
political relations with Britain, 30

primitive, 11, 93
process of writing, 5, 63–4, 66, 73–5,
  80, 81, 83, 84, 87–8, 101, 133,
  134, 135, 136, 137, 146, 154, 155,
  156, 158, 163, 169
representation of in CD's fiction, 64,
  70, 87, 115, 117, 119–21, 130,
  135, 146
Roman, 11
stay in 1846, 1, 13, 15, 30, 45, 55,
  66–9, 72, 75, 73–81, 84, 118, 134,
  137, 139, 140, 145, 150–1, 156,
  158, 162, 169, 172, 174, 175, 177,
  182, 183, 185
theatres in, 64, 136
tourism to, 38–9, 58, 60, 117, 134,
  165
trip to Switzerland in 1844, 11, 17, 22,
  93, 134, 140, 141, 145, 150, 181,
  185
trip to Switzerland in 1845, 22, 69, 91,
  94, 96, 100, 141, 185
trip to Switzerland in 1853, 9–10, 31,
  82, 99, 124, 134, 141, 144, 145,
  177
trips to Switzerland, 5, 7, 10, 15, 30,
  47, 54, 82, 119, 124, 133, 140–51,
  158, 168, 184
walking, 8–9, 63, 69, 73, 76, 80, 89,
  133, 134, 137
weather, 9, 22, 165
swords, 125, 137

Tale of Two Cities, 69, 83, 104, 108–9,
  120, 136, 173, 174, 175, 177,
  184
Tavistock House, 59, 92, 136
tea, 22, 102
teaboards, 55
tears *see* weeping
teeth and dentition, 115
telescope, 155
Tell, William
  character, 8, 13, 45–6, 51, 54–62, 159
  performances, 20, 21, 42–60
Tellgau, 43
telling and not telling, 71, 122
tenderness, 97
Ternan family, 49
Ternan, Ellen, 4, 49, 56, 120–1, 136, 140,
  142, 145, 146–8, 149, 151
Ternan, Fanny, 121
Ternan, Frances, 49
terror, 97
Thalmann, Liselotte, 3

theatre, 11, 15, 18, 22–3, 30, 35–42, 54,
  55, 56, 62, 64, 100, 124, 126, 131,
  166, 183, 184
theatrical tours, 10
Thirteen Cantons sign, 24
Thomas, Ronald, R., *Dickens's Sublime
  Artefact*, 96
Thomson, William, *Two Journeys
  through Italy and Switzerland*, 70,
  72, 153, 183
thoughts, 80, 87, 155
threats, 102, 105
Ticino, 170
ties and tying up, 137
Tillotson, Kathleen, 64, 84
time, 54
Times, The, 128, 129
'To Be Read at Dusk', 66, 77, 91, 108,
  136, 172
Tomalin, Claire, 56, 58, 136
  Invisible Woman, 146
torrents *see* rivers
Tory party, 170
Townshend, Chauncey Hare, 11, 99,
  179–81
toys, 13, 100–2, 117
tragedy, 46, 73
trains *see* transport
tramps and tramping *see* vagabonds
transcendence, 33, 71, 79
transformation, 54, 80, 94, 106, 107,
  108, 117
transport, 53–4, 91, 93, 94, 130, 133,
  141, 145–6, 154, 159, 160
transubstantiation, 109
trauma, 33, 64, 65, 80, 86, 88–9, 165,
  184
travel writing, 65, 66, 70, 71, 117, 130,
  151–4, 183
travellers, 54, 101, 103, 104, 131, 134,
  167, 184
Travelling Abroad, 53–5, 65, 66, 101,
  113, 115–16, 120, 130, 158–60,
  166, 184
travelling, 58, 70, 73, 77, 84, 91, 93, 94,
  95, 101, 106, 130, 133, 135, 140,
  143, 144, 145, 158–61, 184
trials, 92, 123, 127–8
Trollope, Anthony, 121
  Can You Forgive Her? 25
Trollope, Thomas Adolphus, 121
truth, 54, 84, 88, 90, 98, 124
Tschumi, Raymond, 2
tyranny, 42, 43, 50, 51, 54, 56, 57, 59,
  61, 62

214   *Dickens and Switzerland*

ugliness, 105
uncanny, 34, 65, 76, 105, 117, 129, 171, 172
uncertainty, 41, 50
Uncommercial Traveller, 47, 53, 65, 76, 111, 112, 113, 120, 158–61, 184
unreality, 77, 160
upwards *see* rising
Urania Cottage, 177
USA, 2, 12–13, 17, 69, 87, 175, 181, 184

vagabonds, 54, 63, 88, 133, 134, 138
Valais, 170, 173
Vanfasse, Nathalie, 71, 121
vanishing, 140–8, 167
vanity, 62, 137
Vaud, Canton de, 13, 43, 120
vaudeville, 54
Vaudois, 7–8
vegetables, 51
Venice, 69, 77
Vernon, Lord, 55
Vesuvius, 101
Vevey, 9
Victoria and Albert Museum, 181
villains, 46, 51, 52, 53, 56, 76, 78, 103, 122, 165, 179–81
vintage, 34–5, 104–11, 113, 171, 173
violence, 76, 92, 95, 101–2, 111–13, 117, 122–32, 137, 164, 165–6, 172, 176, 180–1
virgin, 14
visuality, 90, 100, 105, 166
volcanoes, 101
Voltaire, 21
voyeurism, 27
vulgarity, 105, 105
vulnerability, 102

wakefulness and waking, 77–8, 86–7, 130, 160, 161
Walpole, Horace, *Castle of Otranto*, 59
wandering, 31, 54, 63, 65, 73, 80, 87, 103, 133, 134, 161
war, 8, 110, 112–13, 172, 174; *see also* Sonderbund War
Wardour, Richard, 24
warnings, 101
Warren's Blacking Warehouse, 87, 89, 118, 184
watches and clocks, 55, 78, 117, 165

water, 80, 91, 95–6, 100, 113–17, 160, 164–8, 170
waterfalls, 21, 77, 90, 91, 95, 105, 115, 116, 165, 166, 178
Watson family, 4
   Watson, John Burgess, 16, 99
   Watson, Lavinia, 58, 137
Watt, Ian, *Oral Dickens*, 31, 107, 172
waxworks, 23
weakness, 61
weeping, 32
Wharton Robinson, George, 121
White Book of Sarnen, 42
wildness, 12, 83, 94, 100
Wilkie, David, 98
Wills, William Henry, 89, 114, 140, 141, 145, 151
wind, 103, 160, 166, 167
wine, 104–11, 117, 147, 164, 171–3
winter, 76, 88, 100, 135, 170
women, 14, 26–7, 52, 58, 61, 64, 87, 97, 101, 102, 106, 113, 115, 116, 128–30, 136, 137, 165, 176, 177, 183; *see also* Swiss women; femininity
wood and wooden, 103, 105, 109, 111, 115, 131, 161, 167
Woolford, Louisa, 36–7
Wordsworth, William, 38
   Prelude, 98–9
   We are Seven, 98
Wraight, Sir John, *The Swiss and the British*, 29, 38
writer's block, 73, 133, 134–5, 137
writing, 41–2, 57, 63–5, 66, 71, 72, 73–5, 76, 80–1, 83, 84, 87–8, 89, 92, 101, 103, 109, 118, 133, 134, 135, 137, 154, 155, 156, 158, 169, 170–1, 172
   plans and planning of, 64, 74, 133, 134, 135, 137, 170–1, 173
Wyss, Johann David, 20
   Swiss Family Robinson, 20, 153

Yarmouth, 14
Yung, Emile, 120–1

Zermatt, 120–1
Zschokke, Johann Heinrich, 24–5
   Aböllino, 25
   Blue Wonder, 25
Zurich, 146
Zwingli, Huldrych, 153